Practices of the Sentimental Imagination

Melodrama, the Novel, and the Social Imaginary in Nineteenth-Century Japan

Harvard East Asian Monographs 277

Practices of the Sentimental Imagination

Melodrama, the Novel, and the Social Imaginary in Nineteenth-Century Japan

Jonathan E. Zwicker

Published by the Harvard University Asia Center
Distributed by Harvard University Press
Cambridge (Massachusetts) and London 2006

Printed in the United States of America

The Harvard University Asia Center publishes a monograph series and, in coordination with the Fairbank Center for East Asian Research, the Korea Institute, the Reischauer Institute of Japanese Studies, and other faculties and institutes, administers research projects designed to further scholarly understanding of China, Japan, Vietnam, Korea, and other Asian countries. The Center also sponsors projects addressing multidisciplinary and regional issues in Asia.

Library of Congress Cataloging-in-Publication Data

Zwicker, Jonathan E., 1973–
Practices of the sentimental imagination : melodrama, the novel, and the social imaginary in nineteenth-century Japan / Jonathan E. Zwicker.
p. cm. -- (Harvard East Asian monographs ; 277)
Includes bibliographical references and index.
ISBN 0-674-02273-4 (cl : alk. paper)
1. Japanese fiction--19th century--History and criticism. I. Title. II. Series.
PL747.5.Z85 2006
895.6'334--dc22

2006005444

Index by Pamela Herzog

♾ Printed on acid-free paper

Last figure below indicates year of this printing
16 15 14 13 12 11 10 09 08 07 06

For my parents Steven and Judith Zwicker

and for Golde Zwicker

Acknowledgments

The intellectual relationships and friendships I developed at Columbia University have left me with an enormous debt of gratitude. To Paul Anderer, who guided my work since I was an undergraduate, I owe more in intellectual and personal terms than I can easily convey; his help, encouragement, and advice have led me to a place neither one of us could have imagined a decade ago. Carol Gluck has been a constant source of guidance and support and has pushed me to engage with problems that I have sometimes taken for granted. Franco Moretti introduced me to the kind of work on literature I always wanted to do but never knew existed; his immense intellect and equally immense generosity have helped show me what to strive for as both a scholar and as a teacher. David Wang has been supportive of my work for a long time now and his own work has greatly inspired me.

I would also like to acknowledge the generous intellectual support I received from fellow graduate students at Columbia especially Peter Flueckiger, Sarah Kovner, Jamie Newhard, and Lori Watt. I owe a special debt of gratitude to Kerry Ross and Jason Creigh who read the entire dissertation and were always both supportive and engaged and the most pleasant of company. Michael Scanlon read every piece of this project many times over, often when the thoughts were only half-formed and the arguments rudimentary; I owe him an immense intellectual debt as well as a personal debt for the great friendship he has shown me over the years I have known him. I would also like to thank

Tim Van Compernolle who a provided very detailed and insightful reading of the manuscript at a critical time.

The bulk of the research and writing of this project was carried out in Tokyo. Kawamura Minato has for years now been supporting my research and generously sharing with me his time, his ideas, and his truly vast knowledge of things both related and unrelated to Japanese literature. Takagi Gen pushed me harder than any of my other teachers and for the past five years I have benefited immeasurably from his knowledge and friendship. During my time in Tokyo, Koakimoto Dan provided me advice and encouragement and I would also like to thank my colleagues among the graduate students at Hōsei and Chiba Universities.

The Michigan Society of Fellows provided an ideal environment for finishing this book and I would like to acknowledge the support I received from James Boyd White, Nancy Florida, and the other fellows with whom I overlapped and from whom I learned so much. I would like especially to thank Chuck Davis, Maya Jassanoff, Stella Nair, Ziv Neeman, Shanan Peters, and Neil Safier for their friendship as well as their advice and encouragement. Since coming to Michigan, I have benefited from the advice and support of Ken Ito and David Rolston and from a wonderful group of young scholars including Miranda Brown, Christi Merrill, James Robson, and especially Henry Em whose friendship and support have meant so much to me. In addition, Kenji Niki of the Asia Library has been an invaluable resource and has helped enormously in obtaining permissions for illustrations.

Over the course of my graduate career and during the researching and writing of this project I have received generous support from Columbia University, from the Jacob Javits Fellowship Program, the Fulbright Program, the Japan Foundation, the Ito Foundation, and from the Hōsei International Fund. A three year fellowship at the Michigan Society of Fellows allowed me much needed time to turn the dissertation into a book and I would like to thank the Center for Japanese Studies and the Japan Foundation for making additional research possible.

Portions of Chapters 1 and 3 were originally published in *The Novel*, edited by Franco Moretti, and I am grateful to Einaudi and Princeton University Press for permission to reprint this material. I would also like to thank the Freer and Sackler Galleries, the Tokyo National Museum, and the Tōyō Bunko for permission to reprint the images that appear in this book.

In recent years, book historians have been especially interested in the role of publishers, editors, and printers in the production of books and so it seems especially fitting for a study that takes seriously the history of print to acknowledge the invaluable role played by John Ziemer and William M. Hammell of the Harvard University Asia Center and by the two anonymous readers whose reports helped clarify and sharpen the argument of this book in numerous places.

My most profound debt of gratitude goes to my family. To my siblings and their families—Laura, Rob, William, and Cecilia; Ben and Michi; Aaron and Stephanie—I would like to express my thanks for making this work possible in ways they probably do not realize. In Golde Zwicker, I have been blessed with a grandmother whose own intellectual appetite has been inspiring and who takes real pride and pleasure in the vocations of the mind. To my parents, Steven and Judith, I owe everything and so to them I dedicate this study. They have provided unconditional support and encouragement always and especially when it was most needed. To my father I owe a special debt: his own work has been my greatest intellectual inspiration, his friendship my greatest support; he has read and commented on this piece more than anyone and has made it better than it otherwise could have been. Above all, Kyongmi and Mara have shaped my work and life in the most profound of ways and for that it is my great privilege to thank them.

Contents

Reference Matter

Figures and Tables

Figures

Tables

Practices of the Sentimental Imagination

Melodrama, the Novel, and the Social Imaginary in Nineteenth-Century Japan

INTRODUCTION

Approaching the Archive—
Numbers, Form, and the Seriousness of Sentiment

> We feel it strange to take seriously books that were never part of a "library."
> But let us not forget that books were originally objects of use—indeed, a means
> of subsistence. These were devoured. Let us use them
> to study novels from the point of view of their food chemistry.
>
> —Walter Benjamin, "Chambermaids' Romances of the Past Century"

In the National Diet Library in Tokyo there is a catalogue of the Meiji Collection that is, like all catalogues, full of data and of numbers. By itself, each entry is a record of the individual, the unique; but taken as a whole, this list of titles represents something very different, a large statistical body in which individuality fades away and we are left not with the unique but with the regular, the repeated, even the monotonous. In one year, half as many titles as in another; twice the number of novels as plays; and so on. Numbers and literature seem to belong to different worlds, to different ways of thinking about the past and the work of the imagination, but out of a simple curiosity about the nature and the scope of the book trade in Japan at the end of the nineteenth century. I started to look at numbers, and from that sampling began this work on the novel in nineteenth-century Japan.

First I made some simple charts (these form the basis of the figures in Chapter 3), and then a more elaborate and exhaustive database of fiction titles published during the Meiji period while working through the microfilms of the Meiji Collection. What I found was quite striking. First, and this was especially true in the early Meiji period, there were a large number of early modern titles—that is, titles published before 1868. That of course makes intuitive sense because the books of one generation do not just disappear overnight. Indeed, anyone who has read Mori Ōgai's *Vita Sexualis* (1909) knows the scene of the colporteur coming to the dormitory and Kanai borrowing works by Kyokutei Bakin (1767–1848, also known as Takizawa Bakin) and Santō Kyōden (1761–1816), and eventually Tamenaga Shunsui (1790–1843), who plays such a decisive role in Kanai's libidinal development. But recent histories of the modern Japanese novel have tended to focus on what Karatani Kōjin has called the "nearness of origins" of Japanese modernity and few of these studies devote more than scant attention to fiction of the early nineteenth century, or even to the presence of that fiction in the late nineteenth- and early twentieth-century literary economy.[1] This is beginning to change, but even now one is much more likely to begin a history of Meiji literature with Tsubouchi Shōyō (1859–1935) or Futabatei Shimei (1864–1909) than with a description of the reception of Bakin or Shunsui.[2]

1. Much of the scholarly work during the past decade on the modern Japanese novel has been shaped by the ideas that Karatani put forward in his book, *Origins of Modern Japanese Literature*, and particularly by his insistence on the "nearness of origins" of Japanese modernity. My own book engages and complicates Karatani's work by taking seriously the literary archive of the early nineteenth century and using this archive to interrogate the idea of literary modernity as it has come—too comfortably—to be adopted by critics in recent years. See Karatani, *Origins of Modern Japanese Literature*, pp. 194–95.

2. Recently, a few literary historians who have turned their attention to the material dimensions of the literary experience have begun to challenge the paradigm of two nineteenth centuries. In *The Book in Japan*, Peter Kornicki describes the historiographical effect of the Meiji Restoration as "tyrannical"; see as well Kornicki's essay on "The Survival of Tokugawa Fiction in the Meiji Period." In Japan, a number of scholars of early modern literature have begun to turn to the diversity of ways that early modern fiction continued to participate in a larger social world after the Meiji Restoration; for the results of some of this research, see the special issue of *Edo bungaku* on the "Edo of the Meiji Teens" (Meiji jūnendai no Edo), guest edited by Robert Campbell. In other fields of historical research on Japan—economic history, for example—the idea of a long nineteenth century is becoming increasingly familiar: two of the best examples are

More striking still was the place assumed by translated fiction in the numbers I had gathered. There were many foreign books translated in the Meiji period but not nearly as many as I anticipated. Literary translations are a constant of the book market but never once are they—numerically—the dominant line. The "opening" of Japan and the "influence" of the European novel on the development of modern fiction have assumed such a large place in the historiographcal imagination that I simply expected more—a lot more. Recent work on translation in nineteenth-century Europe has suggested that many markets were totally dominated by translation, that it was not uncommon for foreign books to account for 80 percent or 90 percent of the total literary output. That is what I expected for Japan, at least for a decade or two. But the real transition is between early modern fiction and the modern novel. Translations are part of the market, but in a very different way than expected.

So I became curious. How many novels were published in the first half of the nineteenth century? And if one were to sketch the literary market of the early nineteenth century, would one find any translations? The fiction of late imperial China, we know, exercised a powerful pull on the literary imagination of the eighteenth and nineteenth centuries; so what exactly was it that changed with the "opening" of Japan? Could one extend these lines backward in time—say to the end of the eighteenth century, maybe even a little further—and, if so, what would one find and how would it change our reading of modern Japanese literary history? Can we chart a history of the novel across a long nineteenth century? And if so, can we consider these early nineteenth-century titles novels at all?

The nineteenth century considered as a whole is, of course, not an object of inquiry familiar to Japanese history. Historiographically, it is conventional to think not of one long nineteenth century but of two short nineteenth centuries: the one extending from the Kansei Reforms of the late 1780s through the Meiji Restoration of 1868 and the other from 1868 until the death of the Meiji emperor in 1912. But this chronology also has built into it an implicit bias for change and it exag-

---

David Howell's *Capitalism from Within: Economy, Society, and the State in a Japanese Fishery* and Kären Wigen's *Making of a Japanese Periphery, 1750–1920.*

gerates the totality of the break between the early modern and modern worlds of print. Behind this chronology is obscured a different history, a history often visible only indirectly through its traces. The idea that history is uneven and that different dimensions of historical experience require different chronologies is now commonplace. Indeed, when the chronologies of such different histories as those of political institutions, literary form, and cultural practice converge as they do in the conventional histories of nineteenth-century Japan, it is often because something has been overlooked. Dazzled by the event, we have somehow lost track of the different calibrations of social life.

Practices of the Sentimental Imagination began, then, as an attempt to think through a set of questions posed by an initial foray into statistics: both fundamental empirical questions about the literature of the early nineteenth century, but also larger epistemological questions of why literary history has told the story of the nineteenth century in the way it has, and of how useful it remains to continue to narrate nineteenth-century Japanese literary history in terms of the paradigm of the opening of a closed country, of a colossal divide at mid-century separating the early modern from the modern world.

There are, historically, perfectly good reasons why Japanese literary history should have embraced this chronology; at the same time, what these questions bring to the surface is the very old problem of disciplinary protocols, assumptions that shape not only the answers we reach but more fundamentally the very nature of our inquiry by limiting the kinds of questions that get asked in the first place. In the field of literary history, for example, some of the most intriguing questions have recently been posed from the perspective of readers and their books, and not only books now considered canonical texts, but as well those that seem often to fall outside the domain of literary history. Recent work in book history has dramatically shown that the subject of most literary history, the canon, constitutes but a tiny fraction of the books produced and consumed at any point in time.

The history of canonical texts provides one picture of the literary past, but not a complete picture and not really the most accurate one. "Literary history is an artifice," Robert Darnton writes in *The Forbidden Best-Sellers of Pre-Revolutionary France*, "pieced together over many generations, shortened here and lengthened there, worn thin in some places, patched over in others, and laced through everywhere with anachronism. It bears little relation to the actual experience of literature in the past."[3] This is the problem now facing literary history: how to develop a more inclusive, perhaps even more accurate, picture of what people actually read in the past—works that were once widely enjoyed and have now all but disappeared from literary history—and how these works were experienced and imagined, and further, how they inflected the literature of their own time and in turn shaped and constituted social and imaginative experience. There are many good reasons for pursuing such a literary history. "Accuracy" itself is, of course, an admirable goal for historical research. For those interested in the social dimensions of literary experience and in the history of reading, such a literary history provides not simply a new set of data but also a broader and more complex context within which to understand the social functions of literature. And for scholars interested primarily in the history of aesthetics it provides a richer historical context within which to examine the central problems of the history of artistic forms: why some works are able to transcend their historical and cultural moment while others disappear forever or are relegated to the status of historical curiosities with no continuing social life.

There are reasons enough for excavating this fuller history of what people read in the past, but the fundamental challenge is how to go about this project. To this there is no simple answer, and it emerges as a central problem—both practical and theoretical—that confronts literary critics and historians of the book. Indeed, recognizing the problem is really the easy part. As Takagi Gen puts it in his recent book on nineteenth-century Japanese fiction: "If we do not investigate that group of works which has been neglected as not being worth looking at [in terms of literary value], then we will be ignoring the majority of nineteenth-century Japanese novels."[4] And "majority" does not really do the problem justice.[5] But how does one write a history of this vast majority, of all those titles that have been written out of literary history?

---

3. Darnton, *The Forbidden Best-Sellers of Pre-Revolutionary France*, xvii.

4. Takagi, *Edo yomihon no kenkyū*, p. 423.

5. See Moretti, "The Slaughterhouse of Literature," p. 207: "The majority of books disappear forever—and 'majority' actually misses the point: if we set today's canon of

How does one write a history that more accurately reflects the "actual experience of literature in the past"?

There have been, among literary historians working on this problem, three kinds of answers. The first and most obvious is simply to read, to read more. This is a noble ambition and obviously the first step, to read books that have been consigned to literary oblivion, to read lost best-sellers and so to resurrect something of the reading experience of times now long past. But there are limits. The only study of which I know that has seriously attempted to read an entire corpus is Wendy Griswold's magnificent study of the Nigerian novel.[6] But this corpus of texts totaled less than a thousand titles. That is a *huge* number, of course, but over seven thousand works of fiction were produced in nineteenth-century Japan. And even a totalizing approach to this body of work would be incomplete: if one were to read a title a day it would take roughly twenty years to complete the research—and this does not include the innumerable titles that have been lost completely

"Reading 'more' is always a good thing," writes Franco Moretti, "but not the solution."[7] What Moretti proposes instead is a new way of approaching this vast corpus of texts: literary history cannot be "what we are already doing, just more of it," it will have to be different, not close reading but *distant reading* secondhand, "a patch work of other people's research, *without a single direct textual reading*. . . . [T]he ambition is now directly proportional *to the distance from the text*: the more ambitious the project, the greater the distance must be."[8] This is the second approach that scholars have taken to the problem of redefining the object of literary history and the result, one imagines, would be something like those books Perry Anderson produced in the field of history, such as *Passages from Antiquity to Feudalism* and *Lineages of the Absolutist State*: monumental and erudite works based entirely on secondary sources.

Literary history would no doubt benefit from this sort of synthetic approach, but the drawbacks are obvious and they suggest that the time

---

nineteenth-century British novels at two hundred titles (which is a very high figure), they would still be only about *0.5 percent* of all published novels."

6. See Griswold, *Bearing Witness.*

7. Moretti, "Conjectures on World Literature," p. 55.

8. Moretti, "Conjectures on World Literature," p. 57.

is not right for literary studies to take this step. As Anderson writes, "no interpretations are so fallible as those which rely on conclusions reached elsewhere as their elementary units of evidence" so that any such project must remain "precarious and conditional."[9] The problem in literary history is compounded by the fact that so little work has been done on noncanonical literature that the building blocks available for this sort of project are not yet suitable for producing a study that tries to redefine the field. It seems extremely unlikely that a work cobbled together out of research on canonical texts would be able to produce a study of what by its very nature it excludes.

The third approach is a hybrid and—one imagines as a result—the least theoretically satisfying. This approach has been to combine the first two: close reading supported by distant reading or vice versa. This strategy entails reading through the archive and then attempting to generalize outward using a variety of methods, some derived from traditional literary history and others, such as statistics and sampling, borrowed from work on the history of the book. Such an approach too, of course, has pitfalls, the most serious of which seems to me the risk of methodological incoherence or a certain slippage between and among various sets of assumptions, methods, and techniques. That said, such a synthetic approach has produced probably the best and most provocative scholarship on the topic of noncanonical texts, for example David Wang's *Fin-de-Siècle Splendor* on late Qing fiction in China and Margaret Cohen's *The Sentimental Education of the Novel* on nineteenth-century France, two books that have inspired my own work.

Even if we accept the idea of a methodological compromise, however, there remains the enormous problem of selection: how to choose which books to read out of the thousands available. "Delimiting the field of inquiry is as important as recovering forgotten material," Cohen writes in *The Sentimental Education of the Novel*, "indeed, without delimitation, there would be no recovery."[10] Antonio Gramsci also turned to this problem of delimiting the field in a section of the *Prison Notebooks* titled "Criteria of Method": "On the question of choice: other than the critic's intuition or the systematic study of all literature (a colossal

9. P. Anderson, *Passages from Antiquity to Feudalism*, p. 8.
10. Cohen, *The Sentimental Education of the Novel*, p. 23.

and almost impossible undertaking for a single individual), the simple criterion appears to be that based on the 'success' of a book in two senses—'success with readers' and 'success with publishers.'"[11]

I have tried to use "success" as the basic method of selection, a way of delimiting the literary field of nineteenth-century Japan. But determining the commercial success of novels is not easy. In the very late nineteenth and twentieth centuries, we have a lot to go on—numbers of printings for individual titles, sizes of print runs, publishers' lists, letters to the editor in newspapers—but very little of this data is available for the early nineteenth century. Occasionally we know something of the sales or print runs of individual titles, but we do not have enough information on the cultural field to create a larger landscape or horizon in which to place these examples. We may know that a title was reprinted several times over a certain period, but we do not really know if this is above or below the average or mean for other books.

The records of lending libraries provide a different source of information but, again, the records are quite fragmentary: there are only two extant catalogues for lending libraries operating in the early nineteenth century. The records of the Daisō lending library are intriguing because they provide evidence that the library held as many as five or six copies of some fiction titles while most titles were not kept in duplicate. In his study of Daisō's catalogue, noting the preponderance of duplicates for *ninjōbon*, a genre of sentimental fiction, Nagatomo Chiyoji notes that "among late Edo period fiction, *ninjōbon* were probably the most widely read" titles at the library.[12] This is not much information to go on, but it is a lead, and when we add to this what we can glean from contemporary accounts of reading or from late eighteenth- and early nineteenth-century catalogues and reviews, we can begin to piece together something of the experience of reading in this century.

What follows, then, is a history of literary successes across the long nineteenth century that traces a genealogy of sentimental and melodramatic fiction from the late eighteenth century to the early twentieth century. I have tried to look at the problem of the long nineteenth century from a series of angles and using the hybrid methodology that I

11. Gramsci, *Selections from Cultural Writings*, p. 113.

12. Nagatomo, *Kinsei kashihon'ya no kenkyū*, p. 159.

have described above: close readings of particular literary texts, and broader, more distant, explorations of the ways in which the texts circulated and lived out their social lives. In the chapters that follow I have tried always to keep these two methodological strands in dialogue but the relative weight given to each varies from chapter to chapter. Chapters 1 and 3 and the Epilogue are examples of more "distant" approaches to literary history while Chapters 2 and 4 focus on close readings of specific texts. I began this introduction with numbers because numbers were what first allowed me to pose the questions that underpin this study; but numbers are only part of the story I wish to tell—or more exactly, numbers allow access only to part of the story that I wish to tell. So numbers and charts appear from time to time in the body of the chapters but numbers should not be seen as the governing concern of this book. As I will explain in more detail in Chapter 1, numbers allow us to pose new questions, but the answers to these questions often necessitate that we turn to other sets of tools, tools more familiar to literary history and criticism such as the close reading of individual works and an attention to form and genre.

Chapter 1 returns to the series of questions raised above: why write the history of the novel in nineteenth-century Japan, why the long nineteenth century and not the familiar short nineteenth century, and why the novel? The next chapter looks at the fiction of sentiment from the late eighteenth through the mid-nineteenth centuries. Here I examine a variety of genres in which the sentimental imagination can be seen in full flight across this period—the libretti of the puppet theater, *sharebon*, *kusazōshi*, and *ninjōbon*—in an attempt to trace the emergence of a nineteenth-century mode of sentiment and melodrama that had begun to diverge from the stark and uncompromising vision of eighteenth-century aesthetics. Chapter 3 considers the history of the importation and translation of texts from the mid-eighteenth century through the first decade of the twentieth century; here I am interested in situating the emergence of a domestic fiction market in relation to the trans-national novelistic trade, the center of which shifted during the nineteenth century from the novels of late imperial China to those of Europe and America. In the final chapter, I trace the genealogy of melodrama and sentiment into the Meiji period, looking at both the continuities of generic practices and the ways in which these continuities were reshaped by—and in their turn helped to shape the experience of—new political and social contexts. In the Epilogue, I turn briefly to the problem of situating the history of the nineteenth-century Japanese novel within a larger history of the novel across a global nineteenth century.

Practices of the Sentimental Imagination is governed throughout by a deep historicist impulse, but it is not a work of New Historicism or of cultural history. In many ways this study began as a reaction against what have become, after several decades of important work, the obvious methodological limitations of New Historicism. The most important of these is the foundational role that anecdote has played in much work of a historicist bent over the last quarter century. Anecdote has a very powerful and appealing narrative function because it allows the historian to capture complex, even contradictory, elements of a historical moment in a vivid and arresting image. The thick description that underpins the anecdote suggests an attention to detail and an allowance for the unevenness of the historical record. But to anyone who works with historical materials and on historical problems, and is therefore daily confronted with the inherent untidiness of any historicism, the very clarity and often schematic nature of the picture that emerges from much New Historicist work suggests an important elision. The myth that underlies anecdotal work is that an anecdote chosen almost at random can stand for an entire age, thus very much effacing the innate intractability of the historical record. Fundamentally, the attempt to choreograph different historical registers runs the very serious risk of rendering once again invisible those histories that are least familiar, most fragile and contingent, and again we are left with the standard historical narrative—thicker, no doubt, and perhaps drawn with more nuance, but not fundamentally challenged or changed.

Recent work in cultural history has pointed in almost the opposite direction: that the different registers of history have different chronologies, different rhythms, different historicities, that the history of reading, for example, is not the same as political or economic history or the history of technology. In many ways, this book is deeply indebted to the methodologies of cultural history and is, I hope, an example of how the insights of cultural history might be extended in new directions. But to take the critique that underwrites much work in cultural history seriously suggests that at one level literary history—and especially a historical attention to form—needs to be uncoupled from larger narratives of the history of culture so that the properly historical character of the formal elements in literary history can be made clear.

Every intellectual project is, of course, defined as much by what it does not do—or what it cannot do—as by what it does. The nature of these limitations is both practical and epistemological. On the one hand, a project is defined in terms of time and resources; on the other hand, it is defined in terms of a specific research program: I look at novels and not plays, tears and not laughter, the nineteenth century and not the eighteenth or seventeenth century. Too often, the distinction between practical and epistemological limits and boundaries becomes blurred or confused and a danger emerges when one tries to justify what are essentially practical limitations as epistemological dictates. Everyone should take responsibility for the intellectual contours of their scholarship, but there is a tendency in academic work to make all of these contours seem natural, even inevitable.

At the end of his chapter on Stendhal in *Mimesis*, Erich Auerbach writes that "we must, unfortunately, forego discussing the rise of modern Russian realism . . . even in the most general way; for our purpose, this is impossible when one cannot read the works in their original language."[13] Every intellectual project should strive for this degree of candor, recognizing that some limitations are inevitable and need not be explained away by attempting to justify every decision—or incision—on epistemological or theoretical grounds. This problem has very much shaped the approach of literary historians to the nineteenth century. In many ways, the *field* of early modern literature is quite different from that of modern literature: there are different disciplinary protocols, different bibliographical conventions, and different types of training; indeed, there is an entire history of how the fields have emerged as so distinct and why they have remained distinct for so long. There are good disciplinary reasons for a study of early modern fiction to end in 1868 and a study of modern fiction to pick up at this point. But these are *disciplinary* rather than *intellectual* reasons, and they should be recognized as such. Too much time and intellectual labor is ex-

13. Auerbach, *Mimesis*, p. 492.

pended in tracing the reasons why a study of the novel circa 1890 should make no reference to the fiction of the 1820s and 1830s despite the fact that we know that titles by writers such as Kyokutei Bakin and Tamenaga Shunsui were being reprinted and read well into the early twentieth century—often by the very writers of this new fiction.

My own work too has been shaped by certain limitations and boundaries. Where these limitations matter I have tried to explain them in theoretical terms—the problems described above: why the novel and not drama, why tears and not laughter, why the long nineteenth century. Chapter 1 is an explicit meditation on some of these problems and I return to them often in the course of the chapters that follow. But there are also practical problems that have shaped my approach to this subject. The *biggest* is simply that there are thousands of titles and no way to read all of them. I have tried to use "success" as a barometer, but it is not perfect, and there are no doubt texts which I have not treated which would be equally well suited—even better suited—to this sort of a study. Furthermore, the longer I worked on this project, the more I understood that Japanese literature in the nineteenth century was situated within a world of literature that extends beyond its boundaries. Where possible, I have tried to draw out the implications of this larger world. In Chapter 3, for example, I have looked at the importation to Japan—and the translation into Japanese—of novels both from late imperial China and from nineteenth-century Europe; in Chapter 4, I have touched upon the problem of the importation of Japanese fiction into colonial Korea; and in my Epilogue, I have tried to situate the history of late nineteenth-century Japanese fiction in the world literary market at the turn of the twentieth century. I have left these questions open because to make summary judgments at this point seems counter-productive and because they are problems to which I intend to return in the future and to which I hope others will turn.

CHAPTER 1

The Short Nineteenth Century, the Long Nineteenth Century, and the Garden of Literary Forms

In the search for tears, we soon encounter the book. . . .

—Anne Vincent-Buffault, *The History of Tears*

Tears, the Book, and the History of the Literary Function

Over the course of the nineteenth century, the Japanese reading public was often invited to tears. Writers frequently invoked tears in prefaces and apostrophes to the reader; in 1787, Tanishi Kin'gyo imagined that some readers of his *Keiseikai tora no maki* "would be moved, others weep, and still others be so captivated by the story that they lose the power to move,"[1] while in the 1799 preface to his *Chūshin suikoden*, Santō Kyōden observed that "when the people of the marketplace see plays or read libretti, should there happen to be instances of loyalty, filial piety, virtue, or chastity they are moved and unable to hold back tears of sorrow."[2] Readers were given models of idealized weeping in the frequent tearful scenes of nineteenth-century fiction: characters might weep upon hearing or telling the unhappy fate of others or shed tears over their own misfortunes. In some texts, tears were ubiquitous

1. Tanishi Kin'gyo, *Keisei tora no maki*, p. 303.
2. Santō Kyōden, *Chūshin suikoden*, p. 83.

while in others a well-timed scene of highly charged emotion served as a delicate counterpoint to the wide-ranging adventures of heroes and villains. At the turn of the nineteenth century, Shikitei Sanba remarked that "recently books of wit are dying out and being replaced by weeping books";[3] at the end of that century, a book reviewer might mention how he was brought to tears by a novel, and readers of serialized fiction were provided the opportunity to shed rather public tears in letters to the editor containing a range of emotions from sympathy to outrage over the fortunes of their favorite characters.

In his essay "History or Literature?" Roland Barthes suggested that "a history of tears" could reveal "as much about those who shed them as about the man who made them flow."[4] Barthes proposed that if literary criticism focused upon "production, communication, and consumption" and concerned itself with "activities and institutions, not with individuals"—if, in other words, it were to become "sociological"—literary history would begin to reveal the "function" of literature "in the general economy of our society."[5] Barthes called this the *history of the literary function.* In the last several decades, through studies on various aspects of the culture of the book—from printing to publishing, from authorship to reading, from colportage to lending libraries—the sociological study of literary texts and the history of the book have produced a remarkable body of work on the social dimensions of literature. This work has, however, tended away from rather than toward the "confrontation of society and rhetoric" that Barthes had in mind as the object of literary history.[6] Instead, the study of literary forms and the history of the book have evolved as two relatively autonomous approaches to texts. It is in this context that Franco Moretti has recently suggested the need for a "bridge" between book history and the morphological study of forms: "There is great diplomacy between book historians and literary historians, but true engagement is still to come."[7]

---

3. Shikitei Sanba, *Kejō suigen maku no soto*, p. 298.
4. Barthes, "History or Literature?," p. 158
5. Barthes, "History or Literature?," p. 161 and p. 172.
6. Barthes, "Rhetorical Analysis," p. 84.
7. Moretti, *Atlas of the European Novel*, p. 143.

This book is an attempt to contribute to such an engagement by looking historically at the situation of fiction in nineteenth-century Japan and by taking seriously the methods both of social history and of formal analysis. Hence the hybrid methodology of this study, with an attention, on the one hand, to numbers and to the quantitative derived from work in social history, and, on the other, a series of close readings of individual texts which examine historical morphology. Numbers are often partial and partisan, "nothing more than symptoms produced by the historian himself," as Robert Darnton once observed in warning against "an overcommitment to the quantification of culture" and urging attention to "the symbolic element in social intercourse."[8] But numbers are also useful particularly for the revision of traditional periodization, and for "calling in question the old postulate that all elements of a society follow a homogeneous and identical evolution."[9] I have relied on numbers—numbers of books published and numbers of books circulated—precisely because they tell a story that has escaped traditional Japanese literary history, because they suggest the need to rethink quite thoroughly the way in which Japanese literary history has been periodized. And this is the primary value of numbers, they "simplify the better to come to grips with their subject"[10] and so make accessible through patterns and series solutions to problems that remain virtually invisible within traditional literary histories.

This is what social history has to offer literary history. What formal analysis has to offer the study of the social is precisely that attention to the *symbolic element in social intercourse.* Tears are clues, and their traces can begin to lead us back into the symbolic world of which they were a part. If a history of tears can indeed tell us as much about those who shed them as about those who made them flow, it is because the production of tears itself has a social dimension, it is "a socially symbolic act." Literary texts afford the historian a glimpse of those "unresolvable social contradictions" to which these texts offer "imaginary or formal 'solutions,'" and so make accessible a register of history different from that made available through the study of institutions or the texts of

8. Darnton, *The Great Cat Massacre*, p. 258.
9. Furet, "Quantitative History," pp. 49–53.
10. Braudel, "History and the Social Sciences," p. 51.

intellectual history.[11] Literary and cultural texts are thus historical documents in the strict sense; by taking form seriously we can begin to have access to ideological worlds long since vanished, worlds to which quantitative history provides no access.

But to move from the traces of tears into symbolic worlds long since vanished—to move from individual texts and solitary acts of weeping to a general history of tears with a genuinely social dimension—the literary historian too has to turn to numbers. Kenneth Burke even suggested replacing "symbolic" with "statistical," arguing that, considered statistically, similar texts "become but different individuations of a common paradigm. As so considered, they become 'symbolic of something'—they become 'representative' of a social trend."[12] "'Statistical' analysis," Burke argued, "discloses the ways in which a 'symbolic' act is 'representative.'"[13] Literary historians thus properly begin with publishers' lists and guild records, with library and auction catalogues, with whatever evidence they have at their disposal. And if the true task of literary history is to enable the historian "to pose questions that the texts gave an answer to, and thereby to discover how the contemporary reader could have viewed and understood the work,"[14] the real empha-

11. See Jameson, *The Political Unconscious*, especially pp. 76–82. Jameson has argued (p. 79) that "by construing purely formal patterns as a symbolic enactment of the social within the formal and aesthetic," it becomes possible to understand the truly social dimension of narrative, the "ideology of form" in which "ideology is not something which informs or invests symbolic production; rather the aesthetic act is itself ideological, and the production of aesthetic or narrative form is to be seen as an ideological act in its own right, with the function of inventing imaginary or formal 'solutions' to unresolvable social contradictions."

12. Burke, *The Philosophy of Literary Form*, p. 18 and p. 19.

13. Burke, *The Philosophy of Literary Form*, p. 25.

14. See Jauss, "Literary History as a Challenge to Literary Theory," p. 28. It is striking that at roughly the same time the *Annales* historians were developing the notion of 'serial history' in France, Jauss and other members of the Konstanz school were turning to the idea of the 'series' as a tool for literary history. Thus, early on in developing his method of historical reception, Jauss writes that: "The theory of the aesthetics of reception . . . demands that one insert the individual work into its 'literary series' to recognize its historical position and significance in context of the experience of literature" (Jauss, "Literary History as a Challenge to Literary Theory," p. 32). In such a literary series, Jauss writes, "an important work, one that indicates a new direction in the literary process, is surrounded by an unsurveyable production of works that correspond to the

sis of literary history has to be on those books whose now unfamiliar titles recur with such frequency in the catalogues of lending libraries and the diaries and letters of readers. "Normal literature," as Franco Moretti has called it, this is the perfect object for a history of nineteenth-century Japanese fiction, a literature essentially without masterpieces.[15]

Japan's Two Nineteenth Centuries

Over the course of the nineteenth century, the Japanese reading public was often invited to tears. But who were these readers and how did they read? The history of reading has gained increasing attention from scholars of literature as literary history moves from an almost exclusive concern with the history of literary production and becomes more interested in the circulation and consumption of texts. But any attempt at a history of the practices of reading remains greatly complicated by protocols and problems of evidence. Most directly, such evidence might take the form of manuscript marginalia, but the existence—and legibility—of such notes varies greatly among different cultural milieu and varies even within the same cultural setting; and then again, the writings of readers are themselves evidence of a practice that has ceased to be consumption and has crossed over to production.

Cultural representations of reading in both literature—in prefaces, apostrophes, and asides—and in the graphic arts—in book illustrations, but also in paintings and prints—offer a wealth of indirect evidence of habits and protocols of reading even if such evidence is itself ambiguous, resisting straightforward interpretation.[16] I have reproduced two such

---

traditional expectations or images concerning reality, and that thus in their social index are to be no less valued than the solitary novelty of the great work" ("Literary History as a Challenge to Literary Theory," p. 12).

15. See Moretti, "The Soul and the Harpy," p. 15.

16. Roger Chartier has addressed this problem in his "Popular Appropriations: Readers and Their Books," p. 94: "When we are confronted with these texts and images that bring popular readers into our view, caution is indispensable. Whatever they might be, these representations never involve immediate and transparent relations with the practices they describe. All are lodged in the specific modes of their production, the interests and intentions that produced them, the genres in which they were inscribed, and the audiences at which they were aimed. To reconstruct the conventions that governed

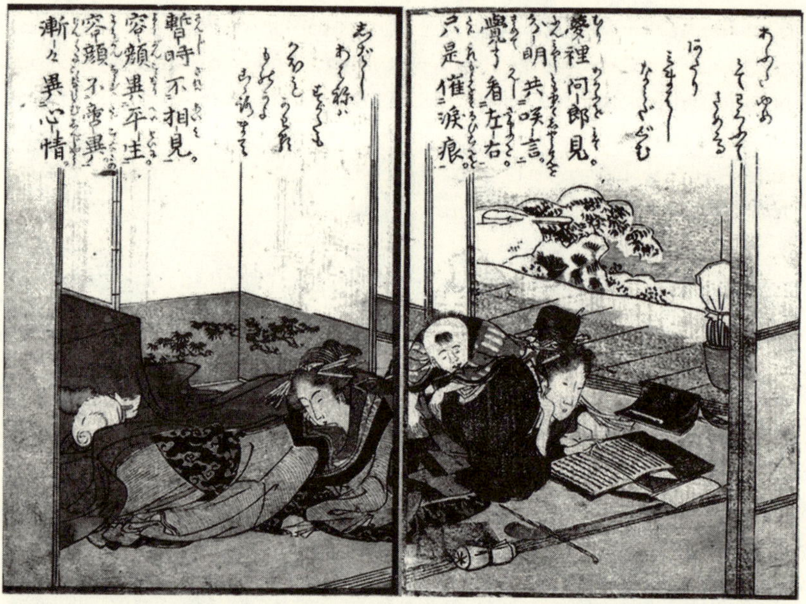

Fig. 1 From Fuji no Karamaro's *Itako zekkushū* (1802), illustration by Katsushika Hokusai. Smithsonian Institution Libraries, Freer Gallery of Art and Arthur M. Sackler Gallery Library Special Collection, Smithsonian Institution, Washington, D.C.

representations of reading from the two historical bookends of this project. The first (Figure 1) is a woodblock print done by Katsushika Hokusai in 1802 as an illustration for the *Itako zekkushū*, a book of verse by Fuji no Karamaro.[17] The other (Figure 2) is oil on canvas, painted by Kuroda Seiki during a sojourn at Gray in the east of France and displayed in the 1891 Salon of the Société des Artistes Français. The painting is now housed at the Tokyo National Museum. The representations appear to illustrate not just two different practices of reading but really two different worlds. First, the world of the early nineteenth century, the world of woodblock printing with its attendant mode of reading. Here the reader is situated in the semipublic world of the demimonde, on the border between the private and public, reclining, a child peering over her shoulder, her companion in tears, distraught over her lover's absence.

---

literate representations of the popular, therefore, we must decipher the strong but subtle bond that ties these representations to the social practices that are their object."

17. For a complete reproduction of the *Itako zekkushū,* see Nagata ed., *Hokusai kyōka ehon.* The book was banned at the beginning of 1803, the printing blocks burned, and its author, Fuji no Karamaro, and his publisher, Tsutaya Jūzaburō, arrested.

Fig. 2 *Reading* (*Dokusho*, 1891), by Kuroda Seiki.
Tokyo National Museum. Image: TNM Image Archives. Source: http://TnmArchives.jp/

Then, the more private world of the modern reader from the late nineteenth century: she sits upright and alone, shut up in a room, closed off from the outside world, the very picture of the post-Romantic reader.

These images appear perfectly to illustrate and to bear out in graphic detail the shift in readerly habits and sensibilities over the course of the nineteenth century that Maeda Ai has detailed in his pioneering work on the history of reading in nineteenth-century Japan. As Maeda writes, there was in the decades following the Meiji Restoration a radical reorganization of print culture and an attendant shift in modes of reading and apprehension—a development Maeda describes as the "emergence of the modern reader." For Maeda, reading moved from essentially a uniform to a pluralistic and individual activity and from a group to a solitary activity, shifts that themselves bear an intimate relationship with the hallmark of the modern reader—silent reading.[18]

Nagamine Shigetoshi has recently expanded on Maeda's argument, suggesting that two factors greatly shaped the emergence of new readerly practices at the end of the nineteenth century. The first is a shift in the sites of reading with the development of new "public spaces"—the train, the prison, the newspaper reading room, and ultimately the public library—in which reading aloud was forbidden and in which (and through which) a generation of readers were gradually trained (we might say disciplined) to read silently.[19] The second is an overall shift from "intensive reading" to "extensive reading" echoing arguments for a *Leserevolution* in eighteenth-century Europe.[20] For Nagamine, these transformations in reading habits were occasioned by the growth of printing and publishing based on moveable type. Over the course of the 1890s, "the absolute number of publications continued to rise due to the steady development of movable type printing," leading to the birth of "a mode of reading as consumption" in which "the book—formerly an object of reverence as a 'sacred text'—was transfigured into a commodity the same as other goods."[21]

Figure 3 is based on Yayoshi Mitsunaga's statistics for the number of book and magazine titles published during the Meiji and Taishō (1912–1926) eras and is intended to give some sense of the publishing activities in the final decades of the nineteenth century and the opening decades of the twentieth century.[22]

---

18. See Maeda, *Kindai dokusha no seiritsu.*

19. Nagamine, *Zasshi to dokusha no kindai*, pp. 35–76.

20. See Nagamine, *Zasshi to dokusha no kindai*, p. 9. Nagamine's terms are *seidoku* 精読 (intensive reading) and *tadoku* 多読 (extensive reading). On the problem of a *Leserevolution* in eighteenth-century Europe, see Engelsing, *Der Bürger als Leser* and Schön, *Der Verlust der Sinnlichkeit.*

21. Nagamine, *Zasshi to dokusha no kindai*, p. 3, p. 8, and p. 5. The term for "a mode of reading as consumption" is *shōhiteki na dokushohō* (消費的な読書法).

22. Yayoshi, *Mikan shiryō ni yoru Nihon shuppan bunka*, vol.5, pp. 279–94.

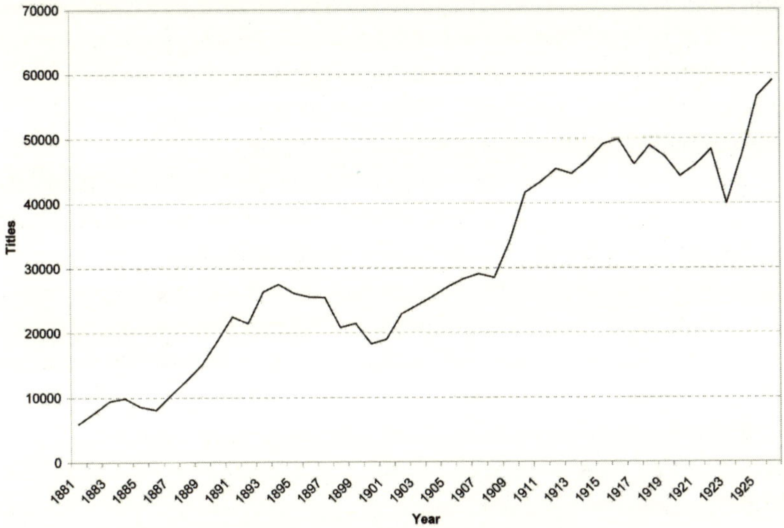

Fig. 3 The Meiji Print Revolution: Book and Magazine Titles, 1881–1926

Yayoshi's numbers, derived from statistics kept by the Police Bureau of the Ministry of the Interior (Naimushō keihokyoku), do indeed suggest a profound transformation in print culture over the final decades of the nineteenth century and the first several decades of the twentieth century; periodical titles of one sort or another alone account for roughly 60 to 75 percent of these titles, largely substantiating Nagamine's claim for the important place of new media like the newspaper and magazine in the readerly world of the early twentieth century.[23]

"The typographical industry set out to conquer the world during these years," Henri-Jean Martin has written of the late nineteenth century and there is no doubt that the history of print in late nineteenth- and early twentieth-century Japan was greatly impacted by this "conquest of the world."[24] But Yayoshi's numbers fail to give any sense of the world before the conquest, that other world suggested by Hokusai's print. What of the first eighty years of the nineteenth century? Or the final years of the eighteenth? What exactly was that culture of the book so completely transformed by the modern press? Many years ago, in his

23. See the preface to Nagamine, *Zasshi to dokusha no kindai*, especially iii.

24. Martin, *The History and the Power of Writing*, p. 454.

history of what he called "the Chinese World," Jacques Gernet warned of a "distortion of perspective" caused by an excessive focus on the history of the late nineteenth century through which "the history of the countries of East Asia fades away almost completely behind that of Western advances and conquests in this part of the world."[25] The best solution to this "distortion" would no doubt be simply to extend Yayoshi's numbers backward, to say 1800 or possibly 1750, but such efforts are hampered by the lack of reliable data before the 1880s. So without being able to reconstruct the entire landscape of the market for books around 1800, we might have to settle for the next best thing: to reconstruct a part of that market and then try to think through that part of the market's broader implications.

There is no reason to assume that any one segment of the book market would necessarily be more representative than any other, but for an inquiry concerned with the emergence of "reading as consumption," it would seem that fiction titles are a good index. Nineteenth-century reading patterns appear to indicate this. Tables 1 and 2, based on Nagatomo Chiyoji's pioneering work on the history of lending libraries in nineteenth-century Japan, suggest the unique place that fiction titles occupy within the two extant catalogues of nineteenth-century lending libraries.[26] Table 1 details the holdings of the Daisō lending library in Nagoya, the largest lending library of its time. Daisō was founded in 1767 and remained in operation through 1898, when its holdings were catalogued for auction. Table 2 details the holdings of a library run by Nakaya Shinzaemon in the spa town of Kinosaki in present-day Hyōgo Prefecture. Nakaya's library was in operation by 1802, and the collection was sold at auction in 1905. These are very different collections, composed of very different holdings, serving, no doubt, very different purposes. What they have in common, of course, is the significant position of fiction titles in their holdings; as Nagatomo himself writes, "It is clear that what we call early modern novels occupied a central position in the holdings of lending libraries."[27]

---

25. Gernet, *A History of Chinese Civilization*, p. 576.
26. See Nagatomo, *Kinsei kashihon'ya no kenkyū*.
27. Nagatomo, *Kinsei kashihon'ya no kenkyū*, p. 156.

Table 1
The Holdings of the Daisō Lending Library

Genre	Number of titles	Percentage	Copies	Percentage of titles with copies
Fiction	3,976	23.8	2,030	51.1
Ihara Saikaku	14	-	-	-
pornography	93	-	-	-
Hachimonjiya	297	-	2	0.7
didactic fiction	82	-	-	-
sharebon	802	-	327	40.8
kibyōshi/gōkan	1,482	-	1,061	71.6
kokkeibon	213	-	127	59.6
ninjōbon	359	-	314	87.5
yomihon	286	-	127	44.4
other fiction	348	-	72	20.7
Medical	352	2.0	-	-
Philosophy/religion	2,093	12.5	-	-
Education	488	2.9	-	-
Classics	300	1.8	-	-
Other	9,525	56.9	-	-
TOTAL	16,734	100.0	4,710	28.1

NOTE: Due to rounding, percentages may not total 100.00.
SOURCE: Adapted from Nagatomo, *Kinsei kashihon'ya no kenkyū*, pp. 153–58.

Table 2
The Holdings of Nakaya Shinzaemon's Lending Library at Kinosaki

Genre	Number of titles	Percentage of total titles
Jōruri	181	55.9
Fiction	90	27.8
Haikai/kyōka	10	3.1
Picture books	16	4.9
Popular religion	2	0.6
Sharebon	5	1.5
Essays, miscellany	20	6.2
TOTAL	324	100.0

SOURCE: Adapted from Nagatomo, *Kinsei kashihon'ya no kenkyū*, pp. 110–16.

In the case of Daisō, not only do these "early modern novels" represent an enormous portion of the library's holdings in absolute terms—nearly double the number of titles for philosophy and religion, more than ten times the number of books on medicine—but more interestingly, the number of duplicate copies of the same books suggests that fiction was differently stocked and circulated, an object of different readerly demands, than were other types of books. And in the case of Nakaya Shinzaemon's library, the numbers are even more striking: if we follow the early modern convention of including *jōruribon*, the libretti of the puppet theater, under the rubric of fiction, 84 percent of the texts available to a patron of the spas at Kinosaki were works of fiction.[28] Nagatomo mentions a book illustrating life in Kinosaki written in the 1840s and depicting patrons of the spa leisurely reading in bed and even while in the bath—and we know, statistically, that these patrons were most likely reading fiction.[29]

So what would a mapping of the nineteenth-century fiction market look like? In Figure 4, I have combined Ekkehard May's statistics (based on Yamazaki Fumoto's research)[30] on the printing of fiction titles between the 1750s and 1868 with my own (based on the National Diet Library's catalogue of works published in the Meiji period)[31] for

---

28. In his *Kinsei mono no hon Edo sakusha burui* (1834), the most important and exhaustive taxonomy of fiction in early modern Japan, Kyokutei Bakin had planned to devote an entire section to authors of *jōruri* 浄瑠璃 and makes no distinction between such works and other genres of fiction such as *akahon* 赤本, *sharebon* 洒落本, *chūhon* 中本, and *yomihon* 読本. Bakin had outlined four volumes for his study but completed only the first volume and part of the second. On reading the libretti of the puppet theater as fiction, see Nagatomo, *Edo no shomotsu to dokusho*, pp. 197–99.

29. Nagatomo, *Kinsei kashihon'ya no kenkyū*, pp. 120–21, and p. 177. The book is *Ehon Kinosaki miyage* written in 1842. Catalogues of lending libraries are, of course, historical records of a peculiar kind. As Moretti has put it in considering the catalogues of English lending libraries "we know what books were on the shelves, but not whether they were read or not. Still, this major limitation makes a study of what was on the market even more significant: if we cannot know what people *did* actually read, finding out what they *could* (or could *not*) read is really all we can do." Moretti, *Atlas of the European Novel*, p. 144.

30. See May, *Die Kommerzialisierung der japanischen Literatur in der späten Edo-Zeit*, pp. 7–8 and Yamazaki, *Nihon shōsetsu shomoku nenpyō.*

31. Kokuritsu kokkai toshokan ed., *Meijiki kankō tosho mokuroku.*

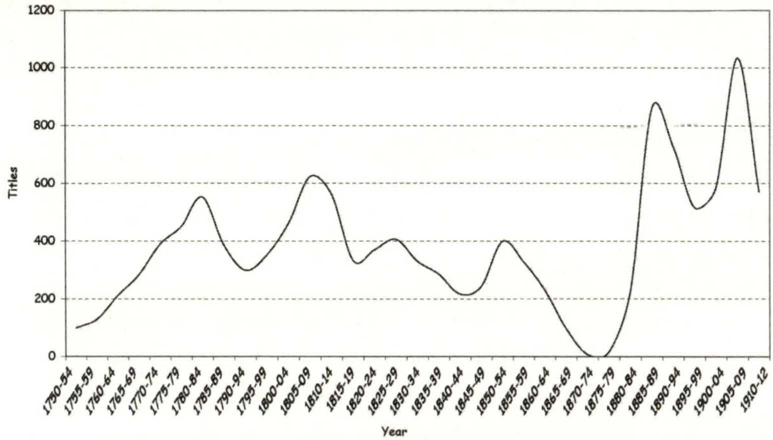

Fig. 4 The Long Nineteenth Century of the Japanese Novel

the period between 1868 and 1912 to show what one segment of the book market looked like across the nineteenth century, across a sort of *long* nineteenth century. This graph has several major limitations. It represents only titles with no indication of the relative size of print runs, and only new titles with no sense of the reproduction or circulation of older titles. So we are not dealing even with the entire market for fiction but with a portion of that market. And then too, this figure has the additional limitations of not including the libretti of the puppet theater (which occupied such an important place in the libraries of the early modern period) and of only representing *book* titles without taking into account the fiction published in dailies (beginning in the 1880s) or periodicals (beginning in the 1890s), two elements of the emerging print culture highlighted in both Yayoshi's numbers and Nagamine's work. Limitations all, and some no doubt more significant than others.

Despite these limitations, however, the graph is immediately suggestive of a basic fact: how *little* the market grew, even in the late nineteenth century. Indeed, there were 1,085 titles published in the first decade of the nineteenth century and 1,243 in the last decade of that century, an increase of 14.5 percent. These numbers are slightly misleading because the 1890s happen to mark a low ebb in the number of new fiction titles published; but even if we take instead the 1,620 titles published in the first decade of the twentieth century, we find only an increase of 50 percent. Such an increase is not insignificant—nor even is an increase of 14 or 15 percent—but neither is it revolutionary, certainly not when compared to the increase of fiction titles between the 1750s and the first decade of the nineteenth century, an increase of some 380 percent. There were certainly more fiction titles in 1900 than in 1800, and this number would no doubt swell if it could take account of larger print runs and a longer shelf life for books, and if it spoke to the number of titles published in magazines and newspapers. Still these numbers suggest that even if there were a printing revolution—even if the total number of book titles published each year doubled or trebled in the three or four decades spanning the turn of the century—this revolution had a relatively small impact on the fiction market, which continued to increase incrementally and remained relatively stable. And more than that, the numbers seem to suggest that whatever changes the market underwent at the end of the nineteenth century—and however it was impacted by new modes of industrial print culture (from the production of paper to the advent of the steam press)—these changes have to be seen as part of the history of a fiction market that goes back at least to the seventeenth century and that took off during the middle of the eighteenth century.

The history of printing in Japan suggests the need for such a long-range approach. As Peter Kornicki has noted, the history of printing in Japan is both extraordinarily long and extraordinarily counter-intuitive: "After the introduction of printing technology in the eighth century, nearly a thousand years elapsed before printing established itself as the principal means for the production of books."[32] Similarly, moveable type was introduced from the Korean peninsula in the late sixteenth century and there was "a period of some 50 years in which moveable type was used extensively for the production of books," but

> moveable type printing had effectively come to an end by the 1650s. . . . As commercial publishers took over from the patronage arrangements of the early part of the [seventeenth] century, they reverted to block printing in order the better to respond to the demands of the market, and it is this familiar technology which governed the production of books for the remainder of the [early modern] period.[33]

32. Kornicki, *The Book in Japan*, p. 112.
33. Kornicki, *The Book in Japan*, pp. 129–30 and pp. 134–35.

It took nearly a millennium for block printing to have a notable impact—and several centuries for moveable type. The history of printing in Japan suggests that technical innovation has rarely had such a revolutionary impact as that suggested for the adoption of moveable type in the late nineteenth century. Indeed, the history of printing in Japan seems uncannily to bear out Fernand Braudel's conceit that "every invention that presents itself has to wait for years or even centuries before being introduced into real life."[34]

Braudel describes the history of technology—of technological change, invention, adoption—as an extremely complex and extremely *slow* process. That is not to say that revolutionary events and moments of paradigm shift do not exist alongside the "slow, mute, and complicated" structures of everyday life, but that such events are themselves embedded within a social framework. Weibe Bijker has proposed the idea of looking at the history of technology through the lens of "sociotechnical ensembles," arguing that "the development of technical designs cannot be explained solely by referring to the intrinsic properties of artifacts" but that "machines 'work' because they have been accepted by relevant social groups."[35] Whatever the impact of new technologies on the history of printing in late nineteenth-century Japan, these technologies were evolving within a set of social formations that had existed in relation to one another since at least the mid-eighteenth century. And whatever the impact of these technologies on social habits and customs, it was bound to be slow, complex, and uneven. Viewed from this perspective, a history of reading focused on the late nineteenth century is itself bound to distort in the very way that Gernet has argued,[36] and we might do well to think of the history of reading practices as more gradual, less revolutionary than is suggested either by the graphic representations I have given above or by Nagamine's argument.

Peter Kornicki has argued that reading for pleasure dates back at least to the seventeenth century and—based on cultural representations of reading—that by the mid-eighteenth century "intimate reading alone,

34. Braudel, *The Structures of Everyday Life*, p. 355.

35. Bijker, *Of Bicycles, Bakelites, and Bulbs*, pp. 14–15 and p. 270.

36. See note 26 above.

and probably in silence, was a common practice."[37] Indeed, the coexistence of various habits and modes of reading is suggested by Terakado Seiken in the preface to his 1832 work *Edo hanjōki*: "In the fifth month of 1831 I happened to fall sick. Unable to sit properly upright and read the works of the sages, I lay idly in bed reading miscellanies to chase away the gloom."[38] Intensive reading of a few sacred works on the one hand and extensive reading of miscellany on the other coexisting, and, more than that, serving complementary roles.

But what then of the readers depicted by Hokusai and Kuroda Seiki, who seem so distant one from another? How could two such representations of reading be more different? Surely something separates the experience of reading at the opening of the twentieth century from reading a century earlier? Roger Chartier suggested caution in approaching these sorts of representations of reading, and this sentiment is echoed by Adrian Johns who, in writing of the "nature of the book" in early modern England, has argued that "it may not really be justifiable to think of a clear and distinct division between modernity and its print culture, on the one hand, and the early modern world . . . on the other. When we probe beyond commonplace representations, this suggestion seems increasingly probable."[39] Indeed, as distant as Kuroda's reader seems from Hokusai's reader, this distance is itself belied by certain traces of continuity—the gendering of the readers, the association of the feminine with the consumption of fiction—that draw attention to a degree of stability over the course of the nineteenth century to which any history beginning in the 1860s or 1880s would be blind.

"Furthermore, There is a Garden of Literary Forms"

In *The History of Reading*, Alberto Manguel remarks that the chronology of reading "cannot be that of political history . . . [but] neither does the history of reading correspond to the chronologies of the histories of

37. See Kornicki, *The Book in Japan*, p. 262 and p. 266.

38. Terakado Seiken, *Edo hanjōki*, p. 4. Over half a century earlier, Itami Chin'en conjured a strikingly similar portrait of reading in the 1779 preface to his collection of short stories *Kara nishiki*: "When sitting, one reads the classics; when lying, one reads novels (*shōsetsu*)." Itami Chin'en, *Kara nishiki*, p. 554.

39. Johns, *The Nature of the Book*, p. 633.

literature."[40] A political history broken at mid-century by the events of 1868; a history of reading—based on a different chronology—extending over the course of a long nineteenth century; and what of the chronologies of literary forms, what of literary history? Several recent histories of the modern Japanese novel have posed the issue of literary historical chronology as a problem of the discursive formation of the concept of "literature" itself, arguing that it was only within a translated or indeed translingual conceptual framework of the late nineteenth century that modern understandings and usages of "literature" and "the novel" emerged in Japan. This insight, which points to the often overlooked or elided role that the historicity of concepts has in the histories that these concepts are themselves supposed neutrally to describe, was, indeed, suggested half a century ago by Nakamura Mitsuo:

> The interest that the history of the novel holds for us is that it has acted out, in the most representative of ways, the comedies and tragedies of Japanese culture. . . . Compared with other arts, the modern Japanese novel occupies a special position. Everyone knows that the special characteristic that runs not just through literature but also through all spheres of art in Japan is that there coexist cultural products of an indigenous tradition with modern forms developed under the influence of the West. . . . What is strange is that among all of these forms it is only in the domain of the novel that we cannot see such a coexistence or contrast. There is no doubt that contemporary Japanese novels are written based on Western notions of literature and that the word "novel" itself only came to be used in its present fashion under the influence of the modern Western novel, but there no longer exist any forms such as Japanese painting (*Nihonga*) or traditional music (*hōgaku*) to oppose it.[41]

Nakamura goes on to quote the novelist Nagai Kafū (1879–1959) that "pure Japanese literature completely died out in the late 1890s. Literature after that point was not Japanese literature. Formally, it was Western literature written in Japanese."[42] Mikhail Bakhtin has written of the novel that "it gets on poorly with other genres. . . . Wherever it triumphs, the other older genres go into decline."[43] And this is essentially what

40. Manguel, *The History of Reading*, p. 22.
41. Nakamura, *Nihon no kindai shōsetsu*, pp. 4–6.
42. Nagai Kafū, "Shin kichōsha nikki" quoted in Nakamura, *Nihon no kindai shōsetsu*, p. 7.
43. Bakhtin, "Epic and Novel," p. 4.

Nakamura is suggesting, that the history of the European novel in Japan (or, what amounts to the same thing, the history of the European novel written in Japanese) is one both of the triumph of the novel *and* of the decline of other genres of fiction. Among the arts, only the novel is unable to coexist with its rivals.

Given the rupture suggested by Nakamura, is it possible to think in terms of a long nineteenth century? Is it possible—or useful—to chart the history of the novel along the same axis as the history of other forms of fiction, forms that emerged in the seventeenth, eighteenth, or nineteenth centuries independently of "Western" notions of literature? Do not terms such as "the novel" and "fiction" impose on genres a normative relationship that is ahistorical and anachronistic? This is Haruo Shirane's argument in a recent essay on the construction of the canon in Japanese literature. "We've come to use the concept of 'the novel' to refer to a wide range of texts," Shirane writes, "we've come to call such genres as *monogatari*, *setsuwa*, *otogizōshi*, *kanazōshi*, *ukiyo-zōshi*, and *kibyōshi* medieval novels or early modern novels. But until [the introduction of various literary concepts from Europe in the late nineteenth century] such genres were regarded as being unrelated to one another."[44] If this is true, then the usefulness of such concepts for a history of nineteenth-century literature is limited or, worse yet, the possibility of writing a history of nineteenth-century Japanese fiction is itself called into question.

The historical record suggests otherwise. For instance, Kyokutei Bakin used the concept of "fiction" (*mono no hon*) to refer to an array of forms of various lengths, formats, and genres in his 1834 work of literary taxonomy *Classification of Recent Fiction Authors of Edo* (*Kinsei mono no hon Edo sakusha burui*). Bakin explains that the etymology of the term goes back to the eighteenth century: "From over a hundred years ago, all narratives in book form (*sōshi monogatari*) have been called *mono no hon* (物之本). That term is a contraction of *monogatari no hon* (物語之本) so as to simplify the rhythm of the word."[45] Bakin's *Classification* covers writers from the Kyōhō period (1716–36) onward and includes entries (often more than one) for all of the major writers of the late eighteenth and early nineteenth centuries—Bakin's friend and some-

44. Shirane, *Sōzōsareta koten*, p. 21.

45. Kyokutei Bakin, *Kinsei mono no hon Edo sakusha burui*, p. 123.

time rival Santō Kyōden, Kyōden's brother Santō Kyōzan, Ōta Nanpo, Ryūtei Tanehiko, Tamenaga Shunsui, Jippensha Ikku, Shikitei Sanba, and, of course, Bakin himself—as well as dozens of other writers of various degrees of fame and infamy. The *Classification* ranges over works of various styles from short comic pieces to long historical narratives and, significantly, was intended to include a section on the libretti of the puppet theater.[46] The most striking feature of Bakin's work is that although it is a classification of *authors*, the primary subdivision of the work is by *genre—akahon, sharebon, chūhon, yomihon, jōruri*—suggesting that not only were these genres understood relationally but that they were understood as themselves part of a larger classificatory system of *mono no hon* or "fiction," a classificatory system designed to encompass a range of works from the eleventh-century narrative of Murasaki Shikibu's *Genji monogatari* (*The Tale of Genji*) to recent satirical writings by Shikitei Sanba.

The history of discourse on fiction in nineteenth-century Japan is complicated by the fact that the late nineteenth century represents in Japan a time of "settlement," a moment in which "old patterns of discourse persist while new arise, both interacting vigorously to produce new discursive situations and perhaps an intensified sense of their historicity."[47] Thus whatever integrity Bakin's notion of "fiction" (*mono no hon*) had within eighteenth- and early nineteenth-century discourse on literature, it had come, by the close of the nineteenth century, to be replaced by the term "novel" (*shōsetsu* 小説) based, as Nakamura puts it, on Western notions of literature. Tomi Suzuki, for instance, looks at the mid 1880s as a moment of "paradigm change": the meaning of the term *shōsetsu*, a lexeme with a history going back almost two thousand years,

46. "Although there are many outstanding works among the recent *jōruri* of Edo," Bakin writes in a note at the front of his study, "the people of the word only remember the titles of the libretti and forget the names of the authors and writers." See Kyokutei Bakin, *Kinsei mono no hon Edo sakusha burui*, p. 6. Not only were such libretti circulated and read as works of fiction—as the holdings of the Daisō and Nakaya libraries suggest—but, by the mid-nineteenth century, they were seen to constitute a genre of fiction in their own right.

47. See J. G. A. Pocock's description of "periods of transition" in "Empire, revolution, and the end of early modernity," p. 311. Carol Gluck refers to the 1880s and 90s in Japan as a "time of settlement"; see Gluck, *Japan's Modern Myths*, especially pp. 17–21.

"changed radically" by having grafted onto it a new set of semantic values as a translation for the concept of the "novel."[48] Such a notion of "paradigm change" fits well with Nakamura's conception of literary history and works to substantiate claims for the totality of a break between early modern and modern worlds of fiction, between *cultural products of an indigenous tradition* on the one hand and *modern forms developed under the influence of the West* on the other. But such a conception puts the problem too simply and does not pay sufficient attention to *the intensified sense of historicity* of words and concepts in late nineteenth-century Japanese discourse.

Before turning to what is for Suzuki the locus classicus of this "paradigm change," *Shōsetsu shinzui*, Tsubouchi Shōyō's meditation on the essence of the novel, written between 1885 and 1886, it is worth pausing for a rudimentary philological exercise, a look at late nineteenth-century dictionaries. First, two early dictionaries from the 1860s, two decades before the publication of Shōyō's essay: Hori Tatsunosuke's *A Pocket Dictionary of the English and Japanese Languages* and Jack Hepburn's original 1867 *A Japanese and English Dictionary* (Table 3).

Table 3
Defining the Novel I: Pre-Meiji Dictionaries

Dictionary	Relevant entries
A Pocket Dictionary of the English and Japanese Languages (1862)	Romance, s. 造リ物語 Fiction, s. 小説モノ Story, s. 小説雑話 Narration, s. 物語
A Japanese and English Dictionary (1867)	Novel, Kusazōshi, sakumono-gatari Fiction, Tsukurigoto; tsukuri mono gatari; Shōsetsumono Narration, Monogatari Story, Hanashi, setsz [sic.], mono-gatari Tale, Hanashi, monogatari

SOURCES: *A Pocket Dictionary of the English and Japanese Languages*, compiled by Hori Tatsunosuke (Edo, 1862); *A Japanese and English Dictionary*, compiled by J. C. Hepburn (Shanghai: American Presbyterian Mission Press, 1867).

48. Suzuki, *Narrating the Self*, p. 19. On the history of the lexeme 小説 in East Asia, see Cho, "Chungguk, Hanguk, Ilbon 'sosol' ui gaenyom," pp. 310–49.

Table 4
Defining the Novel II: Mid-Meiji Dictionaries

Dictionary	Relevant entries
An English-Japanese Lexicon (1895)	Novel, n. 小説、人情本 Romance, n. 小説 Fiction, n. 想像、虚構; 虚説、小説、作リ話シ、虚偏
An Unabridged Japanese-English Dictionary (1896)	Shōsetsu 小説 n. A novel; fiction; story; Syn. Tsukuribanashi Tsukuribanashi 作話、小説 n. A made-up story; fictitious tale; fiction; fable Monogatari 物語 n. 1) Talking; conversation; collocution; gossip. 2) A tale either fictitious or real; a narration; a romance, or novel, or story; a history Mononohon 物本 n. A book, work, or pamphlet Ninjōbon 人情本 n. Novels, love-tales; Syn. Chūhon, Sharebon Chūhon 中本 n. Books of middle size; Books of love stories Saku-monogatari 作物語 n. A fiction; novel Tsukuri-monogatari 作物語 n. A fictitious story; fable; romance; fiction; novel Haishi 稗史 n. A novel, fiction, romance Syn, Kusazōshi, Shōsetsu Kusazoshi 草双紙 n. An illustrated story-book (read mostly by women and children)
A Japanese-English and English-Japanese Dictionary (1903)	*English-Japanese* Novel, n. Kusazōshi, saku-monogatari Fiction, n. Tsukuri-monogatari, tsukuri-mono, saku-mono Narration, n. Monogatari, noberu koto Story, n. Hanashi, setsu, mono-gatari Tale, n. Hanashi, monogatari *Japanese-English* Shōsetsu 小説 n. A story, novel, fiction. Syn. Kukuri-banashi Sakumono-gatari 作物語 n. A fiction, novel Tsukuri-mono-gatari 作物語 n. A novel, fictitious story, romance Kusazōshi 草双紙 n. Storybooks, the name of a kind of fictitious literature; a novel, a pamphlet Mono-gatari 物語 n. History, story, narration Hai-shi 稗史 n. A novel; fictitious storybook; romance

SOURCES: *An English-Japanese Lexicon*, 11th ed., compiled by Y. Shimada (Tokyo: M. Ōkura, 1895); *An Unabridged Japanese-English Dictionary*, compiled by Frank Brinkley (Tokyo: Sanseido, 1896); *A Japanese-English and English-Japanese Dictionary*, 7th ed., compiled by J. C. Hepburn (Tokyo: Z. P. Maruya and Co., 1903).

Both lexemes "novel" and "小説" are used but never as equivalences; "小説モノ" (*shōsetsu-mono*) is given as a translation for "fiction" in Hori's dictionary but the dictionary does not have an entry for "novel" as a noun;[49] Hepburn's dictionary, on the other hand, has an entry for novel but gives as its equivalents "*kusazōshi*" (草双紙) and "*saku-monogatari*" (作物語) and like Hori's dictionary uses "*shōsetsu-mono*" (小説モノ) as a translation for "fiction." Before the 1880s there is indeed no equivalence between "*shōsetsu*" and "novel"; but afterward? Table 4 shows three dictionaries from the 1890s and the first decade of the twentieth century: the eleventh edition of Y. Shimada's *An English-Japanese Lexicon*, Frank Brinkley's *An Unabridged Japanese-English Dictionary*, and the seventh edition of Hepburn's *A Japanese-English and English-Japanese Dictionary*.

"*Shōsetsu*" and "novel" are indeed used as equivalents in one way or another in each of the three dictionaries; but the semantic field also becomes extremely complex and varied. Brinkley's dictionary is the best example of this complexity although it runs through each of the dictionaries. Let us begin with "*shōsetsu*" (小説), which the dictionary defines as "a novel; fiction; story." So far so good, but the definition goes on to give as a synonym "*tsukuribanashi*" and in its definition for "*tsukuribanashi*" the dictionary gives two graphic equivalents, 作話 and 小説, suggesting the deep relationship between both concepts, but then goes on to define "*tsukuribanashi*" as "a made-up story, fictitious tale; fiction; fable" giving several possible equivalents, of which "novel" is not one. Rather, "novel" reappears in several other definitions which are not given as synonyms of "*shōsetsu*": the second definition of "*monogatari*" (物語); the definition of "*ninjōbon*" (人情本), an equivalence Brinkley's dictionary shares with Y. Shimada's dictionary; "*saku-monogatari*" (作物語) and "*tsukuri-monogatari*" (作物語), which are graphically though not semantically equivalent; and "*haishi*" (稗史). "*Haishi*," moreover, links back to "*shōsetsu*" by offering it as a synonym but also branches out in another direction by offering as another possible synonym "*kusazōshi*" (草双紙), defined as "an illustrated story-book (read mostly by women and children)." Brinkley's dictionary is a veritable palimpsest of semantic

49. Hori's dictionary does have an entry for 'novel' used as an adjective, for which it gives *atarashiki* 新シキ.

change. The other two dictionaries are similar. Shimada's gives "*shōsetsu*" (小説) as a translation not only for "novel" but also for "romance" and for "fiction"; Hepburn translates "*shōsetsu*" as "novel" but translates "novel" as "*kusazōshi*" or "*saku-monogatari*" just as in the first edition of his dictionary. And to make matters even more complex, one would also have to trace out the semantic history of the English word "novel" across the nineteenth century, a task more complex, no doubt, than it might at first glance seem.[50]

It is against the backdrop of this dense and complex semantic history that we have to situate any rereading of Shōyō's essay on the essence of the novel so that we might better understand its historicity and its place among older and newer patterns of discourse; and Shōyō's essay is itself—semantically—just as confused and confusing as Brinkley's dictionary. Indeed, Shōyō, at one point or another in his essay, uses virtually every lexeme that appears in the dictionaries above, in ways that often seem contradictory. This has often been considered one of the great shortcomings of *Shōsetsu shinzui* as a work of literary criticism, but contemporary dictionaries allow us to see that there is a reason for this great terminological confusion; Shōyō was not working against the backdrop of a blank semantic field that had been wiped clean by some shift—paradigmatic or otherwise—but against a dense and tightly woven semantic web, labyrinthine in character, in which vocabularies and languages from various discourses overlay each other. This essay dramatizes in the most extraordinary of ways the complexity of the situation facing an author sitting down to write a history and theory of the novel in late nineteenth-century Japan.

Suzuki suggests that *Shōsetsu shinzui*, the title of Shōyō's essay, "usually translated as 'the essence of the novel,' can also mean 'the (Western) novel as the essence of the *shōsetsu*.'"[51] But is Shōyō writing here of the history of the novel in the West? Or in Japan? Or China? In his section on the "development of the novel," Shōyō draws his examples from

---

50. In his book on *Dickens and his Readers*, for instance, George Ford remarks that "the word *novel* continued in the nineteenth century to be so inconclusive, so lacking in qualitative distinctions, that one has almost to summon a semanticist whenever the history of novel criticism is read." See Ford, *Dickens and his Readers*, p. 26.

51. Suzuki, *Narrating the Self*, p. 20.

Norman romance and Saxon ballads; *Sumiyoshi monogatari*, *Ise monogatari*, and *Genji monogatari*; Aesop and the *Zhuangzi*; *Xiyou ji* (*Journey to the West*), *Pilgrim's Progress*, and the *Faerie Queene*. For Shōyō, the rise of the novel does not begin with *Robinson Crusoe* in eighteenth-century England or even some centuries earlier with the Spanish picaresque; rather, the novel "develops" over the course of centuries, even millennia, through a slow process of morphological evolution. Given the nature of Shōyō's project it would have been possible—perhaps even likely—for him to draw a stark contrast between the novel and all other forms of narrative such as myth and romance. Not only does Shōyō fail at every turn to make such distinctions, he takes us in the other direction. The major limitation of Shōyō's work—and the source of his terminological confusion—is also its great charm: at the same time that he uses concepts ahistorically, he does so in an effort to make sense of what was for him an extremely complex empirical reality. And so he began a project to write a theory of the novel that would explain the European novel, early modern Japanese fiction, and the great novels of the Ming and Qing, a project—whatever its merits—the possibilities of which have gone largely unexplored since the late nineteenth century.

Rather than borrowing the notion of a Kuhnian paradigm shift, we might more usefully approach the issue from the perspective of historical semantics. A.-J. Greimas importantly argues for the lexeme as "a locus of an historical encounter." As a structuralist, Greimas insists on the fixed character of the lexeme, but he acknowledges that the lexeme is "of the order of an event and as such is subject to history." Lexemes are in continuous semantic flux, accruing new dimensions over time, disavowing old meanings. "In the course of history, lexemes are enriched with new semes. But that same history—being, to put it most extremely, the difference which separates one action of communication from another (for diachrony can encompass a duration of five seconds as well as five centuries)—that same history may empty the lexemes of some of their semes."[52] Greimas's notion of the historicity of the lexeme is especially useful because it describes the gradual and heterodox processes of semantic change for a particular lexeme—such as "*shōsetsu*" or "novel"—and thus makes legible the palimpsest of

52. Greimas, *Structural Semantics*, p. 41.

Brinkley's dictionary as a document of historical semantics. There is perhaps nothing revolutionary about this notion of semantic change, but in some sense that is the point: semantic change is itself rarely revolutionary and requires a methodology which is attentive to the non-revolutionary character of semic activity.

At the same time, Greimas's notion of the lexeme as being "of the order of an event" despite its "fixed character" is useful because it allows us to situate the problem of the semantic history of the concept of the novel within a framework central to debates in the history of ideas: *event* and *structure*. The language of paradigm change tends to highlight events at the expense of structure. Thus John Pocock, one of the first historians to adapt Thomas Kuhn's work on paradigms to the history of thought and one of the pioneers of a history of concepts which "places illocution at the center," has written that "text and event are for the historian nearly the same thing."[53] As Pocock explains:

> A history of the concept of, for example, 'the state' will in fact be a history of the various ways in which the words *status*, *Staat*, *état*, *estate*, *stato* and so forth have been used. . . . In this history, these words will not have been used on every occasion to convey the concept of the state in any continuous or cumulative sense whatever, so that the history of the language uses and speech acts in which the various cognates of *state* have been involved is not a history of the concept of the state.[54]

The implications of Pocock's work for literary history are extremely important. One might conceive of writing a history of the *novel* or the *shosetsu* or of *mono no hon*, but in each case these will be very different projects and there will be—importantly—virtually no overlap. A history of the "novel" will be a history of the various uses of this concept in the English-speaking world and so will be different from a history of, for instance, *le roman*, *il romanzo*, or *der Roman*. And a history of the *shōsetsu* will again be something different, as Masao Miyoshi's work has long argued. This is to acknowledge that generic distinctions and classifications have their own history and that they are often—and

53. Pocock, "Texts as Events: Reflections on the History of Political Thought," p. 24 and p. 22.

54. Pocock, "Concepts and Discourses: A Difference in Culture?," p. 53

sometimes mendaciously—implicated in the very history that they are supposed neutrally to describe.[55]

The notion of structure takes us in a very different direction, one that may seem, by contrast, to run the risk of being ahistorical. Reinhart Koselleck has highlighted the structural potential of concepts in historical research by arguing that historical semantics allows us to see that "every concept entering into a narrative or representation (eg. state, democracy, army, and party, to cite only general concepts) renders relations discernible by a refusal to take on their uniqueness." Thus concepts "not only teach us of the singularity (for us) of past meanings," as discourse analysis argues, but also contain within themselves a "structural potential" for "dealing with the contemporaneous in the noncontemporary." Concepts are thus useful for historical research because they provide for the historian "*formal categories which are the conditions of possible histories*";[56] they indeed allow for the very possibility of comparative work, whether that work is comparative across geographical or temporal borders.

Both Pocock and Koselleck are writing on the history of political thought; but substitute the word *novel* in the above passages for the word *state*, and what I have in mind will become extremely clear. What Koselleck highlights is the potential that concepts such as "novel" have for *dealing with the contemporaneous in the noncontemporary*, that is, for seeing relations between historical objects that at first glance appear to be of very different worlds. By grouping both early nineteenth- and late nineteenth-century narratives together under the rubric of a single concept, it becomes possible to see them relationally and so to discover the *possibility* of a history that remains virtually invisible when approached from the point of view of texts as events. Koselleck's notion of historical semantics is important because of the potentiality he ascribes to this sort of history: concepts are *formal categories which are the conditions of possible histories.* A history of the novel as a concept would thus have the potential of cutting across various borders—both spatial and temporal—and so allow the historian to discover a potential history—or potential histories—where none has previously existed. And

55. See Jameson, *The Political Unconscious*, p. 107.

56. Koselleck, "Representation, Event, and Structure," p. 113, emphasis added.

it is precisely because at present the history of nineteenth-century Japanese fiction remains only a potential history that Koselleck's notion of structure seems particularly important.

Margaret Doody has recently declared that "the Romance and Novel are one," and that "the separation between them is part of the problem, not part of the solution."[57] Doody is attacking the "parochialism" of Anglophone historians of the novel, a "parochialism [that] betrays itself in the incessant assertion that the Novel should always be separated from the Romance; there is a symptomatic determination to play down the inconvenient fact that other European literary languages make no such distinction."[58] Doody's "true" history of the novel aims "to help us see the range of surviving forest and not merely the individual trees or, at best, small groves. . . . [I]f I emphasize continuities, it is because discontinuity, absolute division, has been harshly and hastily asserted before now."[59]

Two things are striking about Doody's "true" history. The first is the emphasis on *continuities* over a strong inclination to stress discontinuity and division, an emphasis that immediately resonates with anyone involved in the history of nineteenth-century Japan. By going beyond such generic concepts as novel and romance, it becomes *possible* to construct a different kind of literary history, one that traces the history of the novel from antiquity through modernity and one that looks at the vicissitudes of the form in the Mediterranean world of antiquity, in China and Japan, in the Islamic world, in early modern Europe, and so forth. Doody risks being ahistorical (treating "an admittedly protean form as if constantly visible from century to century") because she feels that what is to be gained—a new understanding of the novel, a *truer* history of the novel—is worth the wager.

The second striking feature of Doody's polemic is her choice of metaphors: trees, forests, and groves. E. R. Curtius once wrote of "a boundless realm" that he called *a garden of literary forms*; Vladimir Propp borrowed his central concept of "morphology" from botany; and Barthes once suggested that "there is perhaps a certain *endogenous* devel-

57. Doody, *The True Story of the Novel*, p. 15.
58. Doody, *The True Story of the Novel*, p 1.
59. Doody, *The True Story of the Novel*, xvii–xviii.

opment of the structure of the literary message."[60] It is as if every time literary historians begin to conceive of a history beyond the narrow confines of texts and events (or *texts as events*), they turn to metaphors: metaphors from ecology, botany, biology, metaphors from the *natural* sciences. Why? Because the natural sciences provide a vocabulary and a conceptual framework, a metalanguage, not strictly bound by a purely historical logic or at least by the logic of history. The sciences focus on the structural potential of concepts while virtually ignoring the moments of their illocution; by taking a step outside of history and looking for purely formal patterns in places where traditional history has seen only discontinuity and division, we can begin to conceive of a different type of history that is historical in its own right, but belongs to a different register than the history of texts and events.

To write a history of the nineteenth-century Japanese novel, then, requires an initial wager, a conceptual leap of grouping together—provisionally—under the concept of the novel a set of texts that have traditionally been seen as belonging to two different worlds. Making this initial leap allows the literary historian to discern certain formal continuities, certain patterns, certain trends that were invisible from the perspective of traditional literary history, but which have an integrity across the century that belies the familiar history of rupture. We might begin such a history of form by choosing a relatively well-established morphological category such as Ian Watt's "formal realism," his term for what he has called "the lowest common denominator of the novel genre as a whole."[61] Toward the beginning of his pathbreaking essay on the history of realism in Japanese literature, Etō Jun distinguished between conventional histories of realism in Japan which chart the history of "theories" (*riron*) of realism (and hence begin in the 1880s, after the encounter with Western literature) and an approach which would look primarily at "style" (*bunshō*). Etō examines the "style" of such works as Tsubouchi Shōyō's *Tōsei shosei katagi* (1885–86) and Futabatei Shimei's *Ukigumo* (1887), which had adopted "realism in theory" but which "rely on a static style," and contrasts them with the

60. See Curtius, *European Literature and the Latin Middle Ages*, p. 15; Propp, *Morphology of the Folktale*, xxv; and Barthes, "Rhetorical Analysis," p. 88, emphasis added.

61. Watt, *The Rise of the Novel*, p. 34.

"strangely energetic and vital" style of a passage from Katsu Kokichi's *Musui dokugen* (1842), a work predating the supposed rise of theoretical realism but practicing a stylistic realism.[62] Such a generative approach to the history of realism in Japanese literature allows for the emergence of a different type of historicism, one that calls into question the notion that literary history is reducible to a history of discourse on literature.

Craig Clunas has recently put forward a similar argument in the field of early modern Chinese visual culture; his work is especially instructive in calling attention both to the limitations of criticism that too much privileges discursive structures—aesthetic pronouncements and formulations contemporary with objects of analysis—and to the promise of form and formal analysis in overcoming these limitations. Like Etō, Clunas begins by considering a text, in this case an anonymous sixteenth- or early seventeenth-century painting of a *Lady in a Palace Garden*, which, like Katsu Kokichi's writing, appears to contradict the normal chronology of the history of realism in Chinese art in which "Chinese art . . . reached a point 'beyond representation' at an early date."[63] By recovering objects like *Lady in a Palace Garden* that are "within representation," Clunas is able to offer a critique of those theories of Chinese art "in which mimetic representation is relegated to a decidedly lower status." For Clunas, non-canonical images demand that we fundamentally reexamine the theoretical underpinnings of the canon itself:

> Such theoretical positions are strong in their ability to explicate and historicize the canon of Chinese painting over the past millennium. They are not always as successful in accounting for all the pictures we have surviving from the Ming period, and not even for all the paintings we have, leaving aside the much larger body of graphic work and of pictures in media other than painting. . . . The mainstream of Chinese art-historical theory is good at explaining why these . . . pictures have been excluded from the canon, *but is less helpful in explaining why they were made at all.*[64]

62. Etō, "Riarizumu no genryū," pp. 218–20.

63. Clunas, *Pictures and Visuality in Early Modern China*, p. 10.

64. Clunas, *Pictures and Visuality in Early Modern China*, p. 18 and pp. 20–22, emphasis added.

For Clunas, the goal of such a critique is "not to argue that Chinese painting is *really* like 'this,' instead of like 'that'" but rather to begin to excavate a fuller history of representation which would account for what he calls the "huge art-historical underclass" which "are very much 'within representation,' even if this still implies a distinctive Chinese epistemology and economy of representation."[65] Both Etō's essay and Clunas's book are opening gambits of sorts and each offers a glimpse of what an attention to form promises: the possibility of truly revolutionizing literary history, of shifting its center of gravity away from the canon and its discursive supports and toward an encounter with the huge *underclass* of literary history.

But even as "realism" might seem a useful formal category from which to begin a morphological analysis of the novel, it has, in recent years, come under a series of critiques by such literary historians as Janice Radway, Margaret Doody, and Margaret Cohen.[66] This new literary history has concerned itself less with realism's singular triumph than with its plural failures and has attempted to historicize the history of realism by excavating realism's repressed others: the writings of women, the sentimental register, the fantastic. In her recent revision of the history of the nineteenth-century French novel, Cohen poses the question of "how to write literary history in the wake of poststructuralism," noting that "the most rigorous and influential poststructural analyses are sometimes haunted by the discredited categories of traditional literary history despite themselves": the author, the masterpiece, realism.[67] Instead, Cohen proposes a new way of conceptualizing literary history, "literary history written from the archive," stressing the two meanings of *archive* as "the dusty documents neglected in libraries" and "archive as Foucault defined the term seeking to direct historical inquiry away from individual works to the discursive structures that support them."[68]

65. Clunas, *Pictures and Visuality in Early Modern China*, p. 20 and p. 22.

66. See Radway, *Reading the Romance*; Doody, *The True Story of the Novel* ("it is time to drop the pretence that the primary demand of a long work of prose fiction is that it should be 'realistic,'" p. 16); and Cohen, *The Sentimental Education of the Novel* ("if we unquestioningly equate realism with the modern novel, we give the form a retrospective teleology, perpetuating a narrative of literary history as progress," p. 5).

67. Cohen, *The Sentimental Education of the Novel*, p. 4.

68. Cohen, *The Sentimental Education of the Novel*, pp. 5–6.

Such an approach to literary history has the great advantage of allowing the historian to do away with the master principles of unity in traditional literary history—the author, the oeuvre—and approach the archive from a fresh perspective. It is the perfect approach to nineteenth-century Japanese fiction, which both as a body of texts and as a set of institutions has been essentially written out of traditional literary history. But it is a messy prospect, digging into this "great unread"; Cohen suggests the need to "read around in the archive . . . starting from such untheorized resemblances as similar titles and shared thematic concerns." Cohen thus advocates the practice of "reading for patterns," a term she borrows from Sharon Marcus, which "entails looking for repetition on the level of textual structures and developing a checklist of salient codes."[69] And this is essentially how I approached the archive of nineteenth-century fiction or, I should say, what lead me away from the canon and into the archive in the first place: I noticed again and again the presence—first in late nineteenth-century texts but then too in early nineteenth-century texts—of tears. There were, first of all, the tears shed by the characters of these works, by heroines like Namiko from Tokutomi Roka's *Hototogisu* (1898–1899) or Yonehachi from Tamenaga Shunsui's *Shunshoku umegoyomi* (1832–1833); but gradually, these very visible tears lead to a different register of tears that maintained a ghostly presence at a deeper structural level in these works as mechanisms designed to elicit tears from the historical reader.

Tears are clues, and if pieced together correctly can lead the historian back into a world that has long since vanished and of which only traces remain. Such an approach to literary texts may seem "untheorized," or worse yet, hopelessly naïve; yet it is precisely this untheorized—even naïve—observation that forms the very basis of a more theorized structural analysis.[70] This is especially true of the literature of tears, which has only recently become a subject for literary history.[71] Indeed, with-

69. Cohen, *The Sentimental Education of the Novel*, p. 22.

70. See, for example, Christian Metz on structural analysis and "naïve consciousness" in his *Film Language*, pp. 16–17.

71. This is Franco Moretti's point in his essay on the tearjerker: "the absence of a theoretical tradition makes the starting point of an investigation even more debatable and slippery than usual. . . . In the case of moving literature the preselection permitted by the existence of a theoretical context is not possible. One finds oneself faced with a

out having recourse to this empiricism, this crude but effective "phenomenology of the subject,"[72] literary history is bound to remain wedded to the texts and institutions that it has most thoroughly explored: the masterpiece, the canon.

But "reading for patterns" also runs the risk of being radically ahistorical, of collapsing onto one another the aesthetic and readerly codes of different historical and cultural milieu. "A text always has several epochs," Derrida writes in *Of Grammatology*, "and reading must resign itself to that fact."[73] One need only think of Akutagawa Ryūnosuke's savage parody of Nitobe Inazō in "Hankechi" (1916) to imagine how complicated and how dependent on such codes the interpretation of tears can be. Hasegawa Kinzō, the protagonist of Akutagawa's story, is visited at home by Nishiyama Atsuko, the mother of one of his students. She has come to tell the professor that her son has died the day before and the professor can only marvel at her calm countenance as she relates the news to him: "As their conversation proceeded, the professor became aware of a most unexpected reality. That was that neither the woman's attitude nor her deportment seemed as if she was telling of her own son's death. There were no tears in her eyes. And her voice was unchanged. And in the corner of her mouth there even hovered a smile."[74] At this moment the professor happens to drop his folding fan and as he bends down to pick it up he chances to see that in her trembling hands Nishiyama Atsuko is wringing with all her might a handkerchief to the point that it is about to tear. "On her face is a smile," the professor reflects, "but the whole time she has been weeping with her entire body."[75] The professor is moved by this sight to reflect that it represents something of the "*bushidō* of the Japanese

---

continuum of texts in which one must make two cuts: from here to here, that is, 'moving literature. But why precisely this group of texts and not others? Because . . . only these texts have made me cry. There is no other way. If one wants to put forward a new 'object' for discussion one has to start from very empirical, subjective, and crude premises. One can only begin by asserting that the 'moving' is what makes one cry." See Moretti, "Kindergarten," p. 158.

72. See Metz, *Film Language*, pp. 16–17.

73. Derrida, *Of Grammatology*, p. 102.

74. Akutagawa Ryūnosuke, "Hankechi," p. 273.

75. Akutagawa Ryūnosuke, "Hankechi," p. 275.

woman." But that night, as he resumes his reading of a work by Strindberg that he had put down that afternoon, he encounters a passage in which Strindberg writes of how in his youth people would talk of Lady Heidelberg and her handkerchief: "It was a sort of double performance where on her face would be a smile but with her hands she would be tearing a handkerchief in two. This is what we now call slapstick."[76]

Tears too have their cultural referents and aesthetic codes, and it is a mistake to treat them as if they are natural, everywhere and at all times the same. At the end of "Hankechi," Hasegawa is forced to reflect on this fact that tears have cultural specificity and that one might read the same scene very differently depending on the circumstances surrounding the event and what readerly codes one brings to bear on the text. What is to some quite moving is to others merely slapstick. And indeed, Akutagawa's story contains within it an important point on the question of reading in general. Recent work on the history of reading has focused on the way in which readers actively produce meaning, treating reading as an act of appropriation, a form of "poaching," as Michel de Certeau put it, in which the reader "insinuates into another person's text the ruses of pleasure and appropriation."[77] De Certeau's work has aimed at restoring to the reader a certain degree of historical agency and critiquing the notion that reader response can be accurately deduced from the text itself. The readers conjured by text, implied readers, are different from historical readers who read according to their own programs, with their own motives. And so it becomes immediately apparent how contingent, how vulnerable any act of "reading for patterns" becomes.

But this recent work on the history of reading has tended to highlight the role of the reader at the expense of the text, often ignoring the fact that literature cannot be understood apart from a basic theory of communication and that all communicative messages—even literary messages—have built into them isotopic devices, that is, devices that work toward overcoming interference with the message through its medium or at its moment of reception, devices that ensure that communication takes place. "Communication is," as Greimas once put it,

76. Akutagawa Ryūnosuke, "Hankechi," p. 277.
77. de Certeau, *The Practice of Everyday Life*, xxi.

"the exercise of a certain but limited freedom."[78] So while such notions of readerly appropriation usefully restore *a certain freedom* to acts of reading, it is necessary to recalibrate them in order to understand the *limitations* imposed on that freedom. Certain literary works "aim at eliciting a sort of 'obedient' cooperation";[79] indeed, the existence of such limitations is inscribed in the very notion of "poaching," which posits as the other side of agency, restriction, and coercion. To paraphrase Marx (rather loosely), men read texts but they do not read them *just as they please*; they do not read under circumstances created by themselves, *but under circumstances directly encountered, given, and transmitted.*

We might go on to conceive of a readerly *habitus* in which the reading is "objectively 'regulated' and 'regular' without being in any way the product of obedience to rules."[80] Such a readerly habitus would account for both the "tactics" of the reader (de Certeau) and the "inflexible projects" (Eco) of the texts themselves, allowing the literary historian to work with two sets of data simultaneously: the affective responses of real and particular historical readers (whether from marginal notes, diaries, letters, or book reviews) and the formal structures of the text.

Thus, however useful histories of particular readers have been in making literary history dynamic and forcing literary historians to account for particular historical responses, [81] they are unable to cope with concepts such as the reading public (of which they have been quite critical)[82] or what we might simply call—after Gramsci—*the silent majority*: "Commercial literature must not be disregarded in the history of culture. Indeed it has enormous value precisely in this respect because the success of a work of commercial literature indicates (and it is often the only indication available) the 'philosophy of the age,' that

78. Greimas, *Structural Semnatics*, p. 39.

79. Eco, *The Role of the Reader*, p. 7.

80. See Bourdieu, *The Logic of Practice*, p. 53.

81. The best known of such histories are Carlo Ginzburg's study of the sixteenth century miller Menocchio in *The Cheese and the Worms*; Lisa Jardine and Anthony Grafton's study of Gabriel Harvey, "'Studied for Action': How Gabriel Harvey Read his Livy"; and more recently Kevin Sharpe's study of Sir William Drake in *Reading Revolutions*.

82. See in particular James Raven's "Introduction: The Practice and Representation of Reading in England."

is, the mass of feelings and conceptions of the world predominant among the 'silent' majority."[83] What remains of this silent majority are fragmentary and diffuse archival traces, such as the records of lending libraries or publishing houses (the study of which Gramsci advocated and had hoped to himself pursue had he been freed from prison), and then the archive of the texts themselves, which often (and increasingly) exist in easily obtained critical editions but also commonly and sometimes only in those now fading and fragile material forms in which they were first encountered, read, and often cherished.

"A Community with No Visible Presence": Print and the Social Imaginary

In her study of nineteenth-century French sentimental novels, Margaret Cohen notes how she first found the objects of her study "illegible": "Too often, noncanonical texts are fragments of lost solutions or answers to questions we no longer hear."[84] But when one confronts the archive of nineteenth-century Japanese fiction—or at least of that portion of the archive written and published over the first two thirds of the century—one encounters a different order of illegibility: not only do these texts belong to a different time, the aesthetic and ideological underpinnings of which are often only dimly visible, but the books themselves are often faded and worn and, more fundamentally, they are printed in a cursive style that remains illegible to a reader of modern Japanese. The page of the block-printed Japanese novel is unfamiliar to the modern eye, accustomed as it is to the logic of typography described so wonderfully by Henri-Jean Martin as "small lead blocks lined up like soldiers on parade."[85]

By contrast, the page of the block-printed book seems like the scene of a battle: figures interlocked with one another, bodies intertwined as if engaged in a melee. Of course, the block-printed page, too, has its logic, and like any system of signs, once one has learned the codes of the page, a whole world is opened up. But it is worth pausing over the initial difficulty one encounters upon entering the archive because it is

83. Gramsci, *Selections from Cultural Writings*, p. 348.
84. Cohen, *The Sentimental Education of the Novel*, p. 21 and p. 25.
85. Martin, *The History and Power of Writing*, p. 231.

an exemplary instance of "the book as an expressive form."[86] It would perhaps be too hasty to consider the problem of the semiosis of the text without first considering the semiosis of the book.

In his recent history of the book in Japan, Peter Kornicki suggests that Japanese books became "profoundly visual" over the course of the early modern period. In the first instance, this visuality has something to do with the character of the graphic notation used in block printing which preserves something of the human hand now long lost to the history of typography; Kornicki, for instance, ascribes to early modern Japanese block-printed books a "calligraphic character" which allowed books produced by this method to "enforce a more particularistic relationship between reader and text than was possible with moveable type,"[87] which tends to flatten out and homogenize individuality and idiosyncrasy.[88] A second aspect of this profound visuality is the inclusion of illustrations in a wide variety of texts. As Kornicki argues, readers encounter not only the textual "conventions" and "expectations" of the book but also, and as importantly, the "calligraphic style reproduced in the printed text and with a visual style in illustrations."[89] In this sense, any notion of reading which does not account for the ways in which "readers confronted the visual" may be inadequate to understanding how early modern fiction was apprehended and consumed.[90]

When one approaches the literary archive of nineteenth-century Japan, one is repeatedly confronted by a set of problems related to these *expressive* dimensions of block-printed books. But more than this,

---

86. McKenzie, *Bibliography and the Sociology of Texts*, p. 17.

87. Kornicki, *The Book in Japan*, p. 27 and p. 29. Isomae Jun'ichi provides an extraordinary example of this in his "Kindai ekurichūru no tōitsu."

88. This was one of the central points put forward by Marshall McLuhan in his *Gutenberg Galaxy* and has been extremely influential in Japan in shaping the way that book historians and literary critics have conceptualized the "break" between "premodern" and "modern" print cultures. See for instance Komori, "Shōsetso gensetsu no seisei" especially pp. 6–8; Kōno, *Shomotsu no kindai* especially pp. 26–32; Li, *Hyōshōkūkan no kindai*, pp. 138–62; and Isomae, "Kindai ekurichūru no tōitsu."

89. Kornicki, *The Book in Japan*, p. 58.

90. Kornicki, *The Book in Japan*, p. 58. Two recent books have made this argument rather persuasively for the case of early-modern China. See Hegel, *Reading Illustrated Fiction in Late Imperial China*, especially the chapter "Art as Text," pp. 290–336; and Clunas, *Pictures and Visuality in Early Modern China*, pp. 29–41 and especially pp. 36–37.

one is confronted by an "epistemological problem": whether or not to treat block-printed books as phenomenologically equivalent to moveable-type printed books.[91] If we return to Figure 4 (that chart of fiction titles across the long nineteenth century) we can see how this epistemological problem becomes crucial to any consideration of the novel in nineteenth-century Japan. What the graph does not represent is the fact that we are dealing with two very different orders of books: some of these novels are printed by woodblock, others by moveable type. The entire idea of writing a history of nineteenth-century Japanese fiction is inextricably linked to the epistemological problem that Kornicki raises: are we justified in treating block-printed *novels* as equivalent to *novels* printed with moveable type?

But when one steps back for a moment to reflect, one is struck by a fact so obvious it hardly bears mentioning: whether produced by xylography or typography, we are in fact dealing with books. After all, the book is not the only form of written inscription nor is it in any sense natural. The birth of the codex, writes Henri-Jean Martin in *The History and Power of Writing*, is "undoubtedly the most important revolution in the book in the common era"[92]—more important, that is, than the invention of printing. Writing of the history of printing in China, Tsien Tsuen-Hsuin notes that "printing did not result in much change in the physical appearance of the book. . . . The evolution from the roll form to flat binding in the late ninth or early tenth century, was primarily because of the inconvenience of opening the paper roll for reading; it was not necessarily a result of printing"; the new format of the book, he observes, "made the different parts of the text more immediately accessible than had been possible with rolls."[93] Roger Chartier notes a similar effect: "The reader was liberated by the codex. Resting on table or lectern, the book in quires no longer required the participation of so much of the body. One might thus distance oneself, reading and writing at the same time, moving at one's own pace from page to page, from book to book."[94] Here we might think back to our

---

91. Kornicki, *The Book in Japan*, p. 26

92. Martin, *The History and Power of Writing*, p. 59.

93. Tsien, "Paper and Printing," p. 375 and p. 227.

94. Chartier, "Representations of the Written Word," pp. 19–20.

two readers depicted by Katsushika Hokusai in 1802 and by Kuroda Seiki in 1891. The book, as a medium for print, provides a certain commonality between these two images that are in many ways so strikingly different. And it is precisely the physical difference in the books being read that allows us to grasp the fundamental importance of the book as a form: each reader is indeed indulging in a liberation of the body and we can begin to see how the apparent differences between these two orders of books are belied by certain commonalities of form, which also allow for certain commonalities of bodily practice.

Any discussion of the epistemological problem raised by Kornicki might rightly begin by a return to a consideration of the fundamental form of the book, which is itself common to the traditions of block printing and typography. Even if typography and xylography "enforce" different relations between the reader and the text, we might do well to recognize that the book itself, as a cultural form, has already "enforced" a particular relationship between reader and text that is shared by both traditions. It is indeed only within the field of commonality of the book that we can understand the difference between xylography and typography.

Kornicki is no doubt right to urge caution and to suggest that the history of the book in any culture should not be understood apart from the technologies employed in the production of the book. But the problem of the relationship between typography and xylography reverberates throughout the history of the printed book, not only in Japan but also in the West. In the early modern world, *both* in Asia *and* in Europe xylography and typography coexisted, and it would be a mistake to see a "filiation" between the two.[95] In China, "wood-block engraving . . . became part of ordinary life in the course of the tenth century," but there soon followed the birth of a tradition of moveable type "independent of the European one and also different in technique."[96] And in Europe, block-printed books enjoyed their "moment of greatest popularity" after 1455—after the typographic revolution—suggesting that far from inspiring printing, early modern xylographs are

---

95. Febvre and Martin, *The Coming of the Book*, p. 48; for Febvre and Martin's full argument see also pp. 45–49.

96. Gernet, *A History of Chinese Civilization*, p. 335.

best seen as "a response on the part of wood engravers to the appearance of printing."[97] This point is extremely important. Block printing did not *predate* typography, it did not lead *to* typography, typography did not develop *from* xylography: the two technologies are fundamentally different and have to be seen not in terms of filiation but as competing technologies. And this is true of the history of printing in Europe as well as in China, Korea, and Japan.

It is tempting to see the development of print cultures in early modern Europe and East Asia as reverse negatives of one another: while "the logic of lead" (as Martin described moveable type) was making its triumphant march through Europe at the expense of the woodcut, woodblock printing was being adopted for the large scale production of texts in Asia at the expense of a typographic tradition. There thus developed distinct cultures of the book, each dependent as it was on its own technology. But this apparent symmetry is belied by the complexity of the history of interactions between technology and culture that we see again and again in both European and Asian history.

The problem becomes clear if we consider the issue of the "choice" of block printing, the question of why printing in Japan continued to be dominated by xylography long after the introduction of moveable type. Charles Shirō Inouye has recently criticized Kornicki for placing too much stress on the economic dimensions of the problem and suggests that the question needs to be posed from a broader cultural perspective. Inouye argues that a certain "visual predilection helps explain why the Japanese favored woodblock prints and rejected moveable type printing, which made both the inclusion of illustrations and the preservation of what we might call a calligraphic regard for the written word difficult."[98] Henri-Jean Martin, for instance, has described the triumph of typography over xylography in early modern Europe, where the *logic of lead* "consummated the decline of a certain type of relation between text and image."[99] The print culture of early modern Europe, Martin writes, is marked by a distancing of the image from the text. But an examination of the history of the visual dimensions of the Japanese

97. Martin, *The History and Power of Writing*, p. 214.
98. Inouye, "Japanese Books in Perspective," p. 248.
99. Martin, *The History and Power of Writing*, p. 230.

book—both the history of illustrations and the history of the "calligraphic regard"—reveals that the problem is far more complex.

"Although many early manuscripts of Japanese literature were illustrated," writes Kornicki, "it was only rarely in the centuries before the Tokugawa period that printed books included illustrations. . . . It was probably the Sagabon that established the role of illustration in Japanese printed books, particularly in the case of literary texts."[100] Kornicki continues his description of Sagabon: "the extensive use of ligatures, enabling the print to represent the flow of calligraphy, together with the inclusion of illustrations . . . resulted in books of great beauty."[101] But Sagabon are not block-printed books; rather they belong to the corpus of seventeenth-century texts produced using wooden moveable type. The historical irony of the problem is no doubt apparent: block printing had been used in Japan for almost a millennium but it was only with the use of moveable type in the seventeenth century that illustration became common in printed books. It is almost as if the illustrations of the Sagabon suggested the very possibility of illustrating printed texts. Thus whatever the merits of the arguments that "the inclusion of illustrations was . . . facilitated by the fact that they were produced by the same block-printing process as the text,"[102] we can see that the history of culture is never reducible to the history of technology, and that the history of technology is itself often marked by what seem in hindsight to the historian to be logical contradictions.

But Kornicki's description of the Sagabon contains within it another problem: "The extensive use of ligatures" enables "the print to represent the flow of calligraphy."[103] Again, we are dealing not with block printing but with moveable type. That is to say, one of the remarkable achievements of the Sagabon was to preserve the *calligraphic character* of manuscript while using moveable type. So we have the seemingly inexplicable fact that the avant-garde of the "profound visuality" of early modern woodblock-printed books was in fact not printed by woodblock but by moveable type, produced with a technology of an

100. Kornicki, *The Book in Japan*, p. 57.
101. Kornicki, *The Book in Japan*, p. 132.
102. Kornicki, *The Book in Japan*, p. 58.
103. Kornicki, *The Book in Japan*, p. 132.

order commensurate with that being used in Europe at the same time. To be sure, the exact reproduction of the human hand through moveable type could be achieved only with a great investment of time and material resources; but the history of print suggests that this was in no way a phenomenon limited to the Sagabon. Indeed, Henri-Jean Martin has noted an almost identical phenomenon in early modern Europe.[104]

When posing the epistemological problem that Kornicki identifies we need to be careful not to essentialize the properties of the media of production and reproduction. Both typography and xylography can be—and historically have been—used in a variety of ways to produce a variety of texts; neither in the history of print in Europe nor in that of East Asia are all extant texts easily explained by a single principle. "A technical invention as such has comparatively little social significance," Raymond Williams has written, "it is only when it is selected for investment towards production . . . that the general significance begins."[105] The history of technology is always a history of the uses of technology and cannot be considered apart from the ways that a given technology has been employed within a given society. Instead of concentrating on the essential properties inhering in any specific technology, we would indeed do well to turn to what Marx describes in the opening paragraphs of *Capital* as "the work of history," the discovery of "the manifold use of things."[106]

---

104. See Martin, *The History and Power of Writing*, p. 231: "The first printers did their best to reproduce, as exactly as possible, the manuscripts with which they were familiar. They went as far as to reproduce some of their models line by line, or so it seems: the Bibliothèque municipale of Lyons conserves two copies of the Missel de Lyon, one a manuscript and the other printed in 1482 by Neumeister, which were owned by the same cannon and decorated by the same miniaturist. The two are true twins: unless the viewer is a specialist, they are indistinguishable from one another by the color of their ink or the regularity of their characters, which are slightly larger in the manuscript version."

105. Williams, "Culture and Technology," p. 120.

106. Marx, *Capital: Volume I*, p. 125. "Every useful thing is a whole composed of many properties; it can therefore be useful in various ways. The discovery of these ways and hence the manifold use of things is the work of history." For his part, Fernand Braudel describes the history of inventions as "a misleading hall of mirrors," writing that "technology is only an instrument and man does not always know what to do with it." See Braudel, *The Structures of Everyday Life*, p. 335 and p. 371.

But we must also be careful not to essentialize the cultural dimensions of the problem. Citing a passage from *The Book in Japan* in which Kornicki states that "in this way Japanese books, but very rarely Chinese books printed in Japan, became profoundly visual in the Tokugawa period," Inouye writes that it might be possible to claim rather broadly that "the Japanese book is distinguishable by its visual elements." For Inouye, visuality is central to an understanding of the Japanese book:

> Could it be that richness of visuality was actually the defining characteristic of the Japanese book, setting it apart from other categories? Advancing this issue one step further, assuming that books are expressive of thought and sentiment, could we say that Japanese thought itself is also defined by this visual tendency? If so, how might we characterize this tendency? More concretely, what semiotic configurations could we take to be manifestations of visually oriented thought?[107]

Yet while Inouye attempts carefully to posit a material basis for what he calls "a social semiotics of thought,"[108] his approach tends to dehistoricize, locating difference in the realm of "structures of thought"[109] and thus removing it from a consideration of the history and materiality of the semiotic process.

In the passage above, Kornicki is, of course, referring only to Chinese books printed in Japan, not to Chinese books printed in China, which had long been illustrated. Craig Clunas notes that during the Ming Dynasty, "The private space of the book was exploding with a quantity of pictures greater than at any previous time since the invention of printing almost a 1,000 years previously."[110] Robert Hegel similarly describes a "nearly ubiquitous inclusion of illustrations in books of all kinds during the Ming period."[111] And so it becomes difficult to maintain the particularity of the "visual tendency" of "Japanese thought." One might of course simply rephrase Inouye's argument to include China—could there be an Asiatic mode of *perception*?—or, perhaps better, argue that a certain visual tendency marks the "thought" of all cultures of block

---

107. Inouye, "Japanese Books in Perspective," p. 249.
108. Inouye, "Japanese Books in Perspective," p. 250.
109. Inouye, "Japanese Books in Perspective," p. 251.
110. Clunas, *Pictures and Visuality in Early Modern China*, p. 29.
111. Hegel, *Reading Illustrated Fiction in Late Imperial China*, p. 6.

printing. But such a leap would require an understanding of the historical relation that attained between texts and images in other predominantly xylographic cultures.

In the introduction to his marvelous *Bibliographie Coréenne*, Maurice Courant wrote that in the 1890s, "when the foreigner arrives in Korea" he is immediately struck by the sale of small, rough, and inexpensive books "in provincial towns just as in the capital, at every turn of the street."[112] As Courant writes, the books were everywhere for sale, like other common items for everyday use:

> In Seoul and in the provinces, in dingy and winding alleys one sees little stalls in plain view sheltered from the sun by a coarse canvas; and near the display is a young man with a shaved head and dressed in an unbleached chanvre with a long pleat hanging from the back; he sells hair pins, fur headbands, pocket mirrors, tobacco pouches and tobacco, common pipes, all sorts of boxes, Japanese matches, brushes, ink, paper and books.[113]

Courant gives some sense of the extensive reach of the culture of the book in late Joseon Korea and how widely available block-printed books must have been. But these books were overwhelmingly unillustrated. One might of course proffer any number of tentative cultural explanations for what seem to be the *textual* as opposed to *visual* tendencies of Korean thought, but no doubt such generalizations fall far short of making sense of the historical complexities at issue.

Where is the novel in all of this? Literary historians and critics—from Ian Watt to Mikhail Bakhtin—have long recognized how closely related are the histories of print and the novel in Europe;[114] but what of this history in the rest of the world? Any consideration of the novel as a form would rightly have to begin by revisiting the epistemological problem raised by Kornicki. How are we, that is, to understand the history of woodblock-printed novels in relation to the history of those printed by moveable type? Under what conditions, is it possible—or

112. Courant, *Bibliographie Coréenne*, xxi.

113. Courant, *Bibliographie Coréenne*, xix–xx.

114. Watt, for instance, writes that "the novel is perhaps the only literary genre which is essentially connected with the medium of print." See Watt, *The Rise of the Novel*, p. 196. Bahktin puts the matter a little differently. "Of all the major genres," he writes, "only the novel is younger than writing and the book." See Bakhtin, "The Epic and the Novel," p. 3.

useful—to consider these forms as sharing a certain history? Without such a consideration of the materiality of the text, we run the risk of succumbing to an idealist conception of literary form divorced from its material existence.

The title of this section, "A Community with No Visible Presence," is taken from a line in Roger Chartier's *The Cultural Origins of the French Revolution*, and functions as an entry point into a discussion of the epistemological problems that Kornicki raises—and, more broadly, a consideration of the relation among print, the novel, and the imagination. "Printing," Chartier writes, "made possible the constitution of a public realm that was unreliant on proximity—a community with no visible presence."[115] We should note that Chartier is writing about eighteenth-century France, and therefore about the history of typographic print. The problem I would like to pose is whether Chartier's image of a "community with no visible presence" allows us a way to understand the truly social dimensions of the history of block printing apart from certain fundamental technological differences with typography. This is what seems to be at stake: can we use certain ideas about the book or print culture developed in relation to the typographic tradition of Europe to begin to think about certain problems raised by the history of xylographic print cultures at other historical moments?

In order to ask this question, we need to take a step back from history and address the problem at a more abstract level, at the level of system. In so doing, we are not abandoning history; the idea is that by taking one step back we can take two steps forward. "With the invention of the printed word," writes Niklas Luhmann, "greater, more improbable demands were made of communicative media."[116] It is a marvelous phrase, exactly capturing the difficulties that face the emergence of any *community with no visible presence.* Indeed, Luhmann's notion of improbability turns on its head the idea that the printed word naturally and seamlessly creates a web of social understanding and community: print simply amplifies the possibility of non-communication, the possibility that communicative messages of all sorts of texts will be mis-

115. Chartier, *The Cultural Origins of the French Revolution*, p. 32.
116. Luhmann, *Love as Passion*, p. 2.

understood, misappropriated, misused.[117] So print tends toward the creation of a chaotic system but the system itself takes measures to insure its own functioning. Or, as Luhmann puts it, "the medium itself finds countermeasures," and "the media used for dissemination have their own technique for making selections; they create their own possibilities of maintenance, comparison and improvement."[118] The history of print, Luhmann suggests, will always also be the history of a set of *countermeasures* which allow for the system to reproduce itself. These *countermeasures* lurk in the shadows of the history of every print culture, stowed away as a secret sharer.

Luhmann's work poses a fundamental problem: how can we account for the continued functioning of social systems despite the communicative improbability occasioned by the printed word? How have societies overcome this improbability and continued to function? "An intervening requirement mediates between language and interaction," Luhmann writes, "a supply of possible themes that is available for quick and readily understandable reception in concrete communicative processes. We would like to call this supply of themes culture. . . . Culture is not necessarily a normative content for meanings; perhaps it is more like a limitation of meaning (reduction) that makes it possible to distinguish appropriate from inappropriate contributions or even correct from incorrect uses of themes in theme-related communication."[119]

And the novel is *the* great cultural product of print. The novel provides to a reading public—"unreliant on proximity"—a set of common themes and values that allow a set of imaginary relationships to develop among readers who have never met. Thus the importance

117. See Luhmann, *Social Systems*, p. 337: "One can begin with the fact that an increase in communicative possibilities also increases the probability of conflict. Language creates the possibility of negating and concealing: the possibility of lying, deception, and the misleading use of symbols. Means of dissemination like writing and printing switch off the repression of conflict typical in interaction systems. Moreover the differentiation and specification of symbolically generalized media of communication increases the possibility of demanding acceptance so greatly that rejection would be probable if the medium itself did not find countermeasures." This is a wonderful theoretical explanation for the historical existence of someone like Menocchio, Carlo Ginzburg's sixteenth-century miller, in *The Cheese and the Worms.*

118. Luhmann, *Social Systems*, p. 161.

119. Luhmann, *Social Systems*, p. 163.

that Jürgen Habermas places on the novel in *The Structural Transformation of the Public Sphere.*[120] Or we might think of Benedict Anderson's study of the "imagined communities" of modern nationalism, in which the novel is accorded an extremely important place as a vehicle of the imagination. In some sense, the nation is quite literally *unimaginable* without the novel.[121]

When we turn back to the historical archive of nineteenth-century Japan and examine contemporary accounts of the experience of reading, we can see the traces of the ways in which fiction might offer to overcome the improbability of social existence within a community with no visible presence. In his essay *Genji monogatari tama no ogushi* (1796), Motoori Norinaga provides an example of how such *symbolically generalized media* function in practice. This essay is not simply a reading of the *Genji monogatari*; rather, it is an attempt to establish a general theory of reading based on scenes of reading *in* the *Genji monogatari.* Norinaga begins by carefully noting seventeen scenes of reading that occur in the text and then develops a general theory of reading based on his discoveries. I would like to concentrate on one example that has condensed within it the constellation of issues on which we have been focusing. Norinaga quotes the following passage from the "E-awase" chapter in which Genji shows to Murasaki the diary from his exile at Suma:

> That diary. It was so moving that even one who knew nothing of the incident and looked upon the diary for the first time would be overcome by tears had they even the least sensitivity. How much more so for they who were involved in it.[122]

This scene is interesting not only—nor perhaps chiefly—because of the tears at its center; it is also significant because we can see here the ways

---

120. Habermas, *The Structural Transformation of the Public Sphere*, p. 50 f.

121. See B. Anderson, *Imagined Communities*, p. 25: "The novel . . . provided the technical means for 're-presenting' the *kind* of imagined community that is the nation."

122. Cited by Motoori Norinaga in "Genji monogatari tama no ogushi," p. 241. My translation is of the passage as cited by Norinaga; in his translation of *Genji monogatari*, Edward Seidensticker renders this passage: "[H]e took out the sketchbooks and journals of his exile. Any moderately sensitive lady would have found tears coming to her eyes. For Murasaki those days had been unrelieved pain, not easily forgotten." See Murasaki Shikibu, *The Tale of Genji*, p. 310.

in which texts, and specifically fiction, allow for the transmission of experience beyond the spatial and temporal boundaries of that experience; how fiction allows, that is, for an essentially imaginary operation. *Even one who knew nothing of the incident*—of Genji's exile and the suffering it brought to Genji and Murasaki—would be moved to tears. And for his part, Genji "could almost feel as though he were back at Akashi once more."[123] After going through a dozen or so more examples, Norinaga concludes:

> This is how one feels for the most part when one reads fiction (*monogatari*). One reads so as to take the world of the past (*mukashi no koto*) and apply it to oneself, to compare oneself to it; to imagine (*omohiyari*) the feelings (*aware*) of the people of the past, and compare one's circumstances to theirs; and to understand the pathos of things (*mono no aware*), to comfort oneself in times of sadness. By looking at the feelings of those reading old tales as they appear in the various chapters of the *Genji monogatari*, we can understand how we ourselves must read the *Genji monogatari*.[124]

Already, Norinaga has located in fiction a space for the emergence of a set of imaginary relations. Whether in the first instance between the readers that appear in the *Genji monogatari* and the figures about whom they read, or in the second instance between readers of a later day and the figures of the *Genji monogatari* itself, the principles are equivalent.

There is contained in a letter written by Ōta Nanpo to Yamamichi no Takahiko in 1804 a remarkable example of just this type of reading suggested by Norinaga. Nanpo has just arrived in Nagasaki and is recounting his journey from Edo, south through Kyoto, Osaka, and Kobe:

> I arrived in Osaka on the fifteenth of August. In addition to getting together with old friends, I had a good deal of business, both private and official, so three days had passed before I realized it; I set off on the eighteenth. . . . I was at Suma on the morning of the nineteenth and in the lingering moonlight of the early morning had a look at Sumadera. I wrote the following poem:
>
> *The bright moon. Slowly does it crawl across Suma, pausing briefly in midair above Akashi*

123. Murasaki Shikibu, *The Tale of Genji*, p. 311.

124. Motoori Norinaga, "Genji monogatari tama no ogushi," p. 246.

It seemed to me that this moon was priceless, one of the true pleasures of life. Akashi was very sad, I thought of the *Genji.*[125]

In this letter, Nanpo is referring to exactly that moment in the *Genji monogatari* of which Genji and Murasaki are reading in Genji's diary in the "E-awase" chapter: Genji's sad and lonely exile at Suma in the "Suma" and "Akashi" chapters. Nanpo is practicing a form of reading remarkably close to the one imagined by Norinaga only several years earlier. On the one hand, *Genji monogatari* serves as a grid against which Nanpo interprets his own experience of the moon over the Bay of Suma: it is quite literally through a pattern of imagining the feelings of the characters in that work of fiction and comparing his own circumstances to them that he can arrive at his understanding of the beauty of the sadness of the scene before him, describing it as *priceless, one of the true pleasures of life.* On the other hand, the *Genji monogatari* also provides a vehicle through which Nanpo is able to transmit this experience to his friend in Edo. Takahiko would no doubt be familiar with the "Suma" and "Akashi" chapters—and indeed, Nanpo's letter assumes that he would be—and might perhaps, reading Nanpo's letter and poem, be able to *feel that he was back at Akashi once more,* as Genji had felt when he had looked at the diary of his own exile. Luhmann describes culture as "a supply of possible themes that is available for quick and readily understandable reception in concrete communicative processes";[126] this is exactly what is at work in this letter. *Genji monogatari* is an encyclopedic compendium of such themes upon which readers might draw nearly a millennium later to relate their experiences both to themselves and to others. We can see here exactly how fiction can function by allowing imaginative associations to form across both temporal and spatial distances.

And we cannot understand either Norinaga's theory of reading or Ōta's practice of reading apart from the emergence of a widespread culture of print from the seventeenth century onwards. The historian Yokota Fuyuhiko locates in the seventeenth century a moment he calls the "unfolding world of the book," in which, for the first time, move-

125. Letter written by Ōta Nanpo to Yamamichi no Takahiko on the eleventh day of the ninth month of the first year of Bunka; reprinted in *Ōta Nanpo zenshū*, vol. 19, p. 82.
126. Luhmann, *Social Systems*, p. 163.

able type and then block printing had made the central texts of a long manuscipt tradition easily accessible. Yokota notes that "the great majority of what we now call classical Japanese literature was first widely read in this period,"[127] and that "the 'classics' were liberated from the hereditary systems of scholarship and secret transmission in which they were enveloped throughout the medieval period."[128] Whereas a work like the fourteenth-century *Tsurezuregusa* (*Essays in Idleness*) is conventionally classified as an example of medieval literature, Yokota argues that "in the medieval period, one can see evidence only that it circulated in manuscript among an extremely limited group of people" and "from the broad perspective of a popular readership, it might rather be said to be a piece of early modern literature."[129]

But even as printed texts began to circulate widely beyond systems of secret transmission, it was at precisely this moment that a new (or renewed) attention to orality developed among a diverse group of intellectuals. Thus, as Eric Rath has commented in the case of noh drama, "By making available secret texts on noh, the nascent publishing industry turned private intellectual traditions into public commodities"; but this publishing—this making public—of heretofore secret knowledge resuled in a simultaneous reconfiguration of "the relationship between orality and literacy as they related to professional knowledge" with performers "giving more weight to privately and orally transmitted expertise than to written—and now published—secrets."[130] The deep interpenetration and mutual constitution of orality and print in early modern culture suggests that by the seventeenth century, it was no longer possible to think of orality as something coming before or lying beyond the world of print and books. Even as print forced a reorganization of the practices of professional knowledge in traditions like noh, print also provided an opportunity for, and perhaps gave a sense of urgency to, the development of a scholarly interest in orality among eighteenth-century nativist scholars that culminated in Motoori Norinaga's work on the *Kojiki* (*Record of Ancient Matters*) and the age of

127. Yokota, *Tenka taihei*, p. 340.
128. Yokota, *Tenka taihei*, p. 336.
129. Yokota, *Tenka taihei*, p. 335 and p. 339.
130. Rath, *The Ethos of Noh*, p. 160 and p. 161.

the gods. It is not just that the introduction of writing marks an epochal shift in Japanese history—characterized by what Norinaga sees as the emergence of a new form of consciousness and "the disintegration of social order"[131]—but there is also in Norinaga's *Naobi no mitama* (1771) a specific attention to the arrival of books from China: "After many generations, books crossed over and once they had begun to be read and studied, we learned the customs of that country [China] and gradually there came an age when these customs were mixed in with everything."[132] Norinaga's own intellectual project would be to move back beyond writing in search of the oral traditions of the age of the gods. But to situate this passage historically within a cultural moment that was itself witnessing, and in some respects living in, the wake of a second reorganization of knowledge and consciousness, allows us to see that print not only provided eighteenth-century scholars the tools for the study of the past in the form of printed texts and commentaries, but also provides a context within which we can situate a renewed interest in orality at a moment when orality was itself again reconfigured by the "unfolding world" of the book.

To argue that there was in nineteenth-century Japan a print-dependent mode of imagining community that relied less on physical proximity is not to suggest that we can casually or unreflexively locate at this historical moment an imagined community analogous to that posited by Benedict Anderson in his study of nationalism. Anderson's study addresses only the specifically historical imagining of the community of the nation and the historical emergence of the ideologies of nationalism. Here we encounter again the epistemological problems raised by Kornicki; whether the constellation of relationships—among print, the novel, and the imagination—that Anderson puts at the center of these ideologies can in any way be generalized; whether this constellation can be extended beyond a consideration of the historical ideologies of nationalism; whether it can be used to explore other "communities with no visible presence," other historical ideologies, other *social imaginaries*?

---

131. Burns, *Before the Nation*, p. 91.

132. Motoori Norinaga, "Naobi no mitama," p. 290.

There are two ways to answer these questions. On the one hand, we could insist on the very special relationship that developed among print, the novel, and the national imaginary in eighteenth- and nineteenth-century Europe; such a maneuver would necessarily sever the history of the European novel from the history of other fictional forms and cut the history of nationalism off from the history of other ideologies. The advantage of such an approach is the specific understanding it yields of the relationship among these terms as they developed in the West as well as the insight it affords into the cultural dimensions of colonialism and imperialism as they emerge from or in relation to this constellation of interests.

On the other hand, we could argue that the constellation of relations among print, the novel, and the imagination exists beyond the historical scope of nationalism and the European eighteenth and nineteenth centuries. This approach, of course, runs the risk of blurring important distinctions and of thereby making less rather than more intelligible the meaning of this constellation of relations. By arguing that a similar relationship among print, the novel, and forms of social imagination obtained in nineteenth-century Japan—and obtains, more generally, in the case of block printing—we run the risk of collapsing onto each other modes of imagining and ideological forms which are historically distinct. By doing so, we run the risk of radically misunderstanding history. But such an approach can offer a truly comparative dimension, and so allows us to see the historicity of nationalism as but one form of social ideology or social imaginary. Indeed, if Anderson's study has been criticized for one shortcoming, it is precisely for a historical myopia that forces him to cut off his discussion of nationalism from a broader discussion of the social imagination. "The point is not so much that national identity existed in premodern times," writes Prasenjit Duara, "rather, it is that the manner in which we have conceptualized political 'identities' is fundamentally problematic." Duara argues that "In privileging modern society as the only social form capable of generating political self-awareness, . . . [we] regard national identity as a distinctly modern mode of consciousness: the nation as a whole imagining itself to be the cohesive subject of history." And yet, historically, "individuals and groups in both modern and agrarian societies identify simultaneously with several communities, all of which are imagined; these identifications are historically changeable and often conflicted internally and with each other." Indeed, the very positing of a break between the modern and premodern has created a historical blind spot both by casually ignoring other historically situated social imaginaries and, importantly, by accepting as given "the assumption of modern consciousness as a *unified* episteme marked by an epistemological break with past forms of consciousness." This has tended to create in historical work on Asia—not just on Japan—a willingness too readily to accept an argument for a historical and epistemological rupture in the nineteenth century so that "the nation is *ipso facto* denied any credible links with the past."[133]

Although Duara does not address print culture per se, he has precisely located the crux of the epistemological problem suggested by Kornicki. The epistemological problem raised by a consideration of the technologies of xylography and typography is broadly related to the periodization of modernity, to the distinction between the premodern and modern, and to an epistemological break that historiography sees dividing the modern world from what came before. So Duara's phrase that "the nation is *ipso facto* denied any credible links with the past" resonates immediately with our project. One needs only to recall Nakamura Mitsuo's genealogy of the modern novel: literature written after the 1890s *was not Japanese literature, it was Western literature written in Japanese.*

To address block printing in this manner is to raise epistemological concerns that contain within them the possibility for a critique of the historiography of modernity. Craig Clunas understood this problem very well when he proposed a history of the "work of art in the age of woodblock reproduction," which by considering the history of xylography in China, might disturb "pre-existent assumptions about the 'modernity' of the West"; Clunas's point is not that "'the Chinese' were 'there first'" but rather that "there is no 'there' there, that on the contrary the 'modern' has no single safe home in the West."[134] And

133. Duara, *Rescuing History from the Nation*, p. 54.

134. Clunas, *Pictures and Visuality in Early Modern China*, p. 148. Clunas puts the matter more polemically elsewhere: "All these arguments for a perceived (even if unarticulated) European exceptionalism can only operate by ignoring the fact that in contemporary

indeed, we might note that Walter Benjamin's essay on "The Work of Art in the Age of Mechanical Reproduction"—to which Clunas alludes, of course—itself had contained within it the kernel of this idea: "with the woodcut graphic art became mechanically reproducible for the first time, long before script became reproducible by print. . . . Within the phenomenon [the mechanical reproduction of the work of art] which we are here addressing from the perspective of world history, print is merely a special, though particularly important case."[135] Of course, Benjamin does not specifically address the issue of the mechanical reproduction of script though the woodcut—that is xylography—but by beginning his essay "from the perspective of world history" we can see that he has already understood the ways in which techniques of mechanical reproduction have functioned throughout history. They are not, that is, essentially modern or Western.

By thinking about the history of block printing *from the perspective of world history*, by attempting to situate *the age of woodblock reproduction* within a broader history of print and communicative media, it becomes possible to pose a series of questions relating the history of print to the imaginary institutions of society. It would be naïve to assume that all print cultures function everywhere in the same way or that the ensemble of relations between print and the imagination are stable across temporal and spatial boundaries. This is where history reenters the problem. If we are to account for the specificities of the social imagination of nineteenth-century Japan, we cannot approach the problem

---

China texts and images were being, and what is more *had been* for centuries, reproduced mechanically and disseminated by a highly commercialized printing and publishing industry to an audience spread across the entire empire. . . . If the mere fact of the technology changed things, if the mere fact that 'identical images, maps and diagrams could be viewed simultaneously by scattered readers constituted a kind of communications revolution in itself,' then that revolution had happened in China a couple of hundred years before Gutenberg. The decision to omit this inconvenient fact, and to frame the question of 'printing revolutions' as one affecting Europe alone, is excusable only as a defensive act which has already committed itself to protecting the given of European 'modernity' at almost any cost. Again, the point is *not* to argue that China 'got there first', but to cast doubt on the unilinear and exclusionary nature of the arguments deployed for the single destination of modernity." Clunas, *Pictures and Visuality in Early Modern China*, p. 32.

135. Benjamin, "The Work of Art in the Age of Mechanical Reproduction," pp. 218–19.

from abstractions about print culture in general. Such abstractions serve only as a framework that allows for the development of working hypotheses, that allows us to pose certain questions that are impossible to imagine or at least unlikely to be posed if we insist on a break or rupture between the modern world and its antecedents.

To suggest that we are dealing, in nineteenth-century Japan, with a social imaginary that depended on print—a community with no visible presence—is not to say that we are dealing with imagined communities exactly analogous to those described by Anderson in his study of nationalism; rather, it is to suggest that the national imaginary is but one permutation of a possible ensemble of relations that have historically obtained between print and the imagination. We need only think of the issue of time to understand this problem. In Anderson's study, the imagining of the nation hinges on "simultaneity," on the emergence of "empty, homogenous time." But everything we know about the circulation of texts in early modern Japan suggests that the overwhelming characteristic of print culture was not simultaneity but rather *slowness*. "In contrast to urban lending libraries, which sought out newly published works that their readers vied with one another to read," writes Nagatomo Chiyoji in his history of lending libraries in early modern Japan, "provincial readers were reading books that had been published several years earlier."[136] And Hamada Keisuke notes that since the publishing of large format fiction titles was "limited to print runs of several hundred, such books would circulate passing from one dealer to another. At first, a centrally located lending library would use the books, which might then pass from, say, Osaka to Sakai and from Sakai to Wakayama, and then into the mountains along the River Ki" in a gradual progression outward from center to periphery. "A book might be read over several decades," Hamada continues, "passing through three or four dealers. . . . The speed of such circulation was entirely different from today. It didn't matter if a book was three or five years old. . . . Lending libraries played an important role in the spread of the novel, acting as intermediaries between the work itself and the reader. Lending libraries allow us to consider not just the readers of the city of Edo who rushed after each year's fads but also the readers of the entire

---

136. Nagatomo, *Kinsei kashihon'ya no kenkyū*, p. 80.

country who were years or even decades behind."[137] *Years or even decades behind.* . . . We are dealing with a time scale totally different from the one Anderson considers in his *Imagined Communities*, a scale marked not by simultaneity and uniformity but by slowness and unevenness.

By the beginning of the twentieth century, the speed of circulation had changed considerably. Asaoka Kunio provides two examples of this radical contraction of time in a recent study of a lending library operating in Toriyama-chō, Tochigi Prefecture around the turn of the century. He cites first an article from 1899 called "An Encouragement of Reading," published in a local newspaper, the *Shimotsuke shinbun*, in which the author complains that "In our Tochigi Prefecture, it is almost common practice for books that one has ordered to arrive ten days or even two weeks behind schedule." Asaoka goes on to cite an advertisement from 1906, put out by Koshikumo Minoji, the owner of a provincial lending library, in the same newspaper, in which claimed that he would obtain books and periodicals "as soon as they are ordered, regardless of where they are published."[138] In the latter example, we are dealing with something approaching simultaneity; but even in the first example we can see how much has changed in such a short time: days and weeks rather than years and decades. The frame of reference is totally different.

When considering the ideologies of the modern nation, it is best to keep the idea of simultaneity as a vanishing point; the history of ideology is never really one of simultaneity and uniformity but rather one of unevenness and contradiction. There is a stunning description of these uneven developments in an essay written in 1891 by Nakae Chōmin (1847–1901) on the occasion of his visit to Hokkaido. "Today we lunched in Chikubetsu," Chōmin wrote in a travelogue published in the *Hokumon shinpō*: "There is only a single fisherman's hut there. We entered the hut and sat down by the hearth and exchanged greetings. The master of the house was disheveled, reading a book. He set the book down and answered us. I picked up the book and had a look at it. It was volume nine of the *Hakkenden*. I imagined that the old fisherman

137. Hamada, "Bakin wo meguru shoshi, sakusha, dokusha no mondai," p. 286.
138. Asaoka, "Meijiki kashihon kashidasihi daichō no naka no dokushatachi," p. 6.

and myself and Miyazaki were just like characters in the *Hakkenden*."[139] It is a remarkable scene: Chōmin, the great liberal thinker of the Meiji period, having only just resigned his seat in the Diet (a victim of what Carol Gluck has so vividly described as the "denaturing of politics"), having traveled all day on horseback across the vast expanses of Japan's northern island, warming himself by the hearth in a solitary fishing village. There is a rich irony in this episode: a great exponent of modernity and liberalism finding comfort in Kyokutei Bakin's masterpiece, imagining himself and his companions as canine retainers in the service of a feudal ideal.

But there is another dimension to this scene. Chikubetsu is the last Japanese settlement visited by Chōmin and his companion Miyazaki before passing into the world of the Ainu. And it is also the last scene of reading they encounter before emerging back into the world of what Chōmin calls "Japanese civilization" at Wakkanai where they spend the day reading "novels, military books, and old newspapers."[140] In between these two points is a world without writing, as Chōmin stresses, writing out Ainu names first phonetically and then assigning to them Chinese characters after thinking the phonetic transcriptions "unrefined, somewhat animal like."[141] The scene of reading in Chikubetsu is striking because this old and disheveled fisherman is reading a work published in 1843, a quarter century before the Meiji Restoration, almost half a century before the scene takes place. How different this scene would have been had this fisherman been reading Futabatei Shimei's newly published *Ukigumo* or, perhaps better, had he been consuming a *roman-feuilleton* in a daily, the perfect example of the nexus between the newspaper and the novel, for Benedict Anderson the two great instruments of the imagining of the nation. This scene is not an example of the simultaneous and homogenous deployment of the ideological imaginings of the nation-state evenly across space by the novel acting as "a sort of literary railway," as Franco Moretti has put it, proceeding "to

---

139. Nakae Chōmin, "Nishikaigan nite no kankaku," pp. 35–41.

140. Nakae Chōmin, "Nishikaigan nite no kankaku," p. 40.

141. Nakae Chōmin, "Nishikaigan nite no kankaku," pp. 38–39. There is a sort of irony in this scene too as the translator of *The Social Contract* and the self-proclaimed "Rousseau of the East" enacts a sort of primal staging of the "violence of the letter."

weave the network capable of covering a country in all its extension";[142] rather, it is an example of a literary underdevelopment, a journey back in time toward the world before the letter transposed onto a journey through space.[143] And perhaps, above all, this anecdote reveals a basic but often overlooked reality: that the literature of an age is really composed not only of what is produced by that age but also by what is consumed. As we will see in Chapter 3, a number of early modern novels were reprinted—and read—over the final decades of the nineteenth century, and no history of Meiji literature is really complete without taking them into account.

Practices of the Sentimental Imagination: Melodrama, the Novel, and the Social Imaginary in Nineteenth-Century Japan: beneath my title lies a fiction, the nineteenth-century Japanese novel. If we now turn back to Figure 4, that chart of the novel across the long nineteenth century, we can see some of the implications of this fiction as well as some of its limitations. It is important to stress the provisional nature both of the chart and of the idea of a long nineteenth century extending from the 1780s to the first decade of the twentieth century. There are thousands of titles represented in this graph and historically speaking it is misleading to call them novels or to write of the nineteenth-century Japanese novel; but the chart is useful—and not least of all as a graphic representation—as one way of re-conceptualizing the problem of periodization in terms of literary form. Numbers are blunt instruments, but sometimes blunt instruments are necessary for bringing down the large structures of history. And while the idea of the nineteenth-century Japanese novel is provisional—and in the end will no doubt create conceptual

142. Moretti, "Modern European Literature: A Geographical Sketch," p. 98.

143. This is exactly how Tessa Morris-Suzuki describes the way in which "difference" came increasingly to be perceived over the course of the Meiji period: "Perhaps the most interesting implication of the notion of *bunmei* [civilization] was the way in which it allowed difference to be transposed from the realm of space to the realm of time, so that 'foreignness' increasingly came to be reinterpreted as 'underdevelopment'. . . . So the vision of a world made up of concentric circles, where foreignness increased the further one moved from the centre, came to be replaced by a vision of a single nation where 'development' and 'modernity' diminished the further one moved from the capital towards the geographical extremities." See Morris-Suzuki, "The Frontiers of Japanese Identity," pp. 62–63.

limitations and blind spots if it is to become anything more than a provisional way of grouping certain objects together—it is useful, or even necessary, for precisely the reasons Reinhart Koselleck gives: as a concept, "novel" is a *formal category* which is *the condition* for a possible history of nineteenth-century Japanese literature, or, we might venture to say, for a possible history of nineteenth-century Japan.

At this point, we have only begun to pose the question of the relationship between fiction and the social imagination in nineteenth-century Japan. And at this point it is enough to pose the question. As historians have long understood, reigning paradigms do not simply determine the answers we find, but more fundamentally they control the questions we ask, indeed the questions we are able to ask. In the end, the task of the historian is not to devise new answers to old questions but to ask new questions. That is what I have tried to do by examining a body of texts that not only has largely been ignored but that has never really been grouped together before as constituting an object of historical inquiry. At this point we have only begun to pose the questions; to answer them, we must now enter the literary archive and turn to the texts themselves.

CHAPTER 2

Under the Spell of Tears

Man is always sorcerer to man and the social world is primarily magical.

—Jean-Paul Sartre, *Sketch for a Theory of the Emotions*

A Sociological Experiment

"Scraps of paper containing nothing but the seeds of tears. . . ." This is how Santō Kyōzan described the state in which he received his brother Kyōden's manuscript for the second half of *Iezakura tsugiho no hachiue.*[1] *Iezakura* was Kyōden's final work, only partially complete at the time of his death in 1816 at the age of 55; Kyōzan was asked by the book's publisher to finish the manuscript, which he did in 1821, after being moved to tears by the sight of his brother's ghost.

It is a striking image, these scraps of paper and these seeds of tears. Kyōden was not known as a lachrymose author; indeed, he was essentially on the other side of a rift that began to emerge between the prose of wit and the prose of sentiment in the 1770s and 1780s, a great sentimental divide that marks the birth of a nineteenth-century aesthetic. But a good deal had changed since the 1770s: Kyōden had been imprisoned and his blocks burned;[2] the economics of the book trade, though perhaps not fundamentally altered, had become, in the early decades of the nine-

1. Santō Kyōden and Santō Kyōzan, *Iezakura tsugiho no hachiue*, p. 655.
2. See Kornicki, "*Nishiki no Ura*: An Instance of Censorship and the Structure of a Sharebon."

teenth century, at least exaggerated. There were new readers to contend with, and they had new tastes. To trace an arc in Kyōden's career from wit to sentiment would no doubt flatten the peculiarities and individuality of one of the most prolific and varied literary lives of early modern Japan; but to ask how this career came finally to end in a collection of tearful pages, this is a problem that suggests how literary history can begin to recast itself as a sociology of literary form, looking beyond the author and the oeuvre and toward a more complex and dynamic interaction between the aesthetics and economics of literature.

At the intersection of aesthetics and economics in early nineteenth-century Japan lay tears. Already in the opening years of the century, writers invoked the commercial success of "weeping books" (*nakihon*) as an avatar of changes in the fiction market and in the decades that followed the publication of *Iezakura*, sentimental fiction (*ninjōbon*) would become one of the most popular and lucrative genres of Japanese fiction.[3] The emergence of "weeping books" and the sentimental imagination of the nineteenth century takes place against the background of—or really at the intersection of—several important trends in cultural consumption in the late eighteenth and early nineteenth centuries. The first is a morphological shift within fiction away from the dominant modes of the eighteenth century that placed a premium on sophisticated linguistic play and toward a literature of plot. The second is the striking place that fiction titles came to occupy within nineteenth-century lending libraries and private book collections, suggesting the emergence of a culture of the novel. And the third is the rise to dominance of a culture of the book in which the book assumes an ever more central role in everyday life, transformed from a site of occasional interaction into a common object among the artifacts of daily life. The interrelation among these trends provides the backdrop to this chapter, in which I explore the emergence of an aesthetic of sentiment in the literature of nineteenth-century Japan.

Of the success of a novel in the literary marketplace, Sigfried Kracauer has written "It is the *sign of a successful sociological experiment*, proof that elements have once again blended in such a way as to correspond to the

---

3. On the history of sentiment and tears in nineteenth-century fiction, see Nakamura, "Ninjōbon to chūhonkata yomihon."

taste of an anonymous mass of readers."[4] This is a simple and elegant idea: a book's commercial success, what Kracauer calls its "success as a commodity," is neither entirely inherent in the book itself—in its formal qualities—nor entirely external; rather, it is born of a complex interaction between what the book offers and what the reading public demands. And so a bestseller provides a window onto the world of the reading public—their tastes, their needs, their desires. The history of a bestseller is also the history of its "anonymous readers."

The aim of this chapter is to understand these needs and desires and to begin to develop a history of these anonymous readers. To that end, I take sentiment seriously and in the pages that follow I look closely at two bestselling works of sentimental fiction from the first half of Japan's long nineteenth century: Tanishi Kin'gyo's *Keiseikai tora no maki*, published in 1778, and Tamenaga Shunsui's *Shunshoku umegoyomi*, published in two installments in 1832 and 1833. Between these two readings, I will consider the larger literary and cultural economy in which these two texts participated and pay special attention to the way the book market was itself being profoundly reorganized in the early years of the nineteenth century. Tears emerged in the years around 1800 as a powerful trope in the Japanese novel, and in the decades that followed tearful books would become one of the central genres of Japanese fiction. But tears were not, of course, new to Japanese aesthetics at the opening of the nineteenth century and it is in part by understanding how the function of tears began to change in the final decades of the eighteenth century that we can come to understand both the aesthetic and ideological dimensions of sentiment in the nineteenth-century Japanese imagination.

To writers of sentimental fiction in the nineteenth century, and to Tamenaga Shunsui in particular, the publication of Tanishi Kin'gyo's *Keiseikai tora no maki* in 1778 marked an important event in the history of tears. That same year, in the city of Osaka, a play was staged that, though perhaps less remembered and certainly less commemorated in the history of sentiment, is suggestive of the shape of the sentimental imagination that would become so important for writers in the following decades. In the fourth month of that year, the Takemoto puppet theater in Osaka staged a new play, *Shinjū kamiya Jihei*, by its leading dramatist,

4. Kracauer, "On Bestsellers and Their Audience," p. 91.

Chikamatsu Hanji.[5] The bulk of Hanji's drama was not actually new but a reworking of the famed love suicide of the courtesan Koharu and the paper seller Jihei, immortalized by Chikamatsu Monzaemon in his *Shinjū ten no Amijima* (*The Love Suicides at Amijima*), first staged at the same theater some fifty years earlier in 1721.[6] It was not unusual in the world of the stage for a drama to be revived or rewritten, cannibalized or plagiarized. All things considered, Hanji's version is remarkably faithful to the tragic impulses of the earlier drama. In the final scene of Hanji's 1778 play, Jihei and Koharu rendezvous and the two make their way to Amijima, where they are to be forever bound together by their suicide. Jihei has drawn his sword and in the original *Shinjū ten no Amijima*, he admonishes "let there be no tears on your face when they find you later" before plunging the sword into Koharu and then hanging himself. [7] But at this moment in Hanji's *Shinjū kamiya Jihei*, something rather unexpected happens just as the tragic ending is unfolding; Jihei's brother Magoemon arrives on the scene with the final line of the play: "No! Do not die! The villainy of Tahei and his counterfeiting have been discovered and reported to the authorities and Lord Gozaemon's doubts about you have been dispelled; you are once again son-in-law and father-in-law and he has taken it upon himself to redeem Koharu's contract. And so the dawn broke and the sky brightened and as the sun comes up on this play so all here live in prosperity from one spring to the next."[8]

The appearance of Gozaemon and the averting of the suicides provide, of course, a wonderful twist. But they also underscore the way that the central tragic structure of Chikamatsu Monzaemon's original play is

5. On the staging of *Shinjū kamiya Jihei*, see *Jōruri sakuhin yōsetsu*, vol. 3, p. 596.

6. It is striking that a version of *Amijima* was not staged again until 1776, two years before Chikamatsu Hanji's adaptation; scenes of different versions of the play were subsequently staged almost continuously through the end of the nineteenth century suggesting that it might be more appropriate to consider the story of Jihei and Koharu in the context of nineteenth century rather than eighteenth century aesthetics. See Kokuritsu gekijō chōsa shiryōka ed., *Shinrei Yaguchi no watashi/Natsu matsuri Naniwa kagami/Shinjū ten no Amijima*, p. 123. Donald Keene has noted that "although Chikamatsu [Monzaemon]'s original version has from time to time been revived, it has never displaced [Chikamatsu Hanji's] adaptation in public favor." See Keene, *World Within Walls*, p. 281.

7. Chikamatsu Monzaemon, "The Love Suicides at Amijima," p. 207.

8. Chikamatsu Hanji, "Shinjū kamiya Jihei," p. 56.

reworked in this version, and, in a sense, defused. Whereas Hanji's 1778 play ends with a deus ex machina and the image of the rising sun, Chikamatsu Monzaemon's original had ended with an invocation of tears: "the tale is spread from mouth to mouth. People say that they who are caught in the net of the Buddha's vow immediately gain salvation and deliverance, and all who hear the tale of the Love Suicides at Amijima are moved to tears."[9] The hearer of the tale—and, of course, the audience of the play—are urged to tears not only by the specific tragedy of the love suicide, but also because of what it represents: the impossibility of romantic love, its exclusion from the world of society. We are invited to weep because the play tells us, in no uncertain terms, that the world of socialization and the world of romantic love are mutually opposed and can never be reconciled in this world. Indeed, in *Shinjū ten no Amijima,* love can only be consecrated in death, and thus an ethical world is imagined separate from and opposed to the social world that it attempts to exclude and from which it is, in turn, excluded. It is precisely this inability to locate compromise on either the narrative or social plane that underwrites the tragic vision of the love suicides and it is precisely this uncompromising vision of tragedy to which the compromise ending of Hanji's play responds.

The ethical world established at the end of Hanji's *Shinjū kamiya Jihei* contains a disavowal of the tragic impulses of the original and instead offers a melodramatic compromise, a compromise that will become central to the aesthetic and ethical worlds of nineteenth-century fiction. And indeed, in the same year, but in a different place and in a different genre, Tanishi Kin'gyo would offer his own vision of compromise in a book that would later be seen as an early exemplar of a new genre of sentimental fiction.

Segawa's Ghost

At the end of the eighteenth century, Tanishi Kin'gyo was something of a cause célèbre. His first book, *Geisha yobukodori*, published in 1777, was a sensation; in a marginal note in his copy of the book, dated 1819, Ōta Nanpo would recall how he had read *Yobukodori* some 30 years

9. Chikamatsu Monzaemon, "The Love Suicides at Amijima," p. 208.

earlier, had happened somewhat later upon a copy at a bookstore in Nihonbashi and purchased it, only to lose it later that night after a bout of heavy drinking in Kobunachō. Now, at 71, Ōta wrote, he had finally obtained another copy of the book.[10]

But it was really Kin'gyo's next book, *Keiseikai tora no maki*, that made his reputation both within the critical establishment and among the broader reading public. *Gesaku hyōban hana no origami* contains a review of the novel. Published in 1802, *Hana no origami* reviews and ranks 171 fiction titles published in the final decades of the eighteenth century; *Tora no maki* is the first book reviewed and, along with Santō Kyōden's *Keiseikai shijūhatte* (1790), it is one of only two books which receives the very highest rank. The overall evaluation in *Hana no origami* sums up the book's most salient element: "a flawless plot."[11] And writing in his 1834 *Kinsei mono no hon Edo sakusha burui*, Bakin pointed to two striking and intertwined features of the novel: its ability to entertain—"readers were moved by such scenes as Segawa's ghost and greatly enjoyed the book"—and its ability to make money—"the publisher at the time and even the lending libraries greatly profited from it."[12]

Hana no origami and *Kinsei mono no hon Edo sakusha burui* remark on very different aspects of *Tora no maki*: one praises a formal feature ("a flawless plot") and the other comments upon a sociological or historical feature (the novel's ability to "move" the reading public and its commercial success). Taken together, these two early nineteenth-century readings of *Tora no maki* provide a useful point of entry into the aesthetic and social world of late eighteenth-century Japan because they situate the text at the crossroads of the aesthetic and the social and allow the modern reader to probe one of the fundamental problems of literary history: what is it about the particular formal makeup of this text that allowed it in the late eighteenth century to achieve such a remarkable commercial success

10. Ōta Nanpo, *Ōta Nanpo zenshū: bekkan*, p. 83.

11. See *Gesaku hyōban hana no origami*, pp. 135–82. For the overall evaluation of *Keiseikai tora no maki* see p. 138; for the full critique of the text see pp. 154–55. *Tora no maki*'s rank is "*kyoku-jō-jō-kichi*" (極上上吉); the overall evaluation is "*nukeme no nai tantori*" (ぬけめのないたんとり).

12. Kyokutei Bakin, *Kinsei mono no hon Edo sakusha burui*, p. 96.

and to give birth to a new genre—the sentimental novel—that would dominate the aesthetic world of the nineteenth century.[13]

Bakin provides a starting point for understanding the sentimental logic of *Tora no maki*: the novel's ending, the "moving" scene in which Gokyō is confronted by Segawa's ghost. The scene takes place at an isolated hut on Mt. Masugata, near Mukōgaoka on the western outskirts of Edo, to which Gokyō has withdrawn at the behest of his mother, who opposes his marriage to the courtesan Segawa. In the meantime, Segawa, pregnant with Gokyō's child, has been ransomed against her will by the blind moneylender Kiriyama and falls victim to the machinations of Kiriyama's henchman Kunji. It is while resisting Kunji's advances in the dark of night along the desolate shore of the Tamagawa that Segawa falls to her death, giving birth to a baby boy. Thus the scene is set for the final encounter between Segawa and Gokyō:

The sky suddenly darkened and along with a gentle breeze there appeared at the thatched reed door the seductive voice of a woman—

"Gokyō . . . please open the door," she said in a voice so gentle it would have sounded to anyone overhearing it like scattered notes from a *biwa*.
Gokyō. "A woman's voice on this deserted peak in the dead of night? It must be a fox. I shall shine a mirror on it and expose it."
Segawa. "No, I am no fox. It is I."
Gokyō. "Who?"
Segawa. "It is I, Segawa."
Gokyō. "Segawa? How could you come here in the dead of night?"
Segawa. "I asked at the foot of the mountain."
Gokyō. "Thank you for coming. What are you holding?"
Segawa. "It is the child born to us in our encounters in the floating world . . ."
Gokyō. "No! No! Have you lost all sense of duty that you would put that child in such a position having abandoned wretched me and been redeemed by Kiriyama! Worried sick about your hardships and nearing death, I came to this mountain to recover and thought that perhaps you too worried over me. And though we had no news of each other, I thought I would wait. But at long last, someone from the pleasure quarters came to me and told me that you had been

13. "Sentimental book" is Peter Kornicki's translation for *ninjōbon*; see Kornicki, "*Nishiki no Ura*: An Instance of Censorship and the Structure of a Sharebon," p. 166. On the genetic and generic relationship between *Tora no maki* and the nineteenth-century *ninjōbon*, see Nakamura, "Ninjōbon to chūhonkata yomihon," pp. 459–78.

redeemed by Kiriyama and that you had happily followed him out of the Yoshiwara, easily swayed like a burdock tail."[14]

At this point, Segawa protests that she was ransomed against her will and that the gods and Buddhas know the truth:

I was taken from the pleasure quarters weeping and even though I have had to prolong my life in the face of death, I had wanted once more to see your face and to give you our child and so rid myself of my attachment to this wretched world. And now I have been saved by Buddha. I gave birth to the child on the way and fled from the scene of my own death that in tears I might bring him to you. (p. 327)

Still, Gokyō refuses to believe Segawa and demands that "you now leave." Thus the scene is set for Segawa's final lament:

No, no . . . I am your wife. The pledge we wrote is our proof to each other . . . Why do you doubt my heart, I who have done no wrong, it is too much that you doubt that I was ransomed against my will. Do not doubt me and say to me the single word of 'wife' and then I will take my leave of this world . . . (pp. 327–28)

But it is only after Segawa's spirit has vanished that Gokyō finally understands what has happened and he belatedly calls after her: "Wait, my wife . . . So I will call you wherever you have gone. It was I who was wrong . . . So Segawa has died and I was visited by her ghost who passed me this child." (pp. 328–29)

The scene is predicated on this failed encounter and this recognition that comes too late; it offers a world in which virtue and self-sacrifice are veiled as treachery and deceit and their revelation is postponed by misunderstanding and misrecognition, postponed beyond the point where these human failings can be undone. It is a strikingly dramatic scene—dramatic both in its scenic powers and in its use of dialogue, exchange, and confrontation—and so it is not entirely surprising that both the reviewers in *Hana no origami* and Bakin should turn to the language of the theater to describe this novel.[15] Indeed, Bakin specifically mentions how

14. Tanishi Kin'gyo *Keiseikai tora no maki*, p. 326. All subsequent quotations from *Tora no maki* are from this volume and will be given in parentheses in the text.

15. The word used in *Hana no origami* to refer to "plot" たんとり (段取) is taken from theater criticism and similarly Bakin refers to the novel's "dramatic structure" (こは狂言の首尾整ひて).

different the book is from other *sharebon*,[16] the genre to which *Tora no maki* belonged and which James Araki has described as "essentially sketches" with "typically . . . no plot to speak of."[17] The contrast with Kyōden's *Keiseikai shijūhatte*—the work with which *Tora no maki* is paired in *Hana no origami*—is particularly striking. *Shijūhatte* comprises five discrete sketches, the emphasis of which Araki describes as "minute description, with a light touch of sarcasm, of modish ways in the pleasure quarters."[18] When viewed within the context of late eighteenth-century fiction, within its horizon of literary expectations, it is easy to see why the tragic ending of *Tora no maki* was so striking to contemporary readers; but that the "moving" story of Segawa and Gokyō should have become in the late eighteenth century such a precious literary commodity and that it should have captured so remarkably and perhaps against expectations the desires and needs of the reading public suggests that the history of this novel has contained within it a larger history of the aesthetic and social changes of an understudied and much misunderstood moment in Japanese history.

In his preface to *Tora no maki*, Kin'gyo had imagined that some of his readers "would be moved, others weep, and still others be so captivated by the story that they lose the power to move" (p. 303); and it is, no doubt, of this final scene that he was thinking. In some ways, however, the final scene is but a replay of an earlier scene in the novel. At the opening of *Tora no maki*, the courtesan Segawa is a sixteen-year-old girl named O-Yae, the daughter of a wealthy samurai family. She falls in love with the delicate and handsome Kōjirō—"his appearance recalled the shining prince Genji or a second coming of Narihira" (p. 305)—and the two are forced to elope, each being betrothed to another. They take refuge in Asakusa at the house of Kanhachi and his wife O-Kiku—infamous for "gambling, prostitution, and blackmail" (p. 305). Kanhachi and O-Kiku convince O-Yae, without Kōjirō's knowledge, to sell herself into the pleasure quarters to purchase medicines for her delicate husband. The villainous couple then absconds with the money, leaving Kōjirō to die

16. Kyokutei Bakin, *Kinsei mono no hon Edo sakusha burui*, p. 96.
17. Araki, "*Sharebon*: Books for Men of Mode," p. 38.
18. Araki, "*Sharebon*: Books for Men of Mode," p. 39.

with no news of his wife, and with the assumption that he has been abandoned.

In the second half of the novel, Segawa first approaches the usurer Kiriyama so that she might borrow money again to purchase medicines, this time for the convalescent Gokyō, and this gesture of love eventually leads to her death and to Gokyō's charges of infidelity and betrayal. The tragic structure of the novel is thus repeated in virtually identical terms, and this repetition underscores for the novel's readers both Segawa's uncompromising virtue and the dangers of a world in which virtue can be so easily manipulated by the powers of money.

In each instance, the virtuous Segawa (O-Yae) is tricked into first abandoning Kōjirō and then Gokyō; in each instance, crucially, her virtue is misrecognized as treachery. Nakamura Yukihiko has described *Tora no maki* as a "sentimental tragedy in which true love is opposed by the power of money and the end is death" and this description is both true and also somewhat misleading.[19] True, of course, because the central dramatic structure of the novel opposes Gokyō to the wealthy usurer Kiriyama—in some sense, the very apotheosis of Marx's "power of money."[20] But Nakamura's formula is also misleading because this dramatic structure is not the central problem of the novel, but its vehicle. In the end, Segawa's tragedy is not about money or love but about recognition. What moved readers, to recall Bakin, was not Segawa's death at the hands of Kunji but the scene of her ghost seeking recognition from Gokyō. And we weep not because the power of money has kept Segawa and Gokyō apart—as indeed it had torn Segawa away from Kōjirō—but because her virtue is continually misrecognized, even after her death. The final chapter of *Tora no maki* is moving not because of Segawa's death, which, after all, occurs in the penultimate chapter, but

19. Nakamura, "Ninjōbon to chūhonkata yomihon," p. 460.

20. In his section on "The Power of Money in Bourgeois Society" in *Economic and Philosophic Manuscripts of 1844*, Marx writes: "That which is for me through the medium of *money*—that for which I can pay (i.e., which money can buy)—that I am. The extent of the power of money is the extent of my power . . . Thus what I *am* and *am capable* of is by no means determined by my individuality. I am ugly but I can buy for myself the most *beautiful* of women. Therefore I am not *ugly*, for the effect of *ugliness*—its deterrent power—is nullified by money." See Marx, "Economic and Philosophic Manuscripts of 1844," p. 103.

because Gokyō continues to doubt her fidelity and refuses her final wish to recognize her as his wife—refuses, that is, until it is too late, until her ghost has already disappeared and he is left alone, holding the child that she bore him even in death. Marx famously wrote that tragedy repeated becomes farce, but in this case it is more accurate to say that tragedy repeated becomes melodrama.[21] At the end of the novel, of course, Segawa is dead and the final consecration of her innocence and virtue takes place, as it were, over her dead body. But she has left to Gokyō a baby boy, "a memento for the future" as she puts it, and the child both redeems her virtue and acts as its sign.

But the problem of recognition in *Tora no maki* is not simply narrative, it is also epistemological, and this is why the novel is so effective, so moving. Historically, the production—and, indeed, consumption—of *Tora no maki* needs to be set against the world of the late eighteenth century, a world, to borrow Conrad Totman's suggestive phrase, of eroding stability.[22] In his intellectual history of the eighteenth century, *Visions of Virtue in Tokugawa Japan*, Tetsuo Najita has perfectly captured this world, in which the stability of moral and ethical imperatives has eroded, in which the epistemological structures of a previous generation were beginning to fray under the weight of historical change, and in which "questions arose as to the ethicality of economic passion and, more broadly, whether the course of history in the context of the new commerce might be properly grasped and brought under effective management."[23] It is into this world that the myth of the courtesan Segawa was born, and it is within this context that the narrative and epistemological structures of the novel must be understood.

Tora no maki addresses the problem of "virtue" in a much different way from those texts of the tradition of intellectual history studied by Najita; but the problem is in both instances the same: how to *recognize* virtue in a world that has lost its moral bearings, or as Najita puts it, "how

---

21. "The expressive means of melodrama are all predicated on this subject," writes Peter Brooks in *The Melodramatic Imagination*, "they correspond to the struggle toward recognition of the sign of virtue and innocence." See Brooks, *The Melodramatic Imagination*, p. 28.

22. See Totman, "Part Five: The Erosion of Stability, 1790–1850" in *Early Modern Japan*.

23. Najita, *Visions of Virtue in Tokugawa Japan*, p. 13.

might the seemingly unpredictable and passionate fluctuations in the fortunes of men be brought into moral perspective that would demonstrate knowledge to be accurate, truthful, and thus a reliable basis of action."[24] And it is precisely this epistemological constellation surrounding virtue, knowledge, and action—and, of course, their disjuncture—that forms the narrative basis of *Tora no maki*, precipitating the events that lead first to O-Yae's fall and then to her eventual death as the courtesan Segawa.

Tora no maki is fraught with misrecognition; it is a world in which the signs of virtue remain hidden and action only impels tragedy. But at the end of the novel, we are given a rather different view of the world. We know that Segawa has remained faithful to Gokyō in both mind and body and that virtue is eventually recognized and forms the basis of the emergence of a new vision of virtue and a new ethical order. The world of stability offered at the end of *Tora no maki* is, of course, dependant upon the death of Segawa and is, in a sense, predicated on her exclusion; but her death provides the kernel around which stability crystallizes and by which it is authorized.

It is in this sense that the ghost of Segawa is so different from the ghost of Miyagi in the "Asaji ga yado" chapter of Ueda Akinari's *Ugetsu monogatari* published in Kyoto in 1776, two years before *Tora no maki*. In the chapter, the ghost of a virtuous woman appears "to tell of her long born resentment,"[25] but here the structure of misrecognition/recognition functions rather differently than in *Tora no maki*, where the effectiveness of the scene of Segawa's ghost is predicated on a gap between what the audience sees—the ghost of a virtuous woman seeking the recognition of her lover even in death—and what Gokyō sees—the fox like visage of a fallen woman unmoved by duty, unswayed by compassion. The reader witnesses Segawa's death along the Tamagawa and is party to her journey to Mt. Masugata; the reader does not discover Segawa's virtue and innocence along with Gokyō, but rather witnesses Gokyō's misrecognition and eventual recognition of that virtue. In "Asaji ga yado," these lines of vision are collapsed and we see exactly what Katsushirō sees: in the evening, the visage of his beautiful and

---

24. Najita *Visions of Virtue in Tokugawa Japan*, p. 14.

25. Ueda Akinari, *Ugetsu monogatari*, vol. 1, p. 179. All subsequent quotations from *Ugetsu monogatari* are from this volume and will be given in parentheses in the text.

chaste wife and their home that he left behind on his journey to the capital; in the morning, the ruins and ghostly presence that awaited him upon his return some seven years later.

And in each instance, this narrative structure has certain epistemological or ideological implications: in "Asaji ga yado," deception is entirely internal, a sort of self-deception; in *Tora no maki*, deception is external, impelled by treachery, by false clues, by the environment. In the two narratives, deception hinges on money; but money, in each narrative, has a very different function. And the configuration in the two texts between deception and money is emblematic of the way in which each confronts the epistemological implications of what Najita suggestively calls *the new commerce*. Written within a few years of each other, amidst the ethical and epistemological confusions occasioned by that new commerce, it is not surprising that each narrative should be centrally preoccupied with the problems of money, profit, and desire. And in some sense, but in very different ways, both narratives are deeply suspicious of the powers of money, deeply suspicious of this new commerce.

In very simple but also very allegorical terms, "Asaji ga yado" posits a disjuncture between the stable, almost timeless world of agriculture and the fluctuating and ephemeral world of the merchant, and it is along these fault lines that the narrative runs (p. 129).[26] It is Katsushirō's desire for profit, quite literally his "desire to become a merchant," that leads him to "turn his fields into money" (p. 129), and so leads him away from Miyagi and the world of agriculture in Shimōsa to the world of commerce in the capital. So "Asaji ga yado" turns on the self-deceiving nature of money and desire, a theme that would, of course, be picked up in Mizoguchi Kenji's 1953 screen adaptation of *Ugetsu monogatari*.

Tora no maki takes exactly the opposite approach: money is always external to Segawa; money is deceiving but that deception, too, is external. This is a striking configuration because Segawa is a courtesan and so,

---

26. "Asaji ga yado" opens with the following passage which sets up the contrast between the world of agriculture and the world of commerce: "In the village of Mama in the district of Katsushika in Shimōsa, there lived a man named Katsushirō. His forefathers had long lived here and, owners of many fields, lived in relative wealth and comfort. . . ."

in theory, her body (if not her desires) can be sold in the form of a commodity; but her only "encounter in the floating world," as she puts it, comes with Gokyō, not a client, but a lover. Although both Segawa herself and the fabric of *Tora no maki* are deeply implicated in the world of commerce, the power of money is continually disavowed in favor of a vision of virtue that exists beyond the world of commerce. Kiriyama is able to purchase Segawa's contract, but in the end, he is not able to purchase her virtue or even her body. Thus, the narrative structures of each story—internal for "Asaji ga yado" and external for *Tora no maki*—are themselves reenactments on the plane of discourse of the central epistemological claim of each story.

At the end of "Asaji ga yado," Miyagi leaves behind her as a memento for the future, as it were, not a baby boy but only a poem describing her longing for her husband and her resentment at being abandoned; her story thus dissolves continually back into the world of the written word. The Chinese story on which the "Asaji ga yado" chapter is based, the "Aiqing zhuan" of the *Jiandeng xinhua* (J. *Sentō shinwa*), ends with the ghost's reincarnation as a baby boy, an ending quite similar to that of *Tora no maki*.[27] Akinari's rejection of this ending emphasizes the distance that separates the aesthetic impulses of *Ugetsu monogatari* from Kin'gyo's novel published but two years later. As Dennis Washburn has noted, there is in *Ugetsu* "a concern with the practice of literature for its own sake," which he describes as a "subordination of ethics to art."[28] In *Tora no maki*, this writerly impulse is entirely absent and the ethical dimensions of the story are much clearer. There is perhaps not a subordination of art to ethics, but there is a collusion between story and discourse in the novel—between its narrative and epistemological structures—that produces a story both entertaining and moving, highly effective as a narrative and highly effective in its capacity to stabilize the erosion of the ethical system in the face of the new commerce.

In this sense, the ethical world established at the end of *Tora no maki* is quite close to that offered at the end of Chikamatsu Hanji's *Shinjū kamiya Jihei,* and rather distant from what was proposed by Chikamatsu

---

27. See Keene, *World Within Walls*, pp. 381–85. For the text of the "Aiqing zhuan," see "Aikei no monogatari" in Iizuka tr. *Sentō shinwa*, pp. 151–66.

28. Washburn, "Ghost Writers and Literary Haunts," p. 40 and p. 79.

Monzaemon's original. In *Shinjū ten no Amijima,* love can only be consecrated in death and thus an ethical world is imagined that is separate from and opposed to the social world from which it is excluded. The world of love in *Tora no maki* is not nearly as stark, and it ends with a typically novelistic compromise: the birth of the child and his integration into the social world. This child, in turn, will give birth to another feature typical of the nineteenth-century novel: the sequel.

Tora no maki offers a novel—and novelistic—approach to the problem of the recognition of virtue and the establishment of a moral universe: "novel" because it breaks with the tradition of the monumentalization of virtue found in such texts of the eighteenth century as *Shinjū ten no Amijima,* which end not with recognition and reconciliation of the world of narrative with the social world, but rather with a division of labor between what each world can—and should—hope to achieve; and "novelistic" because it does so by locating the ethical and moral dimensions of the age within a narrative plot, by literally *emplotting* the central epistemological problems of the day within a narrative structure. And so it is not surprising that *Tora no maki*'s "flawless plot" is seized upon as its most salient feature by its reviewers in *Hana no origami.*

In 1826, at the beginning of his career as one of the great nineteenth-century purveyors of sentiment, Tamenaga Shunsui would revisit the world of *Tora no maki,* writing for it a sequel in which Gokyō is at first separated from and then eventually reunited with his son, marrying the boy's nursemaid and forming a conjugal family watched over by the ghost of Segawa. Before turning to Shunsui, however, let us first step back and examine the world of print and commerce in which his career would take shape.

The Sea Cucumber and the Crab

The early nineteenth century was a defining moment in the development of both the aesthetics and economics of early modern fiction. It is a moment perfectly captured by Shikitei Sanba in the preface to his *Kejō suigen maku no soto* (1807):

The sea cucumber laughs at the crab: is he going or coming, coming or going? The crab laughs at the sea cucumber: is it his head or his ass, his ass or his head? And so on. Recently books of wit are dying out and being replaced by weeping books, blue books are becoming red books. While *sharebon* and *aobon* point at *nakihon* and *akahon* and laugh at them for being boorish and sneer at them for being uncouth, the weeping books and *akahon* no doubt laugh at *sharebon* and *aobon* as going too far and being impudent. We can no longer tell the good from the bad and we playful writers have been put on the shelf and can only close our mouths and vainly lament that our time is over. To one side, the lending libraries say that only uncouth books are selling and are all the rage. And having stooped to the lowest level of readers, the publishers' coffers are overflowing. The profit-seeking booksellers are full of greed and will choose anything—be it a refined work or simply a rant against the world—and sell them cheaper than the goods at a penny store, prizing most above all else works that will sell among the boorish and rustic.[29]

Here the literary field of Japan circa 1800 is drawn in striking terms: a rivalry of genres, with wit and sentiment squared off in a zero sum game; the uncouth rustic reader clamoring for tears; the commercial lending libraries and publishers greedily filling their coffers, unable to tell of a work of fiction its head from its ass.

And Sanba was himself intimately familiar with both the aesthetic and economic dimensions of the rivalry between the crab and the sea cucumber. In 1776, Sanba was born the son of a block carver in Asakusa's Tawaramachi district and spent his youth deeply immersed in the book trade. At the age of nine, Sanba apprenticed to Horino Jihei at the publisher and bookseller Gangetsudō, and by his thirties, Sanba was an accomplished author and his father had carved the blocks for a number of his works putting him in what Tanahashi Masahiro describes as a "unique" position as a writer in the early modern period. Sanba would marry twice into the families of publisher-book merchants: first becoming the son-in-law of the proprietor of the Yorozuya, and then, after breaking with the Yorozuya, marrying the daughter of his former mentor at the Gangetsudō. In the years following *Kejō suigen maku no soto*, Sanba would go on to write the works for which he is best known, *Ukiyoburo* (1809–1813) and *Ukiyodoko* (1813).[30]

We need not, of course, take Sanba's account of the book trade at face value. It was, after all, precisely the era in which Sanba was writing,

---

29. Shikitei Sanba, *Kejō suigon maku no soto*, p. 298.

30. Tanahashi, *Shikitei Sanba*, p. 7. Sanba's biographical information is based on Tanahashi's account.

the Bunka period (1804–1818), to which Tsubouchi Shōyō would turn when describing, some eighty years later, the height of discrimination among the Japanese reading public. "In the Bunka and Bunsei eras," Shōyō wrote in the preface to *Shōsetsu shinzui* (1885), "readers were extremely discerning; poorly done novels and stories were naturally overwhelmed by superior works and never emerged into the world, vainly languishing in manuscript or ending up the food of moths should they happen to make their way to the block carver."[31] It is, of course, a matter of perspective, with each writer using the image of a previous age as an instrument to criticize his own cultural and historical moment as what Shōyō calls "deplorable." There is here something of that image of the escalator with which Raymond Williams opens *The City and the Country*, and we should perhaps not be surprised were we to take the escalator back further still to find at earlier moments similar judgments and pronouncements using the past as a convenient stick with which to beat the present.[32]

Yet there is something rather compelling about Sanba's account. His intimacy with the various facets of the book trade—both commercial and aesthetic—did perhaps put him in an unusual position to comment on the state of the cultural field around 1800. And Sanba locates his critique of the fiction market within the framework of institutional changes related to the production, distribution, and consumption of fiction that had gained increasing momentum across the late eighteenth and early nineteenth centuries. One of these was the power of the publisher, the power of capital. The other was the role of the lending library.

As Adam Kern has noted, "the author" had come into something of his own in the late eighteenth century as both a creative and a commercial figure.[33] It is a moment perfectly illustrated by an image of the author that Santō Kyōden offers at the beginning of his *Gozonji no shōbaimono* (1782): the author alone in the creative process, asleep and quite literally dreaming up the entire world of the book (Figure 5).

---

31. Tsubouchi Shōyō, *Shōsetsu shinzui*, pp. 40–41.

32. See Williams, *The Country and the City*.

33. Kern, "Blowing Smoke," pp. 41–47.

Fig. 5 From Santō Kyōden's *Gozonji no shōbaimono* (1782). Courtesy of Tōyō Bunko.

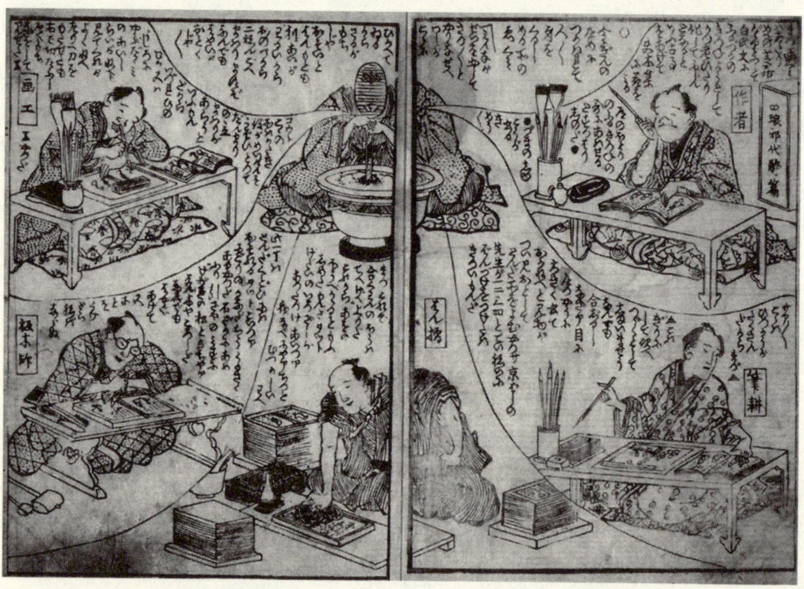

Fig. 6 From Tōri Sanjin's *Takarabune kogane no hobashira* (1818), illustration by Katsukawa Shunsen. Courtesy of Tōyō Bunko.

Tōri Sanjin would offer a rather different picture of the creative process in his *Takarabune kogane no hobashira* (1818): here, the author is shunted off to one side, only one of a number of artisans like the illustrator, calligrapher, and block carver, all controlled by the faceless publisher at the center of the page, his visage covered over by coin. To his side, the copyist laments the disorderly state of the manuscript noting that Kyōden had always clearly numbered the sequences (Figure 6).

We need to be careful not to speak in absolute terms. The book trade was already by the late eighteenth century a place of commerce and commercialism and, as Lucien Febvre and Henri-Jean Martin argue in *The Coming of the Book*, "From its earliest days printing existed as an industry, governed by the same rules as any other industry; the book was a piece of merchandise which men produced before anything else to earn a living."[34] We are not looking in the late eighteenth century at the birth of commercialism in the book trade or the sudden commodification of the book; commercialism in and the commodification of the written word have long and complex histories and to look for their origins at a particular moment would no doubt be to engage in a chimerical hunt.

Sanba's account of this process is striking because of his introduction of the figure of the boorish and rustic reader and that go-between of publisher and reader, the commercial lending library. Something of this problem is already visible—though perhaps only in relief—in the judgments passed out in *Gesaku hyōban hana no origami*. While *Tora no maki* is judged to have "a flawless plot," Santō Kyōden's *Keiseikai shijūhatte* is said to be "adored throughout Edo." Here is the problem in a nutshell: the crab and the sea cucumber, wit and sentiment, and, of course, the city and the country. The split between high and low to which Nakano Mitsutoshi points as the defining feature of nineteenth-century literary culture is thus not simply a split between the publishing worlds of Edo and Kamigata (the Kansai region), and between the poetic arts and the world of fiction; this split is also replicated on a different level within the world of fiction writing.[35] The verbally dense and innovative *Keiseikai shijūhatte* is adored throughout Edo, but for the rustic reader the choice is sentiment and tears, the choice is *Tora no maki*.

34. Febvre and Martin, *The Coming of the Book*, p. 109.

35. See Nakano, *Jūhasseiki no Edo bungei*, pp. 1–67.

But why tears? Why had tears so suddenly become such a lucrative commodity? Why tears and not laughter, for instance, that literary coin on which Sanba would himself trade for most of his career. This is a question to which Sanba does not turn his attention, a question that not only goes unanswered but essentially unasked. And yet this is really *the* question confronting the literary historian engaged with the fiction of Japan's long nineteenth century. "A certain variety of popular novel exists" Gramsci writes, "and it should be noted that, although all of them simultaneously enjoy some degree of success and popularity, one of them nevertheless predominates by far. From this predominance, one can identify a change in fundamental tastes."[36] This is very much the situation in Japan at the turn of the nineteenth century: a certain variety exists—wit, sentiment, humor—but then one comes to dominate, gradually at first, but then decisively. In the years surrounding the turn of the nineteenth century, the weeping book emerged as a dominant form of popular fiction, and this rise to dominance marks the emergence of a new aesthetic imaginary; but this dominance also foregrounds a new social imaginary, a new set of social mythologies and ideologies, and so the history of tears is also, to a large extent, the history of nineteenth-century Japan.

The Cultural Field

Books of wit are dying out and playful writers are put on the shelf. Weeping books are all the rage. And at the center of this mess are the lending libraries. However, we need to be careful not to see in Sanba's description of the cultural field circa 1800 a simple or mechanistic explanation for the rise of the sentimental imagination. It is, of course, tempting to imagine colporteurs roaming the countryside laden with weeping books, pandering to a new class of readers unable—or perhaps simply unwilling—to deal with the linguistic difficulty and atomistic structure of much eighteenth-century fiction. But the historical record is much too fragmentary and fragile to allow this sort of picture to emerge with any clarity or force.

---

36. Gramsci, *Selections from Cultural Writings*, p. 359.

What the historical record does bear out, however, is that there occurred in the final decades of the eighteenth century and the first decades of the nineteenth a dramatic reorganization of the cultural field, and it is against this background that we need to locate the emergence of the sentimental imagination of the nineteenth century. This shift took place along two axes: one was the growing role played by the book in social and cultural life, and the other was the growing significance of the novel within the cultural world of the book. At the center of these two movements—the point at which these two axes intersect—we find the lending library.

At any historical moment there exist a certain variety of popular entertainments, a certain set of options for cultural consumption. Any social or cultural formation is composed of an amalgam of these different entertainments, these different options, and the cultural field is a field of choices. But not all choices are equal, and the cultural consumer does not have even or equal access to each option. The field is indeed structured in such a way to create certain dispositions or inclinations; and crucial to an understanding of any cultural field is an understanding of the economics of the field. The two parts of Table 5 indicate the prices of cultural consumption in early nineteenth-century Japan and are intended to give some sense of the economics of cultural consumption in this period. These prices suggest the unevenness of the field: on the one hand, we have the theater that remains, throughout the nineteenth century, essentially out of reach of most consumers; on the other hand, we have the lending library which makes available to a reader with limited means a large cross section of the cultural imagination, including much of the world of the stage brought to the reader in print. In absolute terms, the book occupies a sort of middle ground; but in terms of access, the unevenness is much greater: to purchase Kyokutei Bakin's five-volume *yomihon*, *Sono no yuki* (1807), would cost roughly 40 times more than to borrow a similar book, Hayami Shun'gyōsai's five-volume *yomihon*, *Ehon sayo shigure* (1801). And to attend a performance at one of Edo's three licensed theaters would cost—even to sit in the *doma* pit section—twice as much still. The world of the stage continued to exercise a powerful pull on the cultural imagination of the nineteenth century through various print media, but for many—indeed most—consumers, the book was the only point of access to the world of Edo's great theaters.

Table 5a
Dispositions I: The Economics of Cultural Consumption, circa 1800

Title	Volumes	Price	% of 1 *koku* of rice
(A) Books borrowed at Nakaya Shinzaemon's lending library			
Kōshoku ichidai otoko, vols. 1–4	4	3 *bu*	0.5
Kōshoku ichidai otoko, vols. 5–8	4	3 *bu*	0.5
Honchō suikoden	10	6 *bu*	1.0
Keisei hangonkō	1	2.5 *bu*	0.4
Ehon sayo shigure	5	3 *bu*	0.5
(B) Books purchased by Matsuzawa Gohei			
Sono no yuki	5	13 *monme* 5 *bu*	22.5
Chinsetsu yumi harizuki (*kōhen*)	6	15 *monme* 5 *bu*	25.8
Akogi monogatari	5	15 *monme*	25.0
Tōkaidōchū hizakurige	3	7 *monme*	11.7
Ukiyoburo	2	4 *monme* 5 *bu*	7.5
Itozakura shunchō kien	3	6 *monme* 5 *bu*	10.8
Suisen tanzen	2	2 *monme* 8 *bu*	4.7

NOTE: Titles listed in (B) were purchased between 1808 and 1813.

SOURCES: Nagatomo, *Kinsei kashihon'ya no kenkyū*, pp. 120–21; Ikeda, "Shimōsa no kuni," pp. 166–95.

Table 5b
Dispositions II: The Economics of Cultural Consumption, circa 1800

Kabuki seat	Price	% of 1 *koku* of rice
Uchi kōshi	25–35 *monme*	41–58
Taifu	30–35 *monme*	50–55
Hira	25–30 *monme*	41–50
Uchi misu	25–35 *monme*	41–58
Soto misu	30–35 *monme*	50–55
Shin kōshi	15 *monme*	25
Hon doma	25 *monme*	41
Mae doma	25 *monme*	41
Hikifune	25 *monme*	41
Kiriotoshi	130 *mon*	3

SOURCE: Shikitei Sanba, *Shibai kinmōzui* (1806).

In Chapter 1, I introduced the catalogues of two commercial lending libraries, the Daisō library of Nagoya and Nakaya Shinzaemon's library at Kinosaki. The catalogues have the major limitation of being compiled when the collections came up for auction at the end of the nineteenth century, and as such they cannot offer any sense of diachronic change or the peculiarity of a particular historical moment. But each catalogue has the advantage of originating from outside the metropolitan center, and indeed together they represent two very different geographies of cultural consumption. Daisō, probably the largest lending library in nineteenth-century Japan, was located in the castle town of Nagoya, the capital of the Owari domain. Nakaya's library was, by contrast, much smaller and was located in the spa town of Kinosaki on the Japan Sea.

Again, we have only these two catalogues, so it is difficult to say how representative each is. But in general, they seem to follow a similar pattern to nineteenth-century European lending libraries. The large urban library, Daisō, with over 16,000 titles, had a great range of types of books available to readers. Fictional works constitute the largest single group of titles, with roughly 28 percent of the total number, but other categories such as education and medicine are also represented in the collection, and there are a large number of philosophical and/or religious works, with 12.5 percent of the total number of titles, second only to fiction. Nakaya's library, on the other hand, with 324 titles, has a very different structure: works of fiction make up 28 percent of the collection, and libretti of the puppet theater constitute another 56 percent; an overwhelming portion of the collection is thus composed of leisure reading, 84 percent of the total number of titles. "A small library doesn't have the same structure as a large library only smaller," Franco Moretti has written of the nineteenth-century European lending library, "it has a different structure."[37] Moretti continues, "Small spaces are not like Noah's Ark, with two of each species; they limit the number of species."[38] And a small number of "species" is exactly what we see in Nakaya's library: it is a veritable menagerie of leisure reading and not much else.

---

37. Moretti, *Atlas of the European Novel*, p. 147.
38. Moretti, *Atlas of the European Novel*, p. 159.

In his study of the French Bibliothèque Bleue, Robert Mandrou notes how it was at the turn of the nineteenth century that the number of fiction titles began to outnumber all other categories in the stocks of French colportage.[39] Perhaps something similar was happening in Japan, and at roughly the same time. But just as large libraries are not simply small libraries only larger, the fiction of the nineteenth century was not simply the fiction of the eighteenth century on an expanded scale. It was a different kind of fiction. This is, of course, what Sanba has in mind in his parable of the sea cucumber and the crab: the rivalry is, after all, not between two "species," not between the novel and devotional literature, for instance, but a sort of internecine struggle among the various forms of fiction. Again, size is not just size: it implies important structural differences.

This moment of transition is captured in a notebook kept by Matsuzawa Gohei of Onigoe village in Shimōsa, in which he details the books he purchased from several Edo book merchants between 1808 and 1813. Matsuzawa's notebook was recently discovered by Ikeda Mayumi, an archivist at the Shiritsu Ichikawa Rekishi Hakubutsukan in Ichikawa City, Chiba.[40] The notebook contains 354 titles purchased by Matsuzawa between 1808 and 1813 and gives extremely detailed information about dates and prices, revealing a part of the early modern book trade that had so far proven elusive. It is a remarkable piece of evidence because it is very historically specific and covers almost exactly the same historical moment that Sanba describes in his parable of the crab and the sea cucumber. As Table 6 suggests, there is a great deal more diversity among the "species" housed in Matsuzawa's library than what we find in the catalogue of Nakaya's lending library. The overwhelming dominance of fiction in both cases is striking—and also somewhat counterintuitive—because the preponderance of fiction titles contradicts most of what we thought we knew about patterns of cultural consumption in early modern Japan: that readers tended to purchase books for everyday use, such as devotional and instructional books, and to borrow fiction titles and entertainment from lending libraries.

---

39. Mandrou, *De la Culture populaire aux 17e et 18e siècles*, p. 185.

40. See Ikeda, "Shimōsa no kuni Katsushika-gun Onigoe-mura Matsuzawa Gohei no Bunka gonen kara jūnen 'shoseki arimonochō'," pp. 166–95.

Table 6
Matsuzawa Gohei's Book Collection

Genre	Number of titles	Percentage of total titles
Fiction	241	68.08
Shinto	3	0.85
Buddhism	4	1.13
Miscellaneous histories	9	2.54
Essays	5	1.41
Geography	5	1.41
Thought	1	0.28
Shingaku	6	1.69
Jōruri	2	0.56
Ōraimono	3	0.85
Dictionary	3	0.85
Politics	1	0.28
Medicine	2	0.56
Rites	1	0.28
Horticulture	1	0.28
Theater	1	0.28
Miscellany	4	1.13
Fables	6	1.69
Educational	7	1.98
Epigraphy	1	0.28
Unknown	41	11.58
TOTAL	354	100.00

NOTE: Due to rounding., percentages may not total 100.00.
SOURCE: Adapted from Ikeda, "Shimōsa no kuni."

This is the pattern Nagatomo Chiyoji discovered in his work on eighteenth-century reading habits using records compiled by a private collector in Osaka in the 1730s,[41] and, again, a similar suggestion was made in the 1850s by Kitagawa Morisada, recalling the fiction of the Bunka period: "It was rare for people to purchase these books for their own collections; in general it was common for lending libraries to collect them, affix a price, and lend them out to various households."[42]

41. Nagatomo, *Kinsei kashihon'ya no kenkyū*, p. 96.
42. Kitagawa Morisada, *Kinsei fūzokushi*, vol. 4, p. 309.

The composition of Matsuzawa's collection of fiction titles is also notable. When broken down by year of publication, 134 of the 245 titles were published in the first thirteen years of the nineteenth century, fifty-nine titles were published in the eighteenth century, and fifty-one titles are of uncertain date. And almost half of the fiction titles—120 in all—are from the nineteenth-century genre of historical fiction known as *yomihon*; by contrast, there is only a single book of wit (*sharebon*), the dominant genre of the late eighteenth century, the genre whose passing Sanba had eulogized at just this moment. So when Sanba lamented that books of wit were dying out and that playful writers were being put on the shelf, this is what he meant.

If we turn to the recently catalogued private library of the Hayashi family, who lived in the post town of Tsumago along the Kiso highway, we see in their collection of books from the middle decades of the nineteenth century a remarkably similar pattern (Table 7). There is a great deal of diversity here—titles in religion, thought, history, and poetry, as well as books on cultural pursuits like tea and gardening—but again there is an overwhelming preponderance of fiction together with libretti from the puppet theater. There are 98 fiction titles, 29 libretti of the puppet theater, and an additional 24 *jōruri nukihon* which contain a single scene "abstracted" from a play. Numerically, this library too is dominated by leisure reading. And, among the fiction titles, there is again a pronounced pattern when broken down by subgenre: only a single example of the eighteenth-century genre of *ukiyozōshi*; only three titles of the comic genre of *kokkeibon*; and then roughly equal numbers of sentimental fiction (*ninjōbon*); historical fiction (*yomihon*); and illustrated fiction (*kusazōshi*); with a large number of illicit manuscript novels depicting recent historical events.

Historians of Japanese fiction have long argued that these genres of fiction circulated differently and were consumed by different kinds of readers: historical fiction was expensive and circulated primarily through lending libraries and was read by men; sentimental fiction was read by women; illustrated fiction by women and children. What evidence that has been mustered to support this schematic understanding has been largely anecdotal and often based on prefaces and apostrophes to the reader contained within the fiction itself. And while these kinds of

Table 7
The Hayashi Family Library

Genre	Number of titles	Percentage of total titles
Religion	2	0.54
Thought/scholarship	16	4.30
Leisure (fiction and poetry)	104	27.96
ukiyozōshi	1	
yomihon	21	
kiritsukebon	8	
kokkeibon	3	
ninjōbon	22	
kusazōshi (*gōkan*)	21	
jitsurokutai shōsetsu	17	
waka (poetry)	5	
haikai (poetry)	1	
zappai (poetry)	1	
kanshibun (poetry)	4	
Performing arts	124	33.33
Music	8	2.15
Pictorial works	19	5.11
Crafts/hobbies	4	1.08
Practical books	47	12.63
Directories	5	1.34
Miscellany/divination	4	1.08
Agriculture	2	0.54
Travel guides	6	1.61
Chinese books	31	8.33
TOTAL	372	100.00

SOURCE: Suzuki et al., *Kinsei kōki ni okeru shomotsu/sōshi nado no shuppan/ryūtsū/kyōju ni tsuite no kenkyū*, pp. 21–93.

paratexts often reveal the author's attitudes towards the reader—and perhaps might even serve as evidence of an imagined or ideal reader—they only rarely, and in exaggerated ways, correspond to the habits and practices of real historical readers.

Indeed, as new evidence of reading, circulation, and collecting come to light, this old framework seems increasingly unable to articulate the complex reality of how nineteenth-century fiction was actually read. In what evidence of collecting and reading we do have, and two of the best examples are the Matsuzawa and Hayashi libraries, we see not readers who fit easily into pre-existing categories based on class or gender or relative distance from the metropole, but readers who seem to avail themselves of the opportunities with which they are presented, readers whose tastes seem to confound the all-too-easy roles that modern historians have tried to ascribe to them, readers whose habits of reading are no doubt shaped by tastes and inclinations—but these tastes and inclinations are now difficult to recover.[43]

The other striking component of the Hayashi library is a collection of forty-one illustrated playbills (*ehon banzuke*) assembled between the 1840s and the 1870s. In addition to the playbills, the Hayashi collection includes a range of other material relating to the theater: two hand-copied kabuki scripts, two actor critiques, and a guide to the genealogy of acting families. Here, we see quite clearly two interesting aspects of the cultural field of the nineteenth century: that although the libretti of the puppet theater were printed, published, sold and read, the scripts of kabuki were not; and that the kabuki theater continued to exercise an important pull on the imagination of nineteenth-century consumers of all kinds, but often this pull was limited to consuming the stage *in print*.[44] Consumers had access to the stage not only in playbills or actor critiques or the truly enormous amount of ephemera that the stage generated—maps, calendars, lists of salaries, rankings of actors, and theatrical genealogies—but also *in novels*. One of the most significant trends within illustrated fiction was the use of actor's likenesses in illustrations, especially from the second decade of the nineteenth century onward. For many consumers, this was the only access available to the world of the stage. As Aoki Kōichirō has argued in his recent study of Meiji-period leisure, it was only begin-

---

43. In *The Order of Books*, Roger Chartier warns of "a narrowly sociographic conception implicitly postulating that cultural cleavages are necessarily organized according to pre-existent social divisions. I think we need to reject this dependence that relates gaps in cultural practices to a priori social oppositions, whether on the macroscopic scale of contrasts between dominant and dominated or between the elites and the people or on the scale of smaller differentiations, as for example among social groups in a hierarchy of conditions, professions or levels, of wealth. . . . The same is true of gender-based and generationally based distinctions . . . and more." Chartier, *The Order of Books*, p. 7.

44. On the publishing of noh texts, see Rath, *The Ethos of Noh*, pp. 159–214 and on the puppet theater see Nagatomo, *Edo jidai no shomotsu to dokusha*, pp. 197–99.

ning in the Meiji twenties—the late 1880s and early 1890s—that "the general public was able, without difficulty, to attend the theater and especially kabuki" following the opening of a number of new theaters and the overall reduction of ticket prices.[45]

Our knowledge of the cultural field of Japan in the nineteenth century is quite fragmentary and, in isolation, many of the pieces seem enigmatic. The holdings of a single lending library or the books of a single reader are, of course, bound in their own ways to be idiosyncratic, shaped both by personal tastes but also by historical accident, by what was available and when. We do not yet have a large statistical body from which to draw general conclusions, but the evidence we do have, when seen as part of a larger whole, provides a suggestive glimpse of nineteenth-century Japanese culture. Taken together with what we know of nineteenth-century lending libraries, the evidence from the titles in the collections of Matsuzawa and the Hayashi family suggests that the generic shift on which Sanba remarked was itself taking place at an important—in some ways defining—moment in the development of the Japanese literary market. In the final decades of the eighteenth century and the opening years of the nineteenth, several different pressures were being brought to bear on the cultural field. There was, within fiction, a formal shift away from the dominant late eighteenth-century mode of wit with its dense and sophisticated linguistic play—the loss of which Sanba so laments—and toward a literature in which plot was central. Then there is the conspicuous place that fiction itself occupied within the overall culture of the book in this period, a position suggested by the number of duplicate fiction titles in the Daisō catalogue and by the overall quantity of fiction titles in the holdings of Nakaya's lending library and the collections of Matsuzawa and the Hayashi family. Both of these trends have to be seen as part of a larger rise to dominance of print itself, in which all the surfaces on which print would appear became important articles of everyday life. These trends were coincident in the sense that they were occurring at roughly the same time; they were also causally interrelated in important ways.

The most striking—and perhaps historically most significant—interrelation among these trends can be seen in the relationship that

45. Aoki, *Meiji Tōkyō shomin no tanoshimi*, pp. 223–24.

emerges between the world of print and the theater. Both Nakaya's lending library and the Hayashi family's collection have huge numbers of libretti from the puppet theater, bearing out Nagatomo Chiyoji's contention that these libretti had become by the late eighteenth century a form of reading matter that circulated like fiction.[46] In both cases, when we add the number of these libretti titles to the number of fiction titles, we find collections dominated completely by leisure reading. When we separate them out, however, the holdings of these libraries reveal a rather peculiar relationship that emerged between fiction and the literature of the puppet theater in the late eighteenth century.

The preponderance of these libretti suggests the importance of the theater in the cultural economy of the nineteenth century; but more significantly these libretti were *printed* and they were *read.* The late eighteenth century is a rather strange time for the puppet theater. On the one hand, most of the great *jōruri* playwrights and theaters defected in these years to the kabuki stage; on the other hand, this was precisely the point at which there occurred a publishing boom in these libretti. As Nagatomo has argued, the libretti themselves began to circulate not as practice scripts for amateurs but as reading material for provincial readers, essentially as fiction. Just as the puppet theater was losing its theatrical audience, it was gaining a new—and greatly expanded—audience of readers. And this has extremely important formal implications both for the theater and for fiction.

In drama, the novel found structure and plot, and historians of early modern Japanese fiction have long written of the dramatization of fiction around the turn of the nineteenth century as themes, tropes, and narrative elements from the theater were incorporated into the novel. But we can also see a sort of countercurrent at roughly the same time, something we might think of as the novelization of the stage, visible, for instance, in the ending of Chikamatsu Hanji's *Shinjū kamiya Jihei* in which Jihei and Koharu are saved at the last instant. It is an astonishing scene reminiscent of the "annulling of gravity" that René Girard has described as essentially the definition of the novelistic ending.[47] This is not to sug-

46. See Nagatomo, *Edo jidai no shomotsu to dokusho*, pp. 197–99.

47. See Girard, *Deceit, Desire and the Novel*, p. 294: "The conclusions of all novels are reminiscent of an oriental tale," writes Girard, "in which the hero is clinging by his fin-

gest that a dramatist like Hanji was consciously writing with a new *readership* in mind, or even that he was aware of the changing nature of cultural consumption occurring at the very moment he was writing; rather, it is to propose that the theater was itself, perhaps ineluctably, moving toward a sort of novelistic aesthetics based on compromise and conciliation.

Kyōden's Tears

Iezakura tsugiho no hachiue, the tearful manuscript that Santō Kyōzan inherited from his brother Kyōden after the latter's death, was itself based on a work of the puppet theater, Suga Sensuke's *Kamiko jitate ryōmen kagami*, staged at the Kita-Horieza in Osaka in 1768 and based on the tragic love suicide of Sukeroku and Agemaki that occurred at the beginning of the eighteenth century. But like Chikamatsu Hanji's rewriting of Chikamatsu Monzaemon's *Shinjū ten no Amijima*, *Iezakura* too omits the most important element of the former work: the love suicide itself. We do not know, of course, the state of the manuscript when Kyōden died, what he had intended for his characters, what "seeds of tears" he had planted; but the book as it was eventually published in 1821—with the first volume ostensibly written by Kyōden and the second volume by Kyōzan—is a remarkably typical example of the nineteenth-century aesthetic of melodrama and sentiment.

At the end of the first volume of *Iezakura*, we are left with a rather messy story, with four plots going on at once. There is the story, with which the novel opens, of the robbery and murder of O-Tsuji, the wife of Wabisuke, a merchant of tea wares. Then there is the story of the retainer Tsuyuemon, his younger brother Tsuyujirō, and Tsuyuemon's servant Senbei, culminating in the theft of the prized sword Asahimaru, Tsuyuemon's ritual suicide, and Tsuyujirō's exile. The third story revolves around the young Sukeroku and his faithful servant Shinpei. And the fourth story features the famed courtesan Agemaki and the rivalry for her affection between Sukeroku and the masterless samurai Kanshin.

The first half of *Iezakura* ends with these four seemingly unrelated stories left very much unresolved. The second half opens with Senbei on

---

ger tips to the edge of a cliff; exhausted, the hero finally lets himself fall into the abyss. He expects to smash against the rocks below but instead he is supported by the air: the law of gravity is annulled."

the way to visit his sister O-Tsuji, only to learn along the way that she has been murdered, her husband has died of illness, and their young daughter O-Machi (Senbei's niece) has been sold into the pleasure quarters to cover her father's debts and that she has become a famed courtesan known as Agemaki. The second volume of *Iezakura* opens with an image of Agemaki weeping before her uncle, recounting her mother's death and the demise of her father's house. And so the first string is pulled and the various strands begin to come together in a fantastic web of coincidence—can we really call it coincidence?—in which the nineteenth-century reader no doubt fully expected all of the disparate elements of the first half of the novel to be seamlessly resolved.

Agemaki entrusts Senbei with the peony *inrō* dropped at the sight of her mother's murder—the sign that will reveal the murderer's identity—and entrusts him with discovering the culprit. All signs point to Kanshin, Sukeroku's rival for Agemaki, but in the end the real villain turns out to be Kanshin's crony Monbei, who had also made off with the lost sword Asahimaru. The story ends happily: Agemaki avenges her mother's death by killing Monbei; Senbei recovers the lost sword to redeem his dead master's honor and in the process discovers that Sukeroku's faithful servant Shinpei is in fact his master's brother Tsuyujirō, who has been under cover searching tirelessly for the sword; Agemaki is granted her freedom by the brothel owner, moved by her virtue and filial piety; and all is set for Sukeroku and Agemaki to marry. However, the final twist in the plot occurs when Agemaki reveals that she is in fact a distant relative and childhood playmate of Sukeroku's and that the two were forbidden in childhood to marry by a fortuneteller because of an accident in which Sukeroku shot Agemaki in the forehead with an arrow leaving a mark that serves as the sign of recognition. So in the end, Sukeroku marries his lover Shiratama and Agemaki marries Kanshin who turns out not to have been a villain after all but merely guilty of bad judgment. And, well, everyone lives happily ever after.

It is a wonderful example of what Peter Brooks has called the "melodramatic imagination," full of false identities revealed, clues and signs of innocence and vice, full of the "aesthetics of astonishment."[48] And it is

---

48. See Brooks, *The Melodramatic Imagination*, especially Ch. 1 "The Melodramatic Imagination" and Ch. 2 "The Aesthetic of Astonishment."

an exceedingly typical example of Kyōden's late illustrated fiction. Indeed, Mizuno Minoru has gone so far as to catalogue the plot elements that typify Kyōden's later work:

> There is the falling in love of a man and a woman and a pledge; there is the jealous love of the villain and the resulting murder; there is the loss of a treasure; the amplification of the villain's brutality; the sufferings of the filial; secret dealings and wicked scheming; the vindictiveness of resentment and mystery; the appearance of a ghost and divine protection; the profligacy of the villain; the hardships of the heroes; the fulfillment of long cherished revenge; the reappearance of the lost treasure; household intrigue and violence; the meting out of punishment; the unexpected reunion of relatives; marriage and a happy ending. All of [Kyōden's] works of illustrated fiction from [1804] on when viewed from the perspective of their materials and plot, are nothing more than slight variations or complications of these narrative elements.[49]

But this very typicalness raises the question of why? What, to put the problem very simply, does this story do? What pleasure does it afford its readers? And why would they read the same story over and over again?

Any serious consideration of the category of popular fiction must surely engage this question of readerly pleasure and the often oblique relationship between repetition and enjoyment. "It is hardly possible," Freud writes in *Beyond the Pleasure Principle*, "to persuade an adult who has very much enjoyed reading a book to re-read it immediately. Novelty is always the condition of enjoyment."[50] *It is hardly possible. . . .* This may be true, but the history of popular literature suggests that it is very possible to persuade a reader to read *almost* exactly the same book over and over again. Novelty is the condition of enjoyment, but not too much novelty, or rather novelty set within certain bounds, certain repetitive structures. The "hunger for redundance," Umberto Eco has called it, is the underlying factor of most of literary history: "the reader continuously recovers point by point what he already

49. Mizuno, *Edo shōsetsu ronsō*, pp. 188–89. In her recent book on early modern illustrated fiction, Satō Yukiko has also remarked on the widespread trope of the virtuous courtesan in nineteenth-century *gōkan*—the genre of illustrated fiction to which *Iezakura* belongs. See Satō, "Chūkō to shinjō" ("Filial Piety and True Love") in her *Edo no e'iri shōsetsu*, pp. 211–26.

50. Freud, *Beyond the Pleasure Principle*, p. 42.

knows, what he wants to know again: that is why he purchased the book. He derives pleasure from the nonstory (if indeed a story is a development of events which should bring us from the point of departure to a point of arrival where we would have never dreamed of arriving)."[51]

In a sense, Eco takes the opposite approach to the pleasures of reading as Freud; or, more exactly, he focuses on a very different aspect of pleasure, not on the pleasures afforded by the story but on the pleasures afforded by discourse, by what he calls "iteration," arguing that "it is precisely on this foreseen and awaited reappearance that our modest but irrefutable pleasure is based."[52] The reader enjoys not the twists and turns of the individual plots—the unmasking of Monbei, the revelation of Agemaki's true identity—but rather the redundancy of the revelation of identity, as such, that links this particular text with a vast array of similar works that trade on the same devices.

Attention to this iterative scheme allows us to move from the discussion of individual texts like *Tora no maki* and *Iezakura* to a broader exploration of the nineteenth-century aesthetic of melodrama and sentiment—of which such texts are but isolated examples—and so to an understanding of the ideological and historical dimensions of this cultural imaginary. There emerges in the fiction of the nineteenth century a striking collusion between the levels of discourse and story, between the iterative scheme of narration and the basic plots of these novels. Both, as it were, tend toward stability. Thus, misrecognition/recognition functions as a formal device in this iterative scheme, satisfying the reader's hunger for redundancy; but it also functions—as we have seen in *Tora no maki*—on an epistemological level, constituting a narrative world in which villainy is punished, virtue rewarded, and stability restored to a morally ambiguous and chaotic world.

At the heart of the social imaginary of nineteenth-century Japan lies the problem of money and its power in the world. As we have seen above in the discussion of Segawa's ghost, it is the central problem in *Tora no maki* as well as the problem that frames *Iezakura.* But the power of money is always raised only to be set aside. This is why the figure

51. Eco, "The Myth of Superman," p. 121 and pp. 119–20.
52. Eco, "The Myth of Superman," p. 117.

of the courtesan is so important in this literature and why the demimonde is its great space: because there is no other space so ostensibly governed by money and no other person more completely subjected to the power of the coin. But what we find in the pleasure quarters is never the triumph of money but always its disavowal. This is the funny thing about courtesans in nineteenth-century Japanese literature: they can never be bought, money is powerless in the pleasure quarters. Money is powerless but it is also all present and pervades these stories from beginning to end. *Iezakura* begins with the murder and robbery of O-Tsuji, which plunges Wabisuke into debt and forces the eventual descent of their daughter into the demimonde, but the story ends with all the characters huddled around Agemaki as she leans on a thousand *ryō* coin. Indeed, the character most closely identified with money, the merchant Monbei, is the one character who is punished; all of the sins and transgressions—the murder and robbery of O-Tsuji and the theft of the Asashimaru—laid on his back, and Agemaki's revenge allows for all of the scores to be settled in one final blow. Money is not just rejected, it is castigated and excised.

In a 1924 essay on Chikamatsu, Mitamura En'gyo wrote that "more than anything else, the monetary system set up by the first Tokugawa shogun was what lead to the collapse of the shogunate."[53] Mitamura was pointing to the symbolic contradiction that the system created between a rigid social structure based on class and a reality in which "from the shogunate through the daimyo and retainers on down, all bowed their heads equally before capital without the slightest resistance."[54] This contradiction lives at the heart of the fiction of Japan's long nineteenth century, it is what animates it, what—we might even say—necessitates it. The fiction of the nineteenth century is so extraordinary because it does exactly opposite of what one might expect: rather than grasping this contradiction, rather than exploring this contradiction and exposing its duplicity, the fiction tends rather to solve the contradiction by disavowing the power of money. Socially, politically, it seems extraordinarily conservative: papering over the great social contradiction and great symbolic lie in order seamlessly to resolve the problem, placing all of the sins of the

53. Mitamura En'gyo, "Chikamatsu no shinjūmono: jiyūren'ai no fukkatsu," p. 16.
54. Mitamura En'gyo, "Chikamatsu no shinjūmono: jiyūren'ai no fukkatsu," p. 16.

world at the feet of capital. It is as if this fiction took it upon itself to do what the shogunate would not: to eliminate the contradiction, to resolve it not in favor of a monetary economy but precisely the opposite, to revert to a world in which money is essentially powerless. Indeed, *Iezakura* ends with the alignment of both the common man and the aristocratic class against the figure of the merchant. The masterless samurai, Kanshin, is redeemed; indeed the villains of nineteenth-century novels are always merchants.

Although the symbolic world of the nineteenth-century novel seems to be serving the ideological interests of the shogunal system, it was precisely this system that emerged as its worst adversary, continually meddling in the affairs of writers and publishers, meting out punishment, confiscating and burning printing blocks. It is as if the *bakufu* (the shogunal government) did not understand what this literature was trying to do; or perhaps, we might speculate, did not approve of what it was trying to do. We are left with a rather strange specter: that the reading public was perhaps more socially conservative than was the government, and that those who were most deeply implicated in the monetary system—including, of course, writers and publishers—were those seeking most ardently for a release.

Freud describes pleasure as "the most obscure and inaccessible region of the mind."[55] It is certainly one of the least understood and most often misunderstood aspects of literary history, in part because literary history rarely directly raises the problem of the pleasure afforded by literature, and in part because literary scholars, when they do approach the problem of pleasure, tend to do so in a confused manner. This is true, for instance, of Roland Barthes's essay on *The Pleasure of the Text*, which is perhaps the most sustained attempt to formulate a theory—if not a history—of pleasure in literature. Barthes draws a distinction between a Freudian notion of pleasure (based on a "tendency towards stability") and a Lacanian notion of enjoyment (exactly that which lies beyond the pleasure principle). Thus for Barthes, the "text of pleasure" is "linked to the comfortable practice of reading," whereas the "text of enjoyment . . . imposes a state of loss," it "discomforts," it "unsettles the

---

55. Freud, *Beyond the Pleasure Principle*, p. 4.

reader's historical, cultural, psychological assumptions, the consistency of his tastes, values, memories."[56]

Barthes's theory of pleasure/enjoyment, however, tends to reinscribe rather than to challenge the fundamental binary opposition between the popular and the avant-garde that underlies most modernist literary theory.[57] Thus Barthes's theory of the pleasures of the text values above all those texts (of modernism) which *unsettle* and *discomfort*, and the popular novel—linked with "the comfortable practice of reading"—becomes nothing more than a deceptive and deceiving tool of ideological domination. This is, of course, exactly the notion of the "popular" given in the most innovative ideological critiques of literature, in which popular narrative has been variously described as a "narcotic" or "opium" (Gramsci), a "mass deception" (Horkheimer and Adorno), or an "ideological domination effect" (Balibar and Macherey).[58]

But the notion of pleasure found in Lacan's rereading of Freud is quite different and allows for a more complex and ambitious understanding of both the pleasures of the text and the pleasures of ideology. In the introduction to *The Ethics of Psychoanalysis*, Lacan writes that "in Freud the characteristic of pleasure, as that dimension which binds man, is to be found on the side of the fictitious. The fictitious is not, in effect, in its essence that which deceives, but precisely what I call the symbolic."[59] Lacan's alignment of pleasure with "the fictitious" is the first step in understanding the pleasures of fiction proper, in that it removes fiction from the realm of the deceptive and realigns it rather with the world of the symbolic—where it properly belongs.

Indeed, the antagonism between the shogunate and the producers of fiction seems to suggest not so much a mass deception as self-deception, a collusion of misrecognition between the producers and consumers of

56. Barthes, *The Pleasure of the Text*, p. 14.

57. This is Franco Moretti's argument when he writes of a "sudden loss of distance [which] has inevitably paved the way to a sort of hermeneutic vicious circle . . . where recent Marxist criticism is really little more than a left-wing 'apology' of Modernism." See Moretti, "The Spell of Indecision," p. 240.

58. See Gramsci, *Antonio Gramsci: Selections from Cultural Writings*, p. 348; Horkheimer and Adorno, *Dialectic of Enlightenment*, pp. 120–67; and Balibar and Macherey, "On Literature as an Ideological Form," pp. 275–95.

59. Lacan, *The Ethics of Psychoanalysis*, p. 12.

the novel. And it is precisely this misrecognition that lies at the heart of the symbolic. "As soon as we enter the Symbolic," Slavoj Žižek writes, "the real secret is no longer what is hidden behind the mask but the 'efficacy' of the mask itself. . . . All the magic . . . is *in the mask itself*—therein consists the basic feature of the symbolic order: there is more truth in the mask, in the symbolic form, than in what is hidden behind it, than in its bearer. If we 'tear away the mask' we will not encounter the hidden truth; on the contrary, we will lose the invisible 'truth' which dwells in the mask."[60] This is the essential property of all forms of magic: magic does not operate in a sort of bad faith in which the sorcerer is, in some sense, outside or above the system of magic; rather, as Claude Lévi-Strauss notes, "the efficacy of magic implies a belief in magic," and this is as true of the sorcerer as it is of the "patient."[61] The same is true of ideology: ideology is not a state of false consciousness but a system of belief, and because of this the critique of ideology has to be concerned not with "unmasking ideology" so much as understanding ideology as a system. The problem with the historical critique of ideology—and of fiction, of the fictitious—is that it starts from a position in which the efficacy of magic is already lost and so it becomes difficult to understand the rules and structures of the system as such. When we read the fiction of the nineteenth century, we wonder how anyone could have been moved to tears by its implau-sible plots and clichéd redundancy. But the point is not to "unmask" this fiction in order to discover the deception that lies at its heart, but rather to ask how this system of belief formed and how it operated, to discover and describe its rules and functions.

By engaging fiction at the level of the symbolic and by taking the pleasures of reading seriously, we can move away from the binary system of the deceiver/deceived that has long governed work on the theory and history of popular culture, and instead pose the question of why popular literature is so popular—why it sells—in a new and

---

60. Žižek, *For They Know Not What They Do*, p. 247.

61. "The efficacy of magic implies a belief in magic," Lévi-Strauss writes in "The Sorcerer and His Magic," "the latter has three complementary aspects: first, the sorcerer's belief in the effectiveness of his techniques; second, the patient's or victim's belief in the sorcerer's power; and, finally, the faith and expectations of the group, constantly which acts as a sort of gravitational field within which the relationship between sorcerer and bewitched is located and defined." See Lévi-Strauss, *Structural Anthropology*, p. 168.

constructive way. The essence of the critique is no longer to "unmask," to understand what lies hidden beneath the system of iteration and redundancy, but rather to understand how the system itself generates pleasure and what is at stake in the pleasures of ideology.

The Sorcerer and His Magic: Tamenaga Shunsui and the Economy of Sentiment

According to contemporary accounts, Tamenaga Shunsui was the most commercially successful writer of the 1820s and 30s. He was widely read and imitated, and almost as widely reviled and vilified. In the 1850s, Kitagawa Morisada wrote of Shunsui, "He was the first to reveal the secrets of love and so dubbed himself the founder of the sentimental novel (*ninjōbon*)." Morisada mentioned too that Shunsui's great work, *Shunshoku umegoyomi*, had "given birth to dozens of imitators" and that Shunsui had himself produced five novels in the *Shunshoku* series: "All in all, five titles, nineteen volumes, a hundred and six books; all nothing more than scribblings on the love of libertines and courtesans."[62] In his study of early modern lending libraries, Nagatomo Chiyoji has noted that in the catalogue of the Daisō lending library in Nagoya there were five copies each of Shunsui's *Shunshoku umegoyomi* and its sequel *Shunshoku tatsumi no sono* (1833–1835); there were 359 titles from the sentimental genre of *ninjōbon* with a duplicate rate of just over 87 percent—the highest among any genre—suggesting, as Nagatomo notes, that "among late Edo period fiction, *ninjōbon* were probably the most widely read" titles at the library.[63]

Even Kyokutei Bakin, who despised Shunsui, had to admit that "he has sold a lot of lewd and obscene books." Bakin continued:

> This has ingratiated him to the proprietor of the Bunkeidō [referring to Chōjiya Heibei, the onetime proprietor of a lending library and a publisher of fiction by both Shunsui and Bakin], who has often told me that Shunsui is now number one among fiction writers; he says that not even [Ryūtei] Tanehiko can compete. For each volume he writes, I am told, he has no plan but simply

62. Kitagawa Morisada, *Kinsei fūzokushi*, vol. 4, p. 310.
63. Nagatomo, *Kinsei kashihon'ya no kenkyū*, p. 159 and p. 155.

follows his brush; yet his readers cherish his works like great jewels and Shunsui thinks himself quite remarkable.[64]

Bakin was himself not fooled. He described Shunsui as "such a fool one would not even think him human," and accused him of "crying out for attention" by using color in the frontispieces of his *Harutsugedori* despite the use of color being outlawed in the Kansei Reforms. Bakin remarked that "he who delights in obscenity will surely be delighted" by Shunsui's fiction.[65] In one of his more petty attacks, Bakin decried Shunsui's "ignorance" of Chinese fiction and in his great *Kinsei mono no hon Edo sakusha burui* accused Shunsui of an act of literary transvestitism in order to sell books.[66] Even after Shunsui's imprisonment in 1842 on charges of violating obscenity laws and his death the following year at age 53, Bakin would not relent, describing Shunsui as "a truly hateful person, one who indulged himself in sex and alcohol and knew not of being sated."[67]

Two strains run through all of Bakin's criticism of Shunsui: one is the vulgarity of his person; the other, the vulgarity of his prose and his crass commercialism. In part, the source of Bakin's hatred of Shunsui can be easily located. Shunsui was a plagiarist and a pirate and Bakin found himself victimized on more than one occasion. And Bakin may have found himself slighted by Shunsui in his *Gedai kagami* (1838), in which Shunsui listed Bakin among the second tier of writers—along with himself—below Santō Kyōden and Shikitei Sanba.[68] But beyond the vitriolic and often quite petty personal enmity between these two literary rivals, one can see in Bakin's attacks the outlines of the historic shift that was occurring across the long nineteenth century: the inexorable slide, as Nakano Mitsutoshi has described, from high art to low art.[69] And the 1830s were the great battleground of this shift, the decade in which the most was at stake and in which those stakes were clearest.

64. Kyokutei Bakin, "*Haishi gedai kagami* hihyō," p. 352.

65. Kyokutei Bakin, "*Haishi gedai kagami* hihyō," p. 352.

66. See Kyokutei Bakin, "*Haishi gedai kagami* hihyō," p. 353 and *Kinsei mono no hon Edo sakusha burui*, p. 117.

67. Kyokutei Bakin, "Chosakudō zakki shō," p. 511.

68. See Tamenaga Shunsui, *Zōho gedai kagami*, p. 138.

69. See Nakano, *Jūhasseiki no Edo bungei*, p. 7.

Bakin, too, was obsessed with money. He wrote about it constantly in his diaries, which are even now the source of much of what is known about the commercial aspects of the book trade in the early decades of the nineteenth century. But like Kyōden and Sanba, Bakin was never fully reconciled to the commercial dimensions of his trade. He would write for money and did write for money, but he complained bitterly about being forced by publishers to turn out picture books when he preferred to work on longer fiction like the *Nansō satomi hakkenden* and *Chinsetsu yumi harizuki.*[70] Shunsui, on the other hand, reveled in his commercialism. Whether or not he masqueraded as a female author to sell books, Shunsui's piracy and plagiarism suggest that he was not averse to less than forthright means of generating money on the literary market. Bakin has left a considerable body of writing: fiction, diaries, letters, essays, works of literary history and criticism; Shunsui, on the other hand, wrote almost exclusively fiction, almost, one imagines, as if he would not set brush to paper unless it was predicated on a monetary transaction. When Sanba wrote at the beginning of the nineteenth century of the tears and commercialism that were overcoming Japanese letters, he could not have imagined the heights to which these would reach during Shunsui's rise to fame in the 1830s and 1840s.

There is a famous passage in Volume 9, Chapter 18 of Shunsui's *Harutsugedori* (1837) in which the hero Chōga wakes up "in a cold sweat" after dreaming that he has been overcome by a band of five or six "fierce looking" ruffians. After the scene, Shunsui adds a brief apostrophe to the reader explaining his penchant for using dream sequences in his fiction:

> An author friend of mine has criticized me saying: you produce no works of fiction in which there is not a dream sequence. Isn't that a rather clumsy trick? My response to this is thus: all of the novels I write deal with nothing but sentiment, and for this reason their plots are all similar. And so, as in drama, I turn all of the scenes that do not fit into this world into dreams. They are dreams but not dreams. In this way, one ought to think that "this is the way things might have turned out!"[71]

70. See Hamada, "Bakin wo meguru shoshi, sakusha, dokusha no mondai."
71. Tamenaga Shunsui, *Harutsugedori*, p. 508.

A clumsy trick that works anyway: it is almost the very definition of magic—and of ideology—one knows that it is only a trick and yet one allows oneself to be fooled. And here, Shunsui brings up what is perhaps the central problem of the aesthetics of sentiment in the nineteenth century: if all of the plots are essentially the same, how do you make them novel? The "hunger for redundancy" demands that fiction be new but not too new, that plots must be similar but not too similar. The problem is how to feed this hunger—in both senses of feed as to satisfy and to amplify—how to make the reader feel content and yet keep the reader clamoring for more. And no writer of the nineteenth century figured out the logic of this feeding as well as Shunsui. He is truly the great sorcerer of sentiment in nineteenth-century Japan.

If we recall here Mizuno Minoru's catalogue of plot elements from Kyōden's work, we would immediately be familiar with the arc of Shunsui's great novel, *Shunshoku umegoyomi.* In this novel, too, we have lovers and jealousy, lost and stolen treasures, machinations, revenge, hidden and revealed identities and, of course, marriage and a happy ending. The main story of the novel revolves around the triangular love relationship between Tanjirō, O-Chō, to whom he has been betrothed since childhood, and the courtesan Yonehachi. As we are told at the beginning of the novel, Tanjirō was adopted into O-Chō's family, the proprietors of the Karakiya house in the Yoshiwara pleasure quarter, and was to become heir of the house. Just after the death of O-Chō's parents, however, Tanjirō is tricked into switching his adoption to the Natsui house; Kihei, the head clerk of the Karakiya, becomes the de facto head of the house and plots to seduce O-Chō; and Matsubei, head clerk of the Natsui house, causes that house to go bankrupt by forging Tanjirō's signature on the bill of sale of a prized tea canister, the Zangetsu, from Lord Hatakeyama to Lord Kajiwara, and then absconding with the money. When the novel opens, Tanjirō is hiding out in Nakanogō, just east of the Sumida River, near present-day Mukōjima. The machinations of the villainous Kihei and Matsubei have left him responsible for a debt of fifteen hundred *ryō* to Lord Hatakeyama for the embezzlement of the proceeds of the sale of the tea canister.

In the ninth chapter of *Umegoyomi*, O-Chō is visited by three men searching for Tanjirō. The men have come from the office of the magistrate and they are on "a most pressing investigation"; if she will not cooperate, they insist, they will charge O-Chō with being an accomplice and, "cruelly threatening her," they begin to "drag her off" to the office of the magistrate to confess. At this point, Tanjirō himself emerges on the scene, but he is bound in ropes and accompanied by several patrolmen (*meakashi*). The situation is hopeless. "W . . . w . . . wait! Tanjirō! Tan-san . . ." O-Chō calls out as she begins to weep. "O-Chō-san! O-Chō! You've been dreaming, wake up!" and as she wakens, O-Chō sees that she is sharing a futon with her "sister" O-Yoshi, it is the dead of night and "she is in a cold sweat, feeling sick."[72] The illustration shows O-Chō, her cheeks stained with tears, in bed with O-Yoshi.

This scene is repeated almost exactly in the very next chapter—except this time it is not a dream. Distraught, O-Chō goes to seek out Tanjirō and tell him of her dream and of the rumors that she has heard from O-Yoshi about the source of Tanjirō's difficulties. "I will sell myself somewhere . . . to raise money for you," O-Chō pleads.

> "What! How terrible! But how could I have you do such a thing?"
>
> "But we must raise money . . . What will happen to you? Me, it doesn't matter if I die" she says, her child's heart all out of sorts, saddened just thinking in this way, "Oh, my darling" she says, and clinging to his waist she begins to weep. (p. 83)

And so the scene continues, until "the battered door is suddenly flung open and forcing their way inside were two blackguards. Tanjirō is taken by surprise; O-Chō is frightened: they resembled in their appearance the men she had seen in her dream that night. Trembling, she sits still at Tanjirō's side." When the men grab Tanjirō's hands, "O-Chō, sadly, pushes her way in between" and pleads with them:

> *Chō*. "Th . . . the money. How much do you need to forbear on Tanjirō?"
> ●. "Ah! The young lady will be the broker? Well, we could perhaps overlook the two of you and leave. But then we would require, in compensation, 50 *ryō*."
> ▲. "Or the young lady could become a courtesan for a year or two. That would settle the matter straight away."
> *Tan*. "No! No, she is like a sister to me, to whom I owe a great deal. I shall never allow it."

---

72. Tamenaga Shunsui, *Shunshoku umegoyomi*, pp. 75–78. All subsequent citations of *Shunshoku umegoyomi* are from this volume and will be given in parentheses in the text.

●. "Then we will be off to the magistrate's office . . ."
▲. "What a nuisance! Tie him tightly," he says, pulling a rope from within his jacket. O-Chō begins to cry.
Chō. "No! Wait. Take me instead of Tan-san. Take the money and just settle the matter."
●. "How lucky you are. What a good girl. Very kind. Out of respect for her wishes" and as he takes O-Chō's hands, a lone samurai appears, with a sedge hat concealing his visage.
Samurai. "Even if Tanjirō may be forgiven, blackmailers can never be pardoned. Do not move!" He was already inside. The two blackguards are staggered as the samurai forces them to the ground and begins to beat them. "You thieves, what are you doing to Tanjirō and this girl?"
●. "Well . . ."
▲. "Well, there is the matter of Lord Hatakeyama's treasure."
Samurai. "That matter is being investigated by me, Honda no Jirō Chikatsune. And I have not requested your help."
●. "Then you are Hatakeyama's . . ."
Samurai. ". . . retainer. And you are a fool!" and with that he removed his deep sedge hat and all are stunned. (pp. 84–86)

The blackguards are driven from the scene and Chikatsune explains that, although his lord knows that Tanjirō's seal was forged, the mistake still lies with Tanjirō, and he would have to repay the debt, but at a rate of only 20 *ryō* a year. And so the problem is settled.

As Shunsui himself suggests, *the dream is a dream but not a dream*, it forces the reader to think: "This is the way things might have turned out!" In a funny way, though, the whole order of dreams and reality is reversed: in "reality" Tanjirō is saved at the last moment by a deus ex machina; in the dream, he is hauled off in ropes. Dreams in Shunsui's novels are not exactly dreams: they are more like glimpses of *reality*. The entire world of the novel functions like a dream, and dreams within this dream restore "reality." And this is why all of Shunsui's characters awake from their dreams in cold sweats: they have glimpsed reality and, in reality, no one is saved at the last moment by a samurai in a deep sedge hat. One is dragged off to the magistrate's office—and the rest is left to the imagination.

This scene is *again* repeated later on in the novel, in an encounter that begins in Volume 3, Chapter 17, and continues—after a brief digression—in Chapter 19, the first chapter of the novel's final volume.

This episode sets in motion the events leading to the final denouement. O-Chō is nursing O-Yoshi back to health at their home in Ko'ume; Tōbei, who has only just rediscovered O-Yoshi (with whom he had many years earlier fallen in love after a fleeting encounter in Sakura), has been called off on business and left the two women alone. Waiting for Tōbei to return, O-Chō is approached one day by a man, "fortyish, his solemn expression tinged with worry," inquiring after Tōbei. When O-Chō explains that Tōbei is away and that she and O-Yoshi are themselves awaiting his return, this man mutters to himself: "Oh, this is too bad. If things go poorly, it will get very sticky. I'm afraid if the matter is taken to the authorities, Tōbei will be headed for a very dark place until the matter is cleared up. I was hoping that we might have simply been able to clear up the matter now, while it is still early" (p. 130). This little monologue sets both women on edge and they plead with him to await Tōbei's arrival. At this point, a second man arrives, calling to the first, "Goshirō!" and this Goshirō, for we now know his name, calls back:

Goshirō. Okahachi? What is it? But I've asked you for just a little more time . . .
Blackguard. But this is not just a private affair!
Goshirō. "Oh, whatever shall I do!" and he begins to stand up. What on earth is going on? [Shunsui interjects] Please read Chapter 19 to find out. (p. 131)

But before we can get to Chapter 19 and find out what happens, there is a rather long digression in Chapter 18: the courtesan Yonehachi, Tanjirō's lover, unexpectedly runs into a rival geisha, Adakichi, outside of Tanjirō's lodging in Nakanogō. This chance encounter grows into a scene of rivalry and mistrust that has nothing to do with the story at hand. Indeed, as Shunsui explains when this thread of the story is picked up again at the end of Chapter 20, "I'm afraid that the circumstances surrounding this quarrel [between Yonehachi and Adakichi] are rather long and I have been unable to tell of them completely in the allotted page length. So I have only given a hint of those matters in the frontispiece to Volume 3 and if I have a bit of spare time in the near future, I will provide the details for my readers as a sequel to this novel. The title shall be: *Shunshoku tatsumi no sono: a prolongation of Umegoyomi* by Kyōjuntei [Tamenaga Shunsui], with illustrations by [Utagawa] Kuninao. Please wait till it goes on sale" (p. 154). The first part of that sequel would go on sale later that year, in 1832, and the novel would be completed in 1834.

When we return, in the first chapter of Volume 4, to the scene in Ko'ume, the various threads of *Umegoyomi* begin to come together. Goshirō is searching for Tōbei, who is suspected of having stolen the money that Tōbei had himself paid to buy out O-Chō's contract from old O-Kuma, to whom O-Chō had indentured herself as a singing minstrel, in order to raise money to help Tanjirō pay off his debt to Lord Hatakeyama. Goshirō agrees that the matter can be settled quietly if the two women can repay some part of the stolen money. O-Chō and O-Yoshi bundle up their money and clothes and other articles and come to fifteen *ryō*, half the stolen amount. With that, the matter is settled.

As Goshirō begins to leave, "shouldering the bundle" of goods, he runs into Tanjirō, who recognizes Goshirō immediately as Matsubei, the head clerk of the Natsui house, who had tricked him into switching adoptions and then bankrupted the house. Matsubei had been working as Tōbei's clerk, and, knowing that his master would be away, conspired with O-Kuma to extort some extra money from O-Chō and O-Yoshi. Just as Matsubei and his henchman Okahachi begin to flee down the footpath, Tōbei himself arrives to catch the two by "the scruffs of their necks." Okahachi twists himself free and tries to escape the scene when he runs across a "great samurai" who easily apprehends him (p. 147).

This "great samurai" is, of course, Honda no Jirō Chikatsune, and it is here for the first time that we learn his true role in the novel. As we know, he is Hatakeyama's chief retainer, but he is in fact engaged in a secret investigation looking for the lost heir of his master's estate, a bastard child who was given up for adoption. This lost heir, it turns out, is none other than Tanjirō, and Chikatsune has been working with his assistant, Tōbei, to uncover the truth. This explains Tōbei's long and unsuccessful seduction of Yonehachi: he has been working with Chikatsune to test this woman's loyalty to Tanjirō and to see if she would be a suitable wife to the heir of the Hatakeyama estate.

But the story becomes even more complex. Tōbei is himself carrying out a secret investigation at the behest of Chikatsune's wife to locate the illegitimate daughter that this great samurai had given up at her birth. This daughter is, in fact, O-Chō. And Tōbei himself learns that both his great love O-Yoshi and the courtesan Yonehachi are in fact the daughters of his father's concubine who had been separated from each other at birth but who were each left with one of a set of three matching sake cups—the third remaining with their mother—that serve as the sign of their identity. The novel ends with a series of marriages: O-Yoshi to Tōbei; Konoito (one of the courtesans of the Karakiya) to Hanbei (who is himself revealed to be the son of the lord Chiba Hannojō); and O-Chō to Tanjirō. This leaves only Yonehachi, the heroine of the novel, who becomes Tanjirō's concubine in a complex narrative arrangement not unlike that proposed by Chikamatsu Hanji at the end of *Shinjū kamiya Jihei.*

Shunsui's novels are complex—exceedingly complex—and this is a feature of his work of which Shunsui was himself well aware. After the rather lengthy excursus in the middle of Chapter 20, in which the identities of O-Yoshi and Yonehachi are revealed, Shunsui adds the following note of apology to the reader:

> If you have not read carefully, there are no doubt elements of the plot that are rather difficult to understand because of failings in my writing. It is my peculiar habit in constructing my works that I reveal only later some elements of the plot that I might have explained up front at the beginning. With me, this is always the case, so I beg that you take your best guesses as you read my novels. (p. 158)

Anyone who has read Shunsui knows that this apology is slightly misleading: no matter how "carefully" one reads, no matter how much the reader conjectures, even guesses, there is no way to figure out how the novel will come together in the end—even if one knows that it will, indeed must, come together in the end. There is a very simple reason for this: *there are no clues*, there is nothing along the way that can be deciphered by the reader. The sake cups are the perfect example of this: in the end they reveal the identity of both O-Yoshi and Yonehachi, but it is not until the very scene in which their identity is revealed that the cups are first mentioned.

Nothing in the novel points to the real solution; rather, everything is intended to lead the reader astray, to make the final denouement even less likely, even less predictable. And this is achieved by the interweaving of different story lines that partake of slightly different temporalities; "temporal transposition" as Viktor Shklovsky calls it:

> In an adventure novel built on several parallel lines of narration, the effects of surprise are achieved by the fact that while one plot line progresses, the other one may proceed at the same or even quicker tempo, during which we cross over to another narrative line, preserving all the while the time of the first line; that is, we find ourselves among consequences whose causes are unknown to us.[73]

We find ourselves among consequences whose causes are unknown to us. This is exactly the situation Shunsui is talking about when he "apologizes" for the clumsiness of his prose: "I reveal only later some elements of the plot that I might have explained up front at the beginning." Except this is not clumsiness. "This device seems perfectly natural," writes Shklovsky, "but it is in fact a definite accomplishment."[74] In this sense, the dream sequence is just one specific example of a more general device. Such devices in Shunsui's novels suggest "what might have been," they lead the reader astray before leading to revelation; they create, as it were, complexity, and complexity is the lifeblood of the novel. Think of the complexity of Kyōden's plot in *Iezakura*, a work that is just a fraction of the length of a novel like *Umegoyomi*, which itself is but one in a series of books that revolves around the same characters. Shunsui's next book, *Shunshoku tatsumi no sono*, develops the side plot of the rivalry between Yonehachi and Adakichi from *Umegoyomi*; his book after that, *Shunshoku megumi no hana* (1836), circles back and picks up the story before *Umegoyomi* starts.

Shunsui's novels generate complexity, except that complexity might not be the right word because, in the end, all of the complexity falls away, dissolved in a flood of tears. What we find in melodrama is not so much complexity as *false complexity*—but this is no less of an "accomplishment" for being false, just a different kind of accomplishment. And it is the very definition of what H. R. Jauss has so wonderfully called "culinary art," which "satisfies the desire for the reproduction of the familiarly beautiful; confirms familiar sentiments; sanctions wishful notions; makes unusual experiences enjoyable as 'sensations'; or *even raises moral problems, but only to 'solve' them in an edifying manner as predicted*

73. Shklovsky, *Theory of Prose*, p. 101.
74. Shklovsky, *Theory of Prose*, p. 101.

questions."[75] This culinary or entertainment art is, for Jauss, the least interesting type of literary production because it demands no change in the horizon of readerly expectations, it "precisely [fulfills] the expectations prescribed by a ruling standard of taste."[76] But for the same reason, this type of art should be of most interest to the literary historian concerned with the social dimensions of literature.

If we return at this point to the obverse relationship between the dream and reality suggested in *Umegoyomi*, we can begin to understand more clearly these social dimensions of the novel. In his study of the melodramatic imagination, Peter Brooks has called attention to the ways in which the melodramatic mode resembles the world of the dream: "Melodrama partakes of the dream world . . . and this is no wise more true than in the possibility it provides of saying what is in 'real life' unsayable. . . ."[77] In *Umegoyomi*, the melodramatic structure of the novel functions as a dream, "saying what is in 'real life' unsayable"; and the dreams in the novel are themselves glimpses of reality. But if, as Brooks suggests, "desire" in melodrama can triumph "over the world of substitute-formations and detours" and "achieve plentitude of meaning," does this triumph simply disappear when the novel is set down? The melodramatic mode can be contestatory, even liberating, because it breaks through all of the social taboos of reality, because it offers a dream world in which anything may be said and in which all virtue is rewarded and all villainy punished; but this contestatory, liberating dimension of the mode is itself over when the dream ends and one is left where one began. And if such is the case, what, one wonders, is it all for?

We have, of course, returned to the problem of the ideological dimensions of commercial literature. In Freud, art induces a "mild narcosis" which "can do no more than bring about a transient withdrawal from the pressure of vital needs, [but] it is not strong enough to make us forget real misery."[78] And this is very much the standard interpretation of popular literature, often viewed as escapist, as a narcotic, as a mass deception. Herbert Marcuse has developed this line of Freud's

75. Jauss, "Literary History as a Challenge to Literary Theory," p. 25; emphasis added.
76. Jauss, "Literary History as a Challenge to Literary Theory," p. 25.
77. Brooks, *The Melodramatic Imagination*, p. 41.
78. Freud, *Civilization and Its Discontents*, p. 30.

thought into the notion that "they can enjoy it—and forget it," which leads us inexorably back to the notion of "culinary art" being just an ideological domination effect.[79] "Phantasy remains pleasant," Marcuse writes, "but becomes useless, untrue—a mere play, daydreaming."[80] But Freud's thought contains the kernel of a very different starting point for interrogating the social dimensions of art, a kernel to which Lacan has pointed when he wrote of the commerce in desire suggested by Freud's notion of sublimation:

> One thing only alludes to the possibility of the happy satisfaction of the instinct, and that is the notion of sublimation. But it is clear that if one looks at the most esoteric formulation of the concept in Freud, in the context of his representing it as realized preeminently in the activity of the artist, it literally means that man has the possibility of making his desires tradable or salable in the form of products.[81]

This is a marvelous description and one quite appropriate to Shunsui. Book historians are fond of talking about literary markets, but here we are confronted by the question of what is really on sale? Books? Or desires? Or desires in the form of books? "The commodity is, first of all, an external object, a thing," writes Marx, "which through its qualities satisfies human needs of whatever kind. The nature of these needs, whether they arise, for example, from the stomach, or the imagination, makes no difference."[82] Books are, as Marx suggests, "commodities of the imagination" and as such they satisfy a certain set of needs—appetites—and it is precisely when we understand that what novels offer should be addressed on the plane of needs that we can begin to move beyond the escapist paradigm for the study of popular culture. Novels provide not escape but sustenance, ideology is not a deformation or deception but one of the most basic of human needs, not unlike food. Althusser, in one of the most perceptive comments ever made on ideology, once likened the unconscious to an engine and ideology to a kind of fuel: if you drain the tank of fuel, you do not get a cleaner burning engine, you get nothing, and the whole apparatus ceases to

---

79. Marcuse, *Eros and Civilization*, p. 145.
80. Marcuse, *Eros and Civilization*, p. 142.
81. Lacan, *The Ethics of Psychoanalysis*, p. 293.
82. Marx, *Capital: Volume I*, p. 125.

function.[83] All of this is to say two things. The first is that ideology is not superfluous, it is a necessity. And second, that we need to get beyond the conception of ideology as being *imposed*—from above, from beyond, from wherever, and who is doing this imposing anyway?—to a conception of ideology as simply part of the fabric of social existence. There is no society outside of ideology. There is nothing outside of ideology.

The ideological dimensions of *Umegoyomi* are very similar to those of early texts in the sentimental tradition like *Tora no maki* and *Iezakura*: Shunsui's novel employs the same Manichean structure of good versus evil, the same system of rewards and punishments. There is again a strong distrust of money and its power, and a final disavowal of money in favor of status—the removal of the various characters from positions in a world of commerce and their restoration to positions within a feudal status society of lords and vassals. The villains are the clerks, Matsubei and Kihei; money is misleading and corrupting. But then there is an added element that is very much absent from earlier recitations of the sentimental and melodramatic conception of the world: there is a distrust of the law. Every time the law appears in the novel, especially in the scenes cited above, it is subject to coercion, corruption, and manipulation. In these scenes, however, we are not really dealing with the law as such—the office of the magistrate is in the end never really present—but with impostures of the law. In a sense, though, this is the point: the law itself is not so much under attack as the manifestation of the law in daily life as capricious and subject to manipulation. Indeed, in the end, the enforcement of the law is left in the hands of *private* interests. And the great symbol of this is, of course, Chikatsune

83. See Althusser, "Letter to D": "We agree that once it is constituted, the unconscious functions as an 'atemporal' structure. I will use a comparison here: once it has been *set up*, and set up to be able to function, an *engine* always 'functions' with *something*. For example, a gas engine functions with gasoline. Now I wonder whether one can't say that the unconscious also needs 'something' to function, and this 'something' is, it seems to me, in the last analysis, *the stuff of ideology*. . . . The unconscious can exploit anything to its ends, but it still has to 'find' something suitable to its ends. To say that the unconscious 'functions with ideological imaginary' is thus to say that it 'selects' in the ideological imaginary the forms, elements, or relations 'suitable' to it." Althusser, *Writings on Psychoanalysis*, p. 75.

in his deep sedge hat. When one arrives at the end of the novel, one sees that although the law has itself been thrown into question, there has been, lurking in the shadows and near at hand, some other force outside the power of money, which literally belongs to a different order of society, which in the end represents what a different ordering of society might look like, a society based on loyalty, immune to the powers of the purse.

Perhaps this seems an odd myth for someone like Shunsui to spin, himself so deeply involved in commerce. He wrote for money and before that operated a lending library and also published books. We know virtually nothing of his private life, but contemporary accounts suggest that he was obsessed with money. And more broadly, as we have seen over the course of the final decades of the eighteenth and opening decades of the nineteenth century, this very ideology of the disavowal of money was itself born in one of the most vibrant areas of the commercial economy, the book trade, and at a time in which the logic of commerce was increasingly tightening its grip on the book trade.

One might imagine that this myth was born of an inherent conflict or contradiction between art and money—this is, after all, the logic of fetishism, to disavow what one is most enjoying—and that the very disavowal of money was in some sense necessary in order to embrace fully the commercial dimensions of print. This seems to be particularly the case with a writer like Kyokutei Bakin. At the same time, there seems to be a much larger social dimension to this ideology of disavowal that extends beyond the writer's study and the printer's workshop. The contradiction we have seen above, between the reality of a money economy and the social myth of a world in which money did not exist, was becoming, over the course of the nineteenth century, increasingly untenable. And more than that, because of the mendacity of the monetary system, the powers of money seemed even more exaggerated, even more out of control. Money was everywhere, but at the same time, money was not supposed to exist. It was as if one would have to wager on the triumph of—or should we say "restoration" of—the old order, or on something entirely different, the total triumph of the coin. Which is to say that the fiction of the early nineteenth century is socially quite conservative: the low always unites with the high to exclude the middle, the villainous merchants that everywhere people the stories of the nineteenth century.

And so, when Shunsui was arrested in 1842, his blocks and books burned, it makes a certain kind of sense. After all, the capricious, even corrupt, nature of the law is one of the central features of Shunsui's works. Although Shunsui's arrest has a certain logic, there is still something enigmatic about it. Shunsui was certainly guilty of piracy and may have "called attention to himself" with colored frontispieces, and he may even have masqueraded as a woman, but it seems unlikely that Shunsui could have been read as transgressive and subversive, let alone as truly seditious. His novels are actually rather conservative, as kitsch often is.[84] We might imagine a very different reading of Shunsui's demise: that it was not the specific content of his works that caused offense so much as the very presence of the works at all, that it was not the particular spells that Shunsui cast that ran him afoul of the law so much as the fact that he was practicing magic at all—or at least that the magic he was practicing quite widely held sway. It is surely no coincidence that the two authors singled out were Shunsui and Ryūtei Tanehiko, the very same writers Chōjiya Heibei had mentioned to Bakin as being the bestselling authors of the day. The authorities seem to have been disturbed not by the specific ideological content of these writers' work but rather by their commercial success, the fact that they had made their own desires salable in the form of products; that they were, so to speak, privately manufacturing ideology. And whether the content of that ideology was seditious or not—probably no one bothered to read the books to find out. But, after all, in some sense, one does not have to read the books, because sedition lies not in the content but rather in the challenge posed by the very popularity of this fiction, the challenge posed to the state's ideological *monopoly*. In his

---

84. In an essay entitled "Love, God, and the Orient: Reading the Popular Sublime," Rita Felski gives a wonderful definition of kitsch as "the *conciliatory* dimensions of mass culture" (emphasis added) and she goes on to discuss at length the conservative dimensions of much popular culture, arguing that "the rehabilitation of the popular text as an object worthy of analysis, may . . . slide into a rhapsodic hymn to its subversive powers" without fully interrogating "the constitution of popular fiction through a tangle of conservative and oppositional, naturalizing and critical discourses." See Felski, "Love, God, and the Orient," p. 118, p. 141, and p. 143.

"Critique of Violence" (1921), Walter Benjamin pointed to this problem, arguing "that the law's interest in a monopoly of violence vis-à-vis individuals is explained not by preserving legal ends but by preserving the law itself; that violence, when not in the hands of the law, threatens it not by the ends that it may pursue but by its mere existence outside the law."[85] And this is equally true—one imagines probably even more true—of ideology. The ends of the specific ideology are, in a sense, irrelevant. It is the mere presence of the mythmaking, ideological character of fiction that makes it so threatening, by its very existence outside the law.

In the end, Shunsui was caught up in a system that he himself had intuited to be capricious and menacing. And there would be no great samurai in a deep sedge hat to save him. This was not a dream, this was reality; and in reality one is dragged off to the office of the magistrate and one is punished for one's transgressions.

Shunsui died in 1843, the year after his arrest. Bakin, on the other hand, lived on another five years and continued to write until the very end. One of his final projects was an illustrated adaptation of the great Ming erotic novel, the *Jin Ping Mei*. This is the untold part of the parable of the sea cucumber and the crab: the place of the Chinese novel in the literary field of nineteenth-century Japan. And it is this part of the story to which we shall now turn.

---

85. Benjamin, "Critique of Violence," p. 243.

CHAPTER 3

The Archaeology of Misplaced Ideas

Comparative literature has the immense merit of combating the false isolation of national literary histories. . . .

—René Wellek, "The Crisis of Comparative Literature"

A World Without Walls

The study of early modern Japanese literature has long been governed by a paradox. On the one hand, it has been described as a "world within walls," to use Donald Keene's metaphor, "cut off from literary influence originating abroad."[1] And yet, despite the language with which he frames his study—"so little foreign literature penetrated the walls with which the Japanese had surrounded their country," and "the literature of this time developed largely without reference to foreign examples,"[2]—Keene himself devotes a dozen or so pages in *World Within Walls* to the "influence" of Chinese letters on the literary imagination of early modern Japan. In his recent history of the book in Japan, Peter Kornicki has put this problem very clearly: "The imports [from China] were insignificant in quantity in the context of a mature publishing industry in Japan that was producing books for a mass home market. But the ties to China

1. Keene, *World Within Walls*, xii.
2. Keene, *World Within Walls*, xii.

remained: they conditioned the literary imagination in the second half of the [early modern] period."[3]

Very few books wielding an enormous influence: this is a somewhat counterintuitive situation, but one that would not be without precedence in literary or cultural history. In some sense, this is the logic of the cultural field that Pierre Bourdieu has described, the importance of books being almost *inversely* proportional to their actual numbers. And it is certainly possible—and, I think, productive—to think of the relation between Japanese writers and Chinese fiction in terms of *distinction* and *symbolic capital.* But when one runs up against the same paradoxes and contradictions in slightly different forms often enough—very few books wielding enormous influence, a closed world within walls whose literary imagination is conditioned by foreign novels—it is worth investing a little time and attempting to untangle some of the problems.

History is often complex, uneven, even contradictory, but occasionally it is we the historians ourselves, despite our best efforts, who create the illusion of contradiction by posing the problem in the wrong terms. The critique leveled at sociology by André Leroi-Gourham over a quarter of a century ago in his *Gesture and Speech* remains a relevant caution against abstracting the social from the material. Too often, Leroi-Gourham points out, we know "more about people exchanging goods for reasons of prestige than about the kinds of exchanges that go on every day, more about ritual observances than ordinary services, more about the circulation of dowry money than about selling vegetables, and much more about how societies think than about how they are structured."[4] And in terms of literary history, it seems fair to say, we know much more about the power of symbolic capital than that of actual capital, we know much more about "influence" than about how texts actually circulated, how they traveled across borders, were translated, read, even enjoyed. Here I would like to turn to what we might think of as the "vegetable selling" of literary history.

In *The Forbidden Best-Sellers of Pre-Revolutionary France*, Robert Darnton has provided a wonderful example of this sort of book history; an example, really, and not a model, because the techniques for unraveling the

3. Kornicki, *The Book in Japan*, p. 299.
4. Leroi-Gourham, *Gesture and Speech*, p. 148.

literary economy of pre-Revolutionary France that he describes are intimately bound up with his archive, the "50,000 letters and several shelves of account books" of the Société typographique de Neuchâtel.[5] This archive does not exist for nineteenth-century Japan, but we have in its place a different archive, consisting of dozens of records related to the trade in Chinese books exhaustively outlined and studied by Ōba Osamu in a series of books published over the last several decades. Since the mid-1960s, Ōba has collected all of the extant materials relating to the early modern trade in Chinese books from various archives throughout Japan and put them together in a thoroughly indexed study. Ōba's work provides a very clear if highly fragmented view of the trade in Chinese books in early modern Japan: clear because the records supply titles, the years that the books arrived in Japan, sometimes prices, very detailed information that makes it possible to begin to think about the traffic in Chinese novels in very concrete terms; fragmented because we have only a scattered handful of each type of record. We know a good deal about the cargoes of particular ships in particular years, but we know nothing at all for other years, even decades. The outline we can assemble is very rich and detailed in some places, but totally blank in others, like Conrad's map of Africa in *Heart of Darkness*. That said, the total or complete archive is a sort of fiction or vanishing point: the historian never really begins with a complete set of data. Rather than arguing for the authenticity of our archive, it seems more useful to set its limits and recognize exactly what it can and cannot reveal.[6]

In the afterword to his most recent book, *Kanseki yunyū no bunkashi*, Ōba writes: "In the study of early modern Chinese imports, I believe that there is virtually no possibility of discovering new primary material produced at the moment books reached Japan. And so, at this point, research will probably turn in the direction of studying the formation collections or to research concerning particular books. In researching

5. Darnton, *The Forbidden Best-Sellers of Pre-Revolutionary France*, xxi.

6. See Foucault, *The Archaeology of Knowledge*, p. 130: "It is obvious that the archive of a society, a culture, or a civilization cannot be described exhaustively. . . . The archive cannot be described in its totality; and its presence is unavoidable. It emerges in fragments, regions, and levels. . . ."

individual books, we need to look into whether or not they were read."[7] Were these books actually read? It is a marvelous question, an enormous ambition belying its deceptive simplicity. After all, it is one thing to show that such and such a book was imported at such and such a time; it is quite another to map out the course of that book's social life once it has cleared customs and the censor's eye and when the paper trail is likely to have ended.

Importing the Novel to Japan: Nagasaki circa 1800

In November 1804, Nikolaj Pjetrovic Rjezanov arrived in Nagasaki. Late that month, Ōta Nanpo wrote to his son, describing his meeting with the Russian envoy:

> On the eighteenth of this eleventh month, I went for the first time to a place called Umegasaki to witness the disembarkation of a group of Russians (roughly nineteen) who had arrived the previous day. I watched all day as they carried their goods to the storehouse. I met their envoy Rjezanov. When the interpreter (Namura Takichirō) said my name "Ōta Naojirō," the envoy repeated "Ōta Naojirō," bowed his head slightly, and shook my right hand. It was the first time I had seen this etiquette. From there, we went inside and sat in chairs. He was a man of the same stature as Yamada Kichizaemon and so I conversed with him by means of the interpreter and he remembered well the Kōdayū incident. From there, I looked around his makeshift lodgings and I saw many rare things. He had many precious images and showed me some paintings. I also saw a book. There were images of the isles of South America, of peoples and flora and fauna and ships and here and there I made mental notes. There was also an image of the Kamchatka port. It looks to be quite a big port. Today, too, a Chinese ship arrived. For now, that's all.
>
> For a lover of curiosities to meet with such marvelous things is the great happiness and pleasure of life. It has brought me some comfort in my illness. Ha, ha![8]

This is a wonderful glimpse of the world of early modern diplomacy: the ships and the cargo, the handshake, and of course the book, that single volume with its images of flora and fauna and foreign lands. It is easy to

---

7. Ōba, *Kanseki yunyū no bunkashi*, p. 341.

8. Letter written by Ōta Nanpo to Ōta Teikichi on the twenty-third day of the eleventh month of the first year of Bunka; reprinted in *Ōta Nanpo zenshū*, vol.19, pp. 118–19.

see how, for a self-described lover of curiosities, this moment might easily rank among the great joys of his life, might even bring him some comfort in a time of illness far from family and home.

But there is another world glimpsed in this letter. Somewhat overshadowed, no doubt, by Ōta's first handshake and his meeting with Rjezanov, there is the arrival of a merchant ship from China. Earlier in the letter, Ōta had described his obtaining of a rare edition of poems by the Northern Song literatus Su Shi, writing that he is "day after day amazed by the rare books and images" arriving aboard Chinese merchant ships.[9] Indeed, Ōta's letters to friends and family from the year he spent in the employ of the office of the Nagasaki magistrate are peppered with little notes and anecdotes about Chinese merchant ships and their precious cargoes of books and images.

Ōta's letter is striking in many ways, but for us it is especially useful as a starting point in considering the early modern trade in Chinese books because it provides a particularly vivid example of one of the cautionary notes that Ōba Osamu has urged in approaching the early modern commerce in books and ideas. "What is recorded in records and diaries that are the materials of history," Ōba writes, "is less the everyday and more the exceptional, the rare, that which leaves an impression and that is the fundamental character of the historical record. That when we talk of foreign trade in Nagasaki we immediately think of the Dutch trade is due precisely to the fact that in reality the Chinese trade was the norm and the Dutch trade appeared uncommon in light of that norm."[10] One of the things that have kept historians from fully recognizing the extent of the early modern trade in Chinese books is precisely its regularity, its everydayness in contrast to the trade of the Dutch East India Company, to the arrival of Russian envoys, or indeed, several decades later, to the arrival of the "Black Ships" from America. It is sometimes precisely the regular that is most difficult for history to see because it is the regular that is most often elided from the historical record or overshadowed by the spectacle of the unique.

There is a corollary to this problem: banned books tend to create a paper trail. Darnton's archive in Neuchâtel was produced precisely

9. *Ōta Nanpo zenshū*, vol. 19, p. 118.
10. Ōba, *Kanseki yunyū no bunkashi*, p. 8.

because it was centered on the illicit trade in "philosophical novels," the forbidden best-sellers of pre-revolutionary France, across the Swiss-French border. "What I was looking for," Ōba writes, "were books that were imported, books that *could be* imported. Such books are the flip side of so called forbidden books, and since to the people of the early modern period they could be imported as a matter of course . . . there was therefore very little effort to record them."[11] That we have an archive at all related to this trade in normal books is due to the fact that from the late seventeenth century onwards, the shogunate had begun to regulate the trade in Chinese books in an attempt to police the import of dangerous books relating to Christianity.[12] The byproduct of this policing is a series of records surrounding the trade in Chinese books that provide a partial view of the normal, legal trade.

Figure 7 is based on Ōba's work on the Nagasaki customs records in *Edo jidai ni okeru Tōsen mochiwatarisho no kenkyū* and summarizes what we know of the trade in Chinese books between 1714 and 1855.[13] Figure 8 compares Chinese imports with domestic book production for the two decades between 1794 and 1815, the one period for which we have relatively consistent data in both categories.[14] The data are, of course, very

---

11. Ōba, *Kanseki yunyū no bunkashi*, pp. 9–10.

12. See Kornicki, *The Book in Japan*, pp. 325–31. In the seventeenth century, Englebert Kaempfer wrote of the curbing of the freedom of Chinese trade: "[L]iberty granted to the Chinese was soon curtailed. For the Japanese learned that the Tartar emperor of China gave the Jesuits, their sworn and banished enemy, easy access and also permitted them to convert his subjects from their heathen beliefs. They further suspected that the books of the padres (that is how they call the Roman Catholic works) printed in China were hidden among the other Chinese volumes that annually arrived in the country and in this manner reached the people, who were easily taken in again and enticed to become Christians. Moreover, the middlemen were themselves suspected to be under the sway of this teaching and be Roman Catholics. It was therefore decided to curb the past freedom of this nation, and to restrict both their trade and their living conditions in the same way the Dutch had to suffer." See Kaempfer, *Kaempfer's Japan*, pp. 224–25.

13. The chart is based on the summary Ōba gives of his findings in *Edo jidai ni okeru Tōsen mochiwatarisho no kenkyū*, p. 227.

14. This figure is based on a composite of figures for titles published in Edo (Tokyo) and Osaka given in *Kyōhō igo Edo shuppan shomoku* and *Kyōhō igo Ōsaka shuppan shomoku*. It does not, therefore, include titles published in Kyoto or locally outside the two major publishing centers.

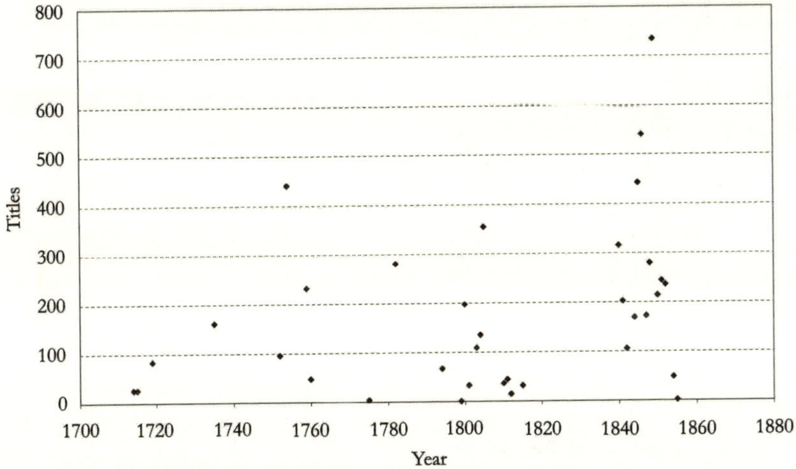

Fig. 7 The Trade in Chinese Books, 1714–1855

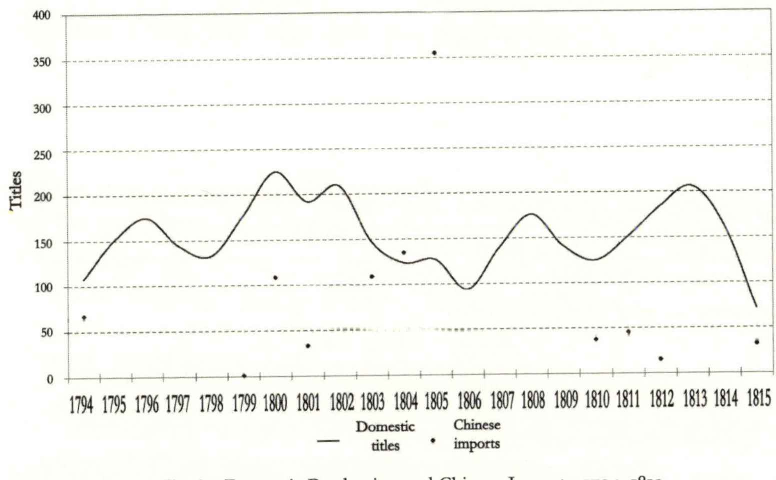

Fig. 8 Domestic Production and Chinese Imports, 1794–1815

incomplete, and it is best seen as a sort of guiding framework; still, the numbers are immediately suggestive of the scale of this trade. A few general points emerge. First, the sketch suggests that the trade in foreign books has a history long predating the Meiji period. Long before Japanese readers got their hands on Bulwer-Lytton, Dumas fils, and Tolstoy, they had been reading *Romance of the Three Kingdoms* and *Water Margin.* Translations and imports have to be seen as forming part of a longer history that stretches from the mid-eighteenth century onward; to start from scratch at Meiji decontextualizes European translations. The second point is the relation between imports and domestic production: although there is no sense in which the book market is dominated by Chinese titles, as the data suggest, the number of Chinese titles making their way into the Japanese book market at the beginning of the nineteenth century is in no way "insignificant."

The comparison with the domestic book trade makes clear that it is no longer really possible to talk about literary "isolation." There were many Chinese titles making their way into Japan and they are not in any sense overshadowed by domestic production; if anything, foreign books probably make up a proportionately larger percentage of the book trade in the early modern period than during the Meiji era. It is from this perspective that we have to view the "opening" of Japan in the 1860s and the translation industry of the mid-Meiji period.

But where are the novels in all of this? Table 8 lists the extant data related to the "four masterworks" of the Ming and the two masterpieces of the Qing.

Table 8
The Masterworks of Late Imperial China

Title	Year of import
Romance of the Three Kingdoms (*Sanguozhi yanyi* 三國志演義)	1727
Journey to the West (*Xiyou ji* 西遊記)	1758, 1861
Water Margin [a] (*Shuihu zhuan* 水滸傳)	1717, 1750, 1804, 1840, 1841, 1846, 1854
The Plum in the Golden Vase [b] (*Jing Ping Mei* 金瓶梅)	1750, 1843, 1851
Dream of the Red Chamber [c] (*Honglou meng* 紅楼夢)	1794, 1804, 1843, 1848, 1852, 1855
The Scholars (*Rulin waishi* 儒林外史)	1850

[a] includes *Illustrated Water Margin* (*Xiuxiang shuihu zhuan* 繡像水滸傳)
[b] includes *A Pocket Jin Ping Mei* (*Xiuzhen Jin Ping Mei* 袖珍金瓶梅)
[c] includes *Illustrated Dream of the Red Chamber* (*Xiuxiang honglou meng* 繡像紅楼夢)

SOURCE: Adapted from Hegel, *Reading Illustrated Fiction in Late Imperial China* and Ōba, *Edo jidai ni okeru Tōsen mochiwatarisho no kenkyū.*

The results are not really surprising: a steady stream of masterpieces from the beginning of the eighteenth century right up until the collapse of the shogunate a century and a half later. The reception of these novels in Japan has been well documented, as has their "influence" on nineteenth-century Japanese letters. In his *Gedai kagami*, Tamenaga Shunsui called *Water Margin* "the greatest of all novels." But we are here talking only about half a dozen titles: important books, of course, some of the great novels of the early modern world, but even so, they would form only a tiny fraction of the hundreds of titles imported each year. This paradigm, with very few titles wielding a tremendous influence, a half a dozen books "conditioning" the literary imagination for several generations, has been central to our understanding of the early modern trade in Chinese books. But what about the *huge underclass* in literary history? What about the *great unread*? Might not there be another trade in normal, regular novels that has essentially be written out of history, overshadowed by the great masterpieces of the Ming and Qing?

Posing the question this way, it is no longer enough just to look through the archive for titles. It is not always clear what one is looking for; once one strays from the well-worn path of canonical titles, it is not always easy to find one's way. And then limiting the search entirely to the Nagasaki customs records would be to engage in a somewhat circular endeavor. These records reveal what titles made it to Japan but they contain no information of what titles *did not* make it to Japan. It is extremely difficult to see the contours of the early modern trade in Chinese novels when approaching the problem entirely from the inside. Table 9, therefore, uses the list of "bestsellers" from Robert Hegel's *Reading Illustrated Fiction in Late Imperial China* as a starting point for excavating the fuller history of this trade.[15]

Water Margin, *Romance of the Three Kingdoms*, *Jin Ping Mei*: that these titles were imported—and re-imported—is totally unsurprising; but *Yu Jiao Li* and *Zui Puti*? Really what surprises is not that this or that title had made it to Japan, but that virtually all of them had. And we have records for only 36 years out of a 136-year period! The chance that 90 percent of these novels would be recorded in this tiny fraction of the

15. See Hegel, *Reading Illustrated Fiction in Late Imperial China*, p. 65.

Table 9
The Bestsellers of Late Imperial China

Title	Year of import
Jin'gu qiquan 今古奇觀	1731, 1805, 1829, 1843, 1844, 1855
Yu Jiao Li 玉嬌梨	1697
Ping Shan Leng Yan 平山冷燕	1725
Dong Zhou lieguo zhi 東周列國志	1730, 1843, 1844, 1849
Yinglie zhuan 英烈傳	1727
Longtu gong'an 龍圖公案	1845
Shuo Tang houzhuan 説唐後傳	1754
Fengshen yanyi 封神演義	1731
Zui Puti 醉菩提	1707
Nan Bei Song zhizhuan 南北宋志傳	1779
Lu mudan 綠牡丹	(no record)
Jing hua yuan 鏡花綠	(no record)
Pai'an jingqi 拍案驚奇	1726, 1801
Haoqiu zhuan 好逑傳	1731

SOURCE: Adapted from Hegel, *Reading Illustrated Fiction in Late Imperial China* and Ōba, *Edo jidai ni okeru Tōsen mochiwatarisho no kenkyū*.

archive is almost unfathomable. One would think that just by chance the records of some might simply have been lost—and this may indeed be the case with the remaining two titles.

But even taken together, the "masterpieces" and the "bestsellers" amount to only 20 titles. In order to expand the sample, Figure 9 looks at three subgenres that Hegel lists: "Historical Novels of the Late Ming Period"; "Qing Military Romance Novels"; and "Qing Scholar-Beauty Romance Novels."[16]

The results are, of course, more mixed. "Scholar-Beauty Romances" do well: we have records for just over 70 percent of the set. Late Ming "Historical Novels" fare comparatively poorly: just under 40 percent;

16. See Hegel, *Reading Illustrated Fiction in Late Imperial China*, p. 45, p. 49, p. 50, and p. 65. For "Historical Novels of the Late Ming Period" there are 8 of 21 titles; for "Qing Military Romance Novels," 5 of 9 titles; for "Qing Scholar-Beauty Romance Novels," 16 of 22 titles; for "Bestsellers," I have followed Hegel's chart (see p. 65) in including the *Sanguozhi yanyi*, *Shuihu zhuan*, *Xiyou ji*, *Jin Ping Mei*, *Rulin waishi*, and *Honglou meng* thus giving 18 of 20 titles.

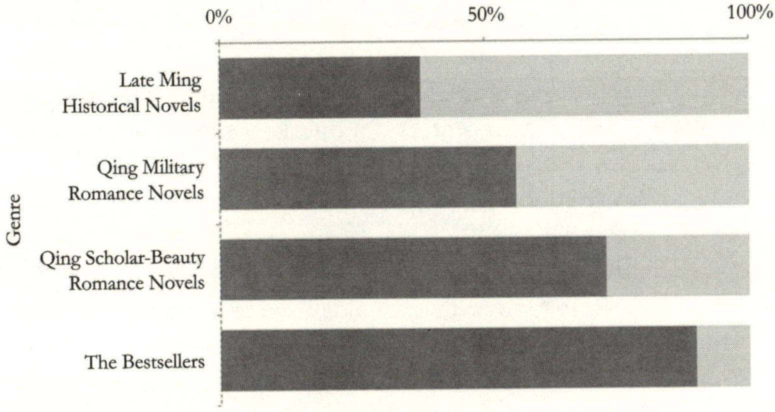

Fig. 9 Importing the Novel to Japan

and "Qing Military Romance Novels" are somewhere in between at 55 percent. But overall, the numbers are extremely high. In his *Edo jidai ni okeru Chūgoku bunka juyō no kenkyū*, Ōba Osamu tells an anecdote in which a Chinese merchant captain shipwrecked in 1826 estimates that some 70 to 80 percent of Chinese titles made their way to Japan.[17] And 70 percent is roughly what the numbers suggest for fiction titles: there are records for 47 of the 72 titles, 65 percent.

The numbers allow us to see that it is no longer really useful to imagine the world of Japanese letters as isolated or closed before the final decades of the nineteenth century; perhaps even more, the numbers should lead literary historians to undertake a more thorough rethinking of the widespread use of concepts such as "foreign" and "indigenous," endogenous and exogenous, in puzzling out the subtleties of literary history. These numbers tell us that virtually the entire literary imagination of late imperial China—one of the richest of the early modern world—was available to the Japanese reading public by the nineteenth century.

And the breakdown by subgenre is suggestive: the numbers are fragmentary but the relative success of scholar-beauty romances is quite evident and somewhat counterintuitive. Nagatomo Chiyoji, for instance, puts military tales at the center of his study of early modern reading

17. Ōba, *Edo jidai ni okeru Chūgoku bunka juyō no kenkyū*, p. 46.

habits and indeed there is good data to suggest that military romances were the most popular prose genre in Japan from the mid-seventeenth century and into the eighteenth century.[18] And of course many Chinese military and historical novels were imported, translated, and circulated in Japan from the eighteenth century on. But the success of the scholar-beauty romances is unequivocal: we have records for 16 of the 22 titles, and some, like the *Jin Yun Qiao*, were imported more than once and had remarkable literary afterlives.

In Vietnam, the *Jin Yun Qiao* became the basis for the *Kim Van Kieu tan truyen*, the verse narrative that would become Vietnam's national epic, written by Nguyen Du in the early nineteenth century. It was imported to Japan in 1754, and in just under a decade, translated as the *Tsūzoku kin'gyōden*, published in Osaka in 1763 jointly by Fujiya Yahei and Kichimonjiya Ichibei, two of the most powerful publishers in eighteenth-century Osaka. In 1805, Santō Kyōden adapted the novel in his *Sakurahime zenden akebono sōshi* and a second, fuller adaptation was made by Kyokutei Bakin between 1829 and 1831, just after the Nagasaki customs records show that 25 copies of the novel were imported in 1828. In the preface to his adaptation, *Fūzoku kin'gyoden*, Bakin wrote that his edition had been commissioned by the publisher Kinrindō, noting that "the *Kin'gyōden*, recently written by a Chinese, had become extremely popular with the reading public since appearing in a vernacular translation in 1763."[19] And Bakin's *Fūzoku kin'gyoden*, too, seems to have been quite popular with readers; in 1839 he complained that it was one of a number of titles being pirated and reprinted:

I have heard that if I do not produce a new work every spring, the Edo booksellers are apt to reissue one of my older illustrated novels, claiming that it has been newly published. Among them, Tsuruya Kiemon's reprint of *Mirugakusuri no hikifuda* [sic] and *Muyō setsuyō nitaji zukushi* [sic] were disclosed to me and furthermore clearly stated that they were reprints so I have no problem with them. But Moriya Jihei's reprinting of *Daishigawara nadeshiko sōshi* [sic] (published by Tsutaya in the Kansei period) and some bookseller or other's reprinting of the *Fūzoku kin'gyoden* (published by Moriya during the Bunsei period) were not disclosed to me and I have furthermore heard that they are masquer-

18. Nagatomo, *Kinsei kashihon'ya no kenkyū*, pp. 188–202.

19. Kyokutei Bakin, *Fūzoku kin'gyoden*, 1 verso.

ading as being newly published. They say that the *Kin'gyoden* falsely claims to be a new work from this spring and that it has been on sale since last winter. And I imagine there are any number of cases of which I have not heard. They say that the trickery has worked to perfection and that all have sold well so I imagine that henceforth more and more of my old works will be falsely republished as new and come out every spring. It is truly a lamentable and hateful situation.[20]

The passage suggests not just the commercial viability of Bakin's adaptation, but also its place within the literary market of the 1820s and 1830s, and the way in which this "foreign" book was published, circulated, read, even pirated and copied much like the other titles that Bakin mentions. But before it could become part of this literary economy, the book would have to make the long journey from Zhejiang—where it was most likely published in the 1660s—through Nagasaki to Osaka and then eventually up to Edo.

The book's translation and publication in Osaka are the beginnings of its social life in Japan. The *Tsūzoku kin'gyōden* was translated by Nishida Isoku and published by Fujiya Yahei and Kichimonjiya Ichibei. How these men obtained the copy of the novel on which the translation was based and what brought them together for its production are not entirely clear. A Kyoto literatus involved in Confucian learning who had studied Chinese with Oka Hakku, Nishida was widely involved in the translation of Chinese fiction in the middle of the eighteenth century: he had begun a translation of *Journey to the West*, the first half of which was published in 1758 but which remained incomplete upon his death in 1764; and he had translated two other novels in 1760 and 1761, one a history of the debauched Emperor Yang of the Sui dynasty and the other, the *Tsūzoku sekijōkien*, based on a chapter of Feng Menglong's *Xingshi hengyan.* It is interesting to note that each translation was published by a different publisher or group of publishers, with no overlap. Unfortunately, we do not know enough about the early modern trade in Chinese books to know whether these novels were obtained by Nishida, who then sought a publisher for the books, or if the publishers had themselves obtained

20. Kyokutei Bakin, "*Haishi gedai kagami* hihyō," pp. 354–55. *Muyō setsuyō nitaji zukushi* should read *Muhitsu setsuyō nitaji zukushi* and *Daishigawara nadeshiko sōshi* should read *Daishigawara nadeshiko banashi.*

copies of the Chinese novels on which these translations were based and then sought out a translator.

At the beginning of the nineteenth century, the Kichimonjiya house was the largest and most powerful publisher in Japan, with branches in both Osaka and Edo. From the 1770s, when Ichibei passed the business onto his 18-year-old son Ietaka, the firm became one of the most important fiction publishers in Japan, and its stocks included many translations and adaptations from both literati and vernacular Chinese fiction. As the grandson of the house's founder, who had brought the firm to dominance in the Osaka book trade, Ichibei was also one of the figures most prominently involved in the production of the *Tsūzoku kin'gyōden.* When Ichibei teamed up with Fujiya Yahei to publish the *Kin'gyōden,* it is unclear what hopes the two men had for the book's commercial success. The advertisement produced for *Kin'gyōden* clearly states that it was the translation of a Chinese novel and that it was meant to be "enjoyed."[21] It is surrounded, in the advertisement, by other works of fiction: it is preceded by several warrior tales, by a five-volume version of the *Tales of Ise,* and a three-volume copy of *The Tale of Genji*'s twelfth chapter—the famous chapter of Genji's exile at Suma, and it is followed by the libretti of two plays written by Kobori Tsuneharu for the puppet theater. But by and large, the catalogue reproduced in the advertisement is composed of titles that represent the stock of Fujiya's trade: instruction books and reference works, philosophical and medical books, and a number of calligraphy manuals.[22]

The advertisement for the novel also mentions that it was illustrated, and these illustrations are one of its most intriguing features. In an essay on the history of the Japanese adaptations of vernacular Chinese fiction, Nakamura Yukihiko brought up the book's illustrations: "I have not done enough research into the book on which the translation is based, but if it was an illustrated book, one would think that the illustrations were copied exactly; they are very Chinese and quite exquisite."[23] We know something more about Qing editions of the *Jin Yun*

21. See Nishida Isoku, *Tsūzoku kin'gyōden,* p. 455.

22. On Fujiya Yahei publishing activities, see Yamaguchi, "Hosoai Hansai to shoshi Fujiya Yahei," pp. 26–37.

23. Nakamura, "Tsūzokumono zatsudan," p. 307.

Qiao than Nakamura knew and we know that they were not, in fact, illustrated.[24] Indeed, there is a copy of a slightly abridged Qing edition at the Naikaku Bunko of the National Archives in Tokyo and it bears no hint of exoticism or refinement. It is a little book with plain brown covers and faded block printing.

That the book's Japanese publishers should have seen fit to add these exotic and exquisite illustrations, so "Chinese" as Nakamura puts it, is suggestive of the way this book circulated—marked as foreign—within the larger Japanese book trade. And indeed, the illustrations in Bakin's *Fūzoku kin'gyoden* published at the end of the 1820s have a similar exotic tinge to them. The plot of the original novel is itself transplanted to a Japanese setting and the characters are all given Japanese names. The illustrations of the text depict these "Japanese" characters. But the frontispieces of each volume are striking: they depict the "Japanese" characters looking into mirrors with "Chinese" reflections.[25] Bakin's manuscript of the novel—which is extant—does not contain these images, although he does sketch out all of the illustrations for the body of the text. So we do not know who came up with such a marvelous idea—Bakin himself, his illustrator Utagawa Kuniyasu, or his publisher Moriya Jihei—but we do know that when the book went on the market in 1828, it did so with this wonderfully exotic touch, making the novel close and comfortable but not too close, not too comfortable—much like translations and adaptations from the early Meiji period.

Indeed, the fate of vernacular Chinese fiction in the opening decades of the nineteenth century—translation, adaptation, often unacknowledged borrowing—is almost exactly that of the European novel in the late nineteenth century; and like the history of the European novel in Meiji Japan, the history of late imperial Chinese fiction in early modern Japan has to be seen as something extending beyond the success of this or that particular work and beyond even the success of translations or adaptations taken as a whole. It is not simply that some several dozen Chinese titles made their way into the literary market of nineteenth-

---

24. For a bibliographic description of extant Qing editions of the *Jin Yun Qiao*, see Ōtsuka, *Zōho Chūgoku tsūzoku shōsetsu mokuroku*, pp. 75–76.

25. On this technique of *mitate* in woodblock prints, see Hockley, *The Prints of Isoda Koryūsai*, p. 48.

century Japan after being imported, translated, and then adapted; more profoundly—and not surprisingly—the Chinese novel, much like the European novel after it, provided a model to be imitated. "Compared with Japanese entertainment reading," Nakamura Yukihiko has written, "Chinese vernacular fiction possessed a far superior narrative element. That excellence lay, of course, primarily in the fineness of the story and its structure as entertainment. For those writers who were stimulated by Chinese vernacular fiction to begin working on new forms of the novel, they started by learning and copying this."[26]

As I have suggested in the previous chapter, Japanese fiction was at something of formal crossroads at the beginning of the nineteenth century, caught somewhere between the prose of wit and the prose of sentiment. One might recall here *Gesaku hyōban hana no origami* further to illustrate the Japanese literary field at the turn of the nineteenth century. The two books that receive the top rank—*Keiseikai tora no maki* and *Keiseikai shijūhatte*—could not be more different in style, tone, and of course, structure: *Tora no maki* is a "sentimental tragedy" (to use Nakamura Yukihiko's description) with "a flawless plot," whereas *Shijūhatte* comprises five independent sketches centered on the relations between the men and women of the licensed quarters and is praised by the reviewers as being "adored throughout Edo."

Thus, even as the vernacular Chinese novel was entering the Japanese literary market in the late eighteenth century, there was already emerging a formal split within Japanese letters between the prose of wit and the prose of sentiment, between the verbally dense and ornate but structurally loose prose of the eighteenth century and the plot driven "weeping books" of the early nineteenth century. But to draw a simple and sharp break between the indigenous and the foreign is to miss the complexity of the situation: much of the culture of wit was itself based on Chinese literati fiction. And so in Japan, the split between the cultures of wit and sentiment was itself, in part, a reenactment of a split within Chinese fiction between the literati and vernacular traditions. At the close of the century, the European novel would simply accentuate this split.

In the end, the *Jin Yun Qiao* seems finally to disappear from the historical record around 1891 when it is recorded, in the form of the *Fūzoku*

26. Nakamura, "Yomihon hassei ni kansuru shomondai," p. 363.

Kin'gyoden, among a number of Bakin's works available in the catalogue of a commercial lending library in Osaka.[27] And that catalogue contained a great many other "foreign novels," among them the works of Jules Verne, Bulwer-Lytton, and Inoue Tsutomu's translation of *Robinson Crusoe*. It is significant that the traces surrounding the social life of the *Jin Yun Qiao* should disappear at just the moment the Meiji market for European translations was beginning to take off. Patterns of cultural consumption were beginning to change in Japan at the end of the nineteenth century, and as the remarkable history of the *Jin Yun Qiao* shows, many of the devices and patterns of cultural production and consumption that drove that later market—translation, adaptation, piracy—were already present in the late eighteenth and early nineteenth centuries.

Robinson Crusoe Stories

In 1857, a decade before the Meiji Restoration, Keika shooku, an obscure and unremarkable firm, published a slender volume, 40-odd pages, titled *Robinson hyōkōkiryaku* (*An Abbreviated Account of Robinson's Wanderings*). This book, a translation of Defoe's *Robinson Crusoe*, is the earliest published translation of a European novel into Japanese. Donald Keene has remarked how fitting a book it was for the task: "We cannot fail to be struck by the peculiar aptness of this work as the first European novel to be translated into Japanese just as Japan itself was about to venture forth into an almost unknown world."[28] From a different perspective, it is equally striking that the history of the European novel in Japan should have begun with a book that has long been hailed—from Watt to McKeon—as the origin of the English novel, as if someone had decided to start from the beginning.

Of course, literary history is never so neat, and although we might read an allegorical significance into the arrival of the European novel in Japan, in some sense we can learn much more if we approach the anecdote on a mundane level. Little is known of the circumstances surrounding the translation: how Yokoyama Yoshikiyo, a student of the minor poet and national learning scholar Inō Hidenori and the book's

27. See Asaoka, "Meijiki Ōsaka no kashihon mokuroku," pp. 23–30.

28. Keene, *Dawn to the West*, p. 60.

translator, obtained the Dutch edition of Defoe's novel on which he would base his translation; how that Dutch edition reached Japan; and whether it had entered Japan as part of the mid-nineteenth-century trade in foreign books or as a personal effect. The Nagasaki customs records, which may have cleared up the final point and held clues to deciphering the others, are only fragmentary, and without reliable records from which to start, it will probably be impossible to reconstruct the events leading up to the production of the Keika edition.

It is tempting to see in a translation something of the history of a book's reception, taking changes and emendations as clues to how a narrative is incorporated into a new setting, both geographical and linguistic. The Keika edition is peppered with little explanations reminiscent of the glosses that often accompanied Chinese novels: York, we are told in the first sentence, is a place name in England, and London, we discover on the following page, is its capital; we also learn about other incidentals, such as "the name of English money" being pounds sterling. But the most striking feature of the translation is its brevity. Indeed, Crusoe's entire diary, which was the backbone of the original 1719 edition and long considered one of the most significant formal developments of the novel in terms of representing "everyday life," is completely eliminated. In the Keika edition, the journal is only mentioned twice, and indeed it is rather cleverly dispensed with: "Because of the scarcity of ink, he recorded only remarkable events." As Stuart Sherman has pointed out, the whole point of the diary in Defoe's book is to record the everyday, the *unremarkable*, to show that everyday life can become the stuff of narrative. To record only the *remarkable* events is to abandon the entire diurnal premise of the novel.[29] In the diary's place, so to speak, we get an expanded role for Friday in the Japanese version. Indeed, the space devoted to Crusoe's first 26 years on the island—the time he spends alone—is limited to seven pages in the Keika edition. Of course, the entire "abbreviated account" spans only 40 pages, so this might not be entirely surprising; but schematically, the Keika edition places a very different weight on the various elements of the narrative. In Defoe's novel, roughly 14 percent of the narrative is devoted to the years before Crusoe's shipwreck: that portion of the

29. Sherman, *Telling Time*, p. 25 and pp. 223–67.

story detailing his early years, his journey to London, his capture at Sallee, his enslavement and escape, and his voyage to Brazil. Just over half of the novel is devoted to his life on the island before Friday arrives. And another third of the novel is devoted to the story from the arrival of Friday to Crusoe's return to England. In the Keika edition, this ratio becomes roughly one quarter, one quarter, and one half, with the two ends of the novel filled out and the middle proportionately shrunk. Thus when it appeared in Japanese translation in the middle of the nineteenth century, the novel was much less like that book which Defoe had written in the early eighteenth century and much more like an adventure novel, as if the narrative could not be assimilated as it stood and had to be recast in a more easily intelligible form.

When we step back for a moment and look more carefully at the history of this translation, we learn that this view is mistaken, or at least partially mistaken. It is well known that the translation is based on a nineteenth-century Dutch edition; indeed, the title page reproduces the Dutch: *Beknopte Levensgeschiedenis van Robinson Crusoe.* The first thing that strikes us about the translation is that the book that has been unanimously hailed as the origin of the English novel was translated not from the English but from the Dutch. There is extant in the University of Michigan's Hubbard Collection an edition of *Beknopte Levensgeschiedenis van Robinson Crusoe* published by J. Zender of Dordrecht in the 1830s, with color illustrations that clearly served as the basis for Kawakami Tōgai's illustrations for the Keika edition. Zender's edition, which is otherwise merely one of a number of Dutch editions published in the 1830s and 1840s, is remarkable (like the Keika edition) for its brevity: only 25 pages. This is in contrast to William Taylor's 1719 edition, which was 364 pages, and to mid-nineteenth-century English editions, which are often 400 or 500 pages long, depending on page size and typography.

And so whatever abridgement or editing of Defoe's novel we see in the Japanese version had already been carried out in the Dutch edition before the novel arrived in Japan.[30] The translation tells us rather less about the work's reception in Japan than we might have hoped, but per-

---

30. The glosses for England, London, pound sterling and so on, however, are not in the Zender edition but were added by Yokoyama to the Keika edition.

haps it can teach us something more compelling: that the arrival of the English novel in Japan is already a part of a much larger story of the spread of the novel across Europe and eventually throughout the globe, and that in the course of their wanderings, novels are often circulated and read in ways in which they were never intended. That the transformation of *Robinson Crusoe* into an adventure story should have taken place in Holland rather than Japan only reinforces the importance of looking at the history of the European novel in Japan as part of this larger history of what Michael Valdez Moses has called the "global history of the novel."[31] And, of course, the backbone of this global trade in the novel—both in Europe and beyond—was formed not by tales of everyday life but by adventure stories and sentimental novels.[32]

A little book, published by a little firm, translated by a minor figure, the Keika edition of Defoe's novel has remained a minor footnote in the history of the novel in Japan: although it anticipated the translation industry that would come 20 or 30 years down the road, it was an isolated incident, a historical anomaly. Viewed from the perspective of traditional literary history, the Keika edition of *Robinson Crusoe* is rather uninteresting: it spawned no imitators, for instance, creating no intertextual relations, no anxieties of influence. The novel probably had a very limited readership—while there are sixteen extant copies of the 1857 edition, no copies of the book were recorded in the holdings of the Daisō library, the largest commercial lending library of the nineteenth century, when the collections were cataloged for auction in 1899; and the novel was not even really understood to be a novel at all, but was taken to be an autobiographical account, which, Mitsukuri Genpo explains in his preface, "is always used in the rearing of Western children as a basis of instruction."[33] The novel was produced, but it was unique, it had a very limited social life, and so what it can explain of literary history is quite limited.

Yoshikiyo's translation is often mentioned, but little discussed. Viewed in a different light, however, the translation is interesting indeed:

31. Moses, *The Novel and the Globalization of Culture.*

32. See Moretti, *Atlas of the European Novel*, pp. 176–77. The data on which this argument is based is on pp. 178–79.

33. Yokoyama Yoshikiyo, *Fukkokuban Robinson hyōkōkiryaku*, p. 8.

although it cannot yield a wealth of information and data directly, the circumstances surrounding this "unique event" can suggest very productive ways for rethinking the material history of the European novel in Japan, if one is willing to believe that these circumstances were not in fact unique. Taken as part of a larger history of translation, the Keika edition suggests that during the life of a text, it is often subjected to various forms of mediation—linguistic, textual, contextual—that are not immediately apparent from looking only at the two bookends of that social life, the original and the final product. The extent to which the history of the life of books as things is available to later historians varies, of course, but it is clear that in the end it will be much more rewarding not simply to turn back to the original edition to see what relation the translation or reproduction bears in terms of a normative fidelity, but archaeologically to trace the mediated and complex middle passage of a book as best we can. It is true that we have not achieved the harmonious circuit from author through publisher and bookseller to the reading public and back again to the author that is the goal of one kind of book history, but in the process we have discovered some valuable clues to the history of the European novel in nineteenth-century Japan, and perhaps as significantly, we have found that there are other circuits and networks through which books travel that take them far afield, and that books participate in a social life that is far more complex and mediated than literary history often admits.

In one of his late essays, posthumously published in *Bungaku tekusuto nyūmon*, Maeda Ai, discussing the early years of the Meiji period and the introduction of Western culture, writes that "for the ordinary Japanese, 'the West' was encountered not first of all at the level of ideology or institution but at the level of *things*."[34] Maeda goes on to mention soap and umbrellas and handkerchiefs; but for many "ordinary Japanese," their first encounter with the West was with material objects of a very different sort, with books. And indeed, we can learn a great deal about the history of Meiji literature from this perspective of treating books as *things*, as "material objects [with] symbolic forms" to use D. F. McKenzie's phrase.[35]

34. Maeda, *Bungaku tekusuto nyūmon*, p. 41.
35. McKenzie, *Bibliography and the Sociology of Texts*, p. 22.

There are, perhaps, two ways to make a history of the European novel in nineteenth-century Japan from this perspective. One would be to trace the history of a single book as a kind of test case: where it came from, how it got to Japan, who translated and who published it, how it was distributed, and ultimately who bought and read it. This approach would be anecdotal, but it would have the virtue of being meticulous and attentive to the various stages in the social life of a book, mapping out in real historical space one of the communication circuits that Robert Darnton has suggested as one model for book history.[36] The other approach would be very different: not to look at any one book in its historical singularity, but rather to survey all the extant translations and come up with some general trends. While both projects are appealing in their own ways, the latter, quantitative approach offers a significantly different vantage point from traditional literary history; and yet, if in the end, one cannot tell how a single book actually got to Japan, all of the numbers and trends would be somewhat hollow. Not hollow in the sense of being worthless, but certainly not representative of the materialist strain in literary history that Maeda's work had suggested.

The history of the translation of *Robinson Crusoe* is one example of this sort of anecdotal history, but this example is generally considered anomalous because the translation was so early, because it had so little afterlife, because the history of translated literature would really start anew two decades after this one-time historical dead end. This is true, of course, but if we take the lessons of Yoshikiyo's translation and use them to interrogate more closely that later history, then the anomaly begins to seem overstated.

Before turning to the numbers and looking more broadly at the history of translated literature in Meiji Japan, let us first look at two more anecdotes. I would like to consider six books published between the 1880s and the first decade of the twentieth century. Only six books out of some 700 translated during the Meiji Period: not an overwhelming number by any stretch of the imagination, but enough perhaps to extend the range of questions we might ask. Rarely do Meiji translations explain

---

36. See "The Communication Circuit" in Darnton, *The Kiss of Lamourette*, p. 112, which also appears in *The Forbidden Best-Sellers of Pre-Revolutionary France*, p. 183.

the history of their own production; but on occasion, something of that history emerges. Two translations of works by William Le Queux, the master of the Edwardian spy novel, were published in Tokyo in 1908, and each reveals something of how the translator ended up with the novel and how he came to translate it. Ike Setsurai, the translator of Le Queux's *England's Peril*, mentions in his preface that he encountered the book first during a trip to French Indochina. He was on board a ship named the *Hanoi* traveling from Hong Kong to Haiphong when he happened to glance through several European novels in his cabin. Le Queux's novel piqued his interest and appealed to his sense of adventure, so Setsurai translated it himself after his return and sent a copy of another of Le Queux's novels, *Confessions of a Ladies Man*, to his friend and protégé Ikuta Kizan. Late in 1908, these two spy novels joined an ever growing group of detective, sentimental, and adventure novels flooding the Meiji literary market, and like so many others would have seeped seamlessly into the great mass of translated literature had they not revealed in their prefaces something of how they came to be translated.

The other four books all appeared at the end of the 1880s from the publisher Hiedō. Like the Le Queux translations these novels are unremarkable save that each mentions in its preface that it was obtained by an "F. Yano" from an acquaintance in Singapore, a Mr. Joseph Clark. "F. Yano" turns out to be Yano Fumio, better known by his pen name Yano Ryūkei, a pioneer of political fiction in the 1870s and a prominent journalist. Joseph Clark of Singapore remains a bit of a mystery and is probably bound to remain one. Indeed, each time one tries to chart the history of a translated book, one runs up against a sort of "Joseph Clark," an enigma that will not yield to historical scrutiny. But if we accept these limitations and instead focus on what we can learn about the social life of these texts, we can begin to piece together a partial but richly suggestive history. When we map, in real historical space, the geography that emerges from the prefaces and introductions to these novels, something of that history begins to emerge. Hong Kong, Singapore, French Indochina, or, in the case of *Robinson Crusoe*, the Dutch East Indies: we are no longer dealing with Japan and the West but with a complex and meandering history marked by the great ports-of-call of the colonial world.

Partha Chatterjee once likened European "Reason" to a parasite that has "traveled the world piggyback, carried across oceans and continents by colonial powers eager to find new grounds for trade, extraction, and the productive expansion of capital."[37] The European novel seems to have traveled in much the same way. Edward Said's work has long suggested the importance of the imaginary geography of imperialism to the history of the European novel; here, we come up against the real historical geography of the European novel in the nineteenth century, and not surprisingly, it also bears an intimate relation to the geography of imperial expansion and power. This history is, of course, effaced once the novel appears in translation, and all of the mediation and complexity disappear behind the relationship that the translation bears to the original work; but if one wants to situate the history of translation historically, then we must think in ways that are not bounded by dualisms such as Japan and the West, original and reproduction.

Pondering the question of "why Italian books are not read . . . why they are considered 'boring' and foreign books 'interesting,'" Antonio Gramsci suggested in the 1920s that Italian literature was "subject to a foreign hegemony."[38] And, as Franco Moretti's recent work on literary markets in nineteenth-century Europe has argued, Italy was not alone: most of southern, central, and eastern Europe were under a sort of foreign literary hegemony, an almost total dominance of English and French novels: "In the crucial century between 1750 and 1850, the consequence of centralization [of the literary market] is that in most European countries the majority of novels are, quite simply, *foreign books.* Hungarian, Italian, Danish, Greek readers familiarize themselves with the new form through French and English novels: and so inevitably, French and English novels become *models to be imitated.*"[39] It does not take a great leap of imagination to add India, China, and Japan, extending Moretti's argument beyond Europe.

Indeed, perhaps the most striking feature of nineteenth-century literary history, and particularly of the global history of the novel, is a sort of great centralization across much of the globe. This is where quanti-

37. Chatterjee, *Nationalist Thought and the Colonial World*, p. 168.
38. Gramsci, *Selections from Cultural Writings*, pp. 348–49.
39. Moretti, *Atlas of the European Novel*, p. 187.

tative methods become important: by treating books as *things*, quantitative data allow access to a comparative dimension of literary history that is difficult when anecdote remains the primary mode of literary history. There is no doubt that numbers flatten out the peculiarities and individuality of their objects, but this function is also part of their value, they "simplify the better to come to grips with their subject" and so make accessible, through patterns and series, solutions to problems that are virtually inaccessible through the methods of traditional literary history.[40]

Figure 10, "The Rise of the Novel," is based on the index to the Meiji period collection of the National Diet Library in Tokyo, and it charts the number of titles published over time for three categories: reprints of Edo fiction, literary translations, and modern novels written in Japanese.[41] Not surprisingly, perhaps, the Japanese novel takes off after a slow start and reprints of the previous dominant form, early modern fiction, drop off sharply after an initial period of dominance. But where are foreign books in all of this? This is where it gets interesting because foreign literature never achieves—numerically at least—the sort of hegemonic position described by Gramsci. A few points: the last time

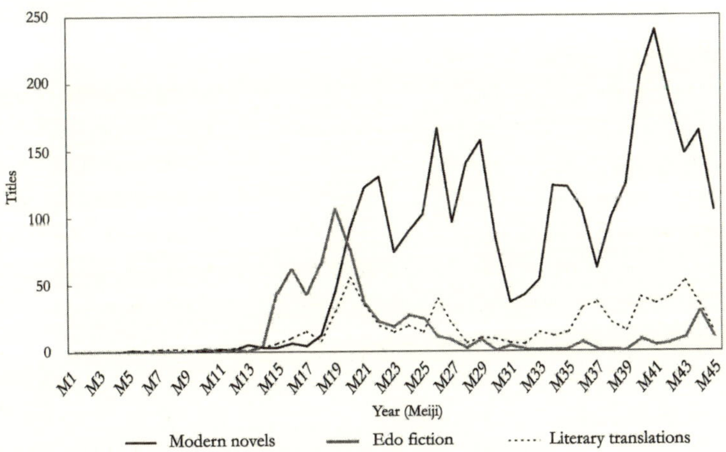

Fig. 10 The Rise of the Novel

40. Braudel, "History and the Social Sciences," p. 51.
41. Kokuritsu kokkai toshokan, *Meijiki kankō tosho mokuroku.*

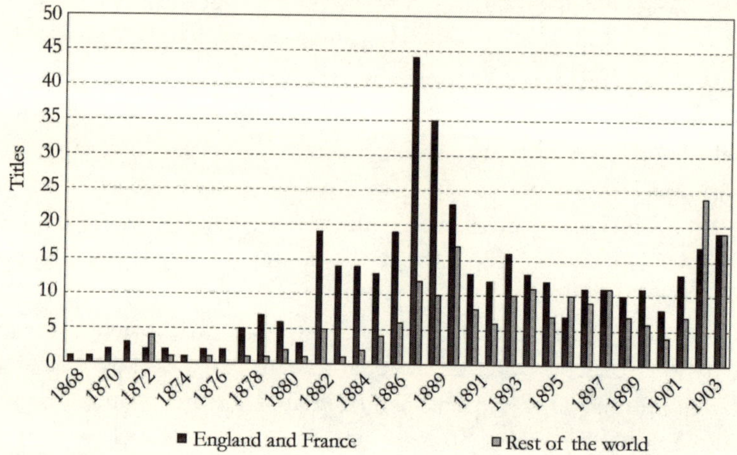

Fig. 11 The Meiji Translation Industry: The Novels of Industrial Capitalism

there are more foreign novels published in Japan than Japanese novels is 1885; the first time there are more foreign novels than reprints of early modern fiction is 1893; and the largest portion of the total number of titles that translations make up is 36 percent in 1904—not insignificant, to be sure, but far from hegemonic.

These numbers tell us that the tremendous stress laid on the importance of translated novels in literary histories of modern Japan is overstated. This is perhaps not surprising when we recall how in his pioneering work on the history of mentalities in Meiji Japan, Irokawa Daikichi argued that because most cultural and intellectual history has been written "with intellectuals at the center," to maintain that "modern Japan suffered to an abnormal degree from an inferiority complex or anxiety about the West does not imply that those feelings were shared by the entire nation."[42] What Irokawa's work has shown is that this emphasis on inferiority and "anxiety" has tended to misunderstand and misrepresent the cultural history of Meiji Japan.

Figure 11 is based on Takuma Izuko's chronology of translations in the *Meiji hon'yaku bungakushū* and breaks down the translated novels by

42. Irokawa, *The Culture of the Meiji Period*, p. 75.

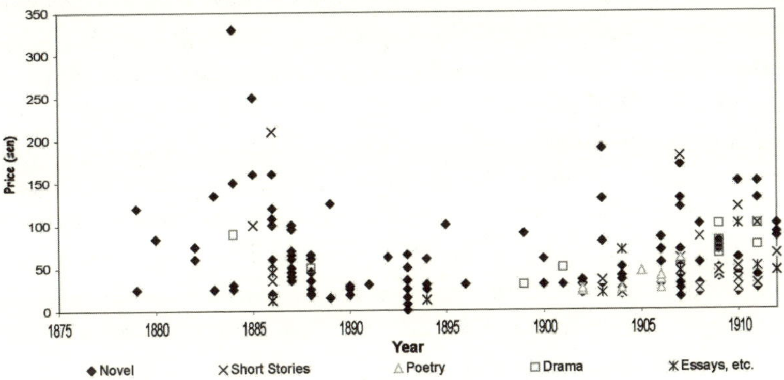

Fig. 12 A Dualist Structure: The Literary Field in Meiji Japan

country of origin, contrasting those from England and France—the "core" in Moretti's formulation—with those of the rest of the world, the semi-peripheral and peripheral countries.[43] What is so suggestive about this graph is not that British and French imports dominate the early years of the Meiji period—this we might have expected—but that they do not in the later years. To be sure, only once do these "peripheral" and "semi-peripheral" imports attain an absolute majority—in 1902—but the total dominance, the "hegemony," of the British and French ends in the late 1880s. Pierre Bourdieu writes of the emergence of a "dualist" structure in the literary market of late nineteenth-century France;[44] something similar appears to happen in the Meiji translation market.

This becomes clearer if we keep Figures 10 and 11 in mind as we look at Figure 12, which plots the first 240 titles from the National Diet Library index. Here, the translations are broken down by genre and price rather than by country, but a very similar pattern emerges: uniformity in the first half of the Meiji period and diversity in the second.

Taken together, the second and third graphs are quite striking: through the late 1880s, the market for translations is dominated almost entirely by British and French novels; after 1890 or so, there are consid-

43. Kimura, ed., *Meiji hon'yaku bungakushū*, pp. 411–35.

44. See Bourdieu, *The Rules of Art*, pp. 47–173.

erably more imports from Russia, Scandinavia, Central and Southern Europe, and also proportionately more poetry, drama, and essays.

And when we turn back to the first graph, we see that this great mass of translations form a sort of *basso continuo* beneath Japanese novels, mimicking the larger swings of these domestic products, but numerically never challenging for hegemony. The graph seems to suggest that once the modern Japanese novel attains dominance circa 1890, translated literature becomes a sort of niche market catering to various curiosities and tastes but no longer wooing the hearts of the mass of the reading public. In this context we can see the rise of Shirakaba after 1910. A dualist structure indeed.

Two significant trends emerge when we consider translated works quantitatively: the first is that these translations are part of a much larger market, and the second is that in the late Meiji period we seem not to be dealing with a single market but with two markets, or a fractured market. Certainly, "hegemony" is not something easily quantified: does it take 75 percent, 60 percent, a simple absolute majority? And then again, sheer quantity does not speak to the quality of the encounter. Numbers are blind to the depth and strength of hegemony. Even Irokawa, who is suspicious of an overemphasis on elites and intellectuals, persists in describing Japan's encounter with the West as "traumatic and disruptive to a degree that is rarely found in the history of cultural intercourse."[45] Surely, these numbers do not tell the whole story, or worse yet they conceal something very important.

Rather than attempt to mitigate what the numbers suggest with anecdotal accounts of the "trauma" of the encounter between Japan and the West, we might gain a greater purchase on this encounter, so long misunderstood, if we are willing to take the numbers seriously without attempting to explain them away or make excuses. For all the limitations of quantitative history, its great strength, as François Furet has argued, is in the revision of "traditional general periodizations" and the "calling in question the old postulate that all elements of a society follow a homogeneous and identical evolution."[46] And this is really

45. Irokawa, *The Culture of the Meiji Period*, p. 51.
46. Furet, "Quantitative History," p. 53 and p. 49.

what the numbers suggest: "a plurality of social times."[47] We need not get rid of the trauma and all of the anxiety and inferiority that accompany it, but simply displace it a bit and specify its parameters. The sort of cultural anxiety that critics have ascribed to Meiji readers and writers, and of which the Shirakaba writers are such a wonderful example, did exist; but as Irokawa suggests, the history of anxiety is a history of elites and intellectuals. The great mass of detective novels and tearjerkers translated over the Meiji period betray no hint of unease, and it is difficult to imagine the Meiji reader as overcome by trauma and self-doubt while consuming William Le Queux, Edmondo de Amicis, and Jules Verne. For most, the West was not first encountered at the level of ideology or institution, but at the level of the potboiler.

Toward the beginning of *Capital*, in the section on "The Fetishism of the Commodity and Its Secret," Marx notes that political economists "are fond of Robinson Crusoe stories."[48] So it seems fitting to bring this Robinson Crusoe story to conclusion by asking what the political economist might teach us about literary history, that is to say, by thinking about books as commodities participating in a literary market. Here, material history meets historical materialism in an effort not just to trace the social life of things, but also to understand their logic and historical significance. First, let us recall Marx's description of the commodity quoted in the previous chapter. "The commodity is, first of all, an external object, a thing," Marx writes, "which through its qualities satisfies human needs of whatever kind. The nature of these needs, whether they arise, for example, from the stomach, or the imagination, makes no difference."[49] And, a little further on, he describes commodities as "social hieroglyphics," as "sensuous things which are at the same time suprasensible or social."[50] It is probably not necessary for our purposes to dwell at length on Marx's language, but the rich suggestiveness of his idiom is no doubt apparent. Because at the same time Marx stresses the physical dimensions of the commodity—its "thing-

47. See Braudel, "History and the Social Sciences," p. 26.

48. Marx, *Capital: Volume 1*, p. 169.

49. Marx, *Capital: Volume 1*, p. 125.

50. Marx, *Capital: Volume 1*, p. 167 and p. 165.

ness"—he also locates this physical thing within a web of social interaction, indeed of social meaning.

For Marx, of course, Crusoe's island is a preeminent example of a non-commodity economy, a form of production with no social dimension. But the history of Robinson Crusoe as a novel suggests that despite this stance at the narrative or discursive level, the book itself was participating historically in an ever-expanding web of commodity production and distribution—both as part of the global history of the novel and eventually as part of a dynamic literary market domestic to Japan. In *The Modern Prince*, Gramsci writes that "in historical reality" the hegemonic relation of forces tends to be mixed "horizontally and vertically so to speak—according to economic and social activities (horizontally) and according to territory (vertically), combining and splitting up differently."[51] Gramsci's language is almost an exact model in theory of what is empirically suggested by the anecdotal and quantitative evidence of the literary market of nineteenth-century Japan—a highly complex system with both such horizontal and vertical dimensions. Literary history must account for both of these historical dimensions, although I have been suggesting from the beginning that they are, in many ways, very different projects. On the one hand, the literary historian would have to track down the "Joseph Clarks" of literary history and begin to map out a history of the European book trade in Asia, of which Japan was a part; on the other hand, we would have to recognize that even by the time of the publication of *Robinson Crusoe* in 1857, there was already a complex literary market operating in Japan that, most scholars agree, was firmly established by the eighteenth century. Treating books as commodities allows us to think at once along these two axes—the vertical and the horizontal—and so to discover both the significance of the international book trade for the history of Japanese literature and the significance of the Japanese book trade for the histories of other literatures. Books are things, but they are also more than things, they are commodities of the imagination. As we come to realize that the consumption of these commodities was shared by readers in Europe and Asia, we should take pause and begin to move away from the binary and traumatic models of the cultural intercourse of nation-centered literary history and toward

51. Gramsci, *The Modern Prince & Other Writings*, p. 170.

a more integrated and comparative history of the European novel in nineteenth-century Asia.

Books from Nanjing, Books from Paris

An optical illusion lies at the heart of nineteenth-century Japanese history, a sort of anamorphosis in which one sees very different images depending on the angle of perception. From one perspective, we see an epochal divide initiated by the hegemonic presence of the West; from a different angle, however, we see a long nineteenth century marked by a continuity of importation and translational practice. The more we focus on one image, the more obscured becomes the other. The problem is not to decide which of these images is the true image and which the false, but to recognize that they stand in relation—the one to the other—and as long as we train our eye on one perspective alone, we are bound to succumb to the power of the illusion.

Perhaps an archaeological approach to nineteenth-century Japan might best reveal the illusion: because archaeology dispenses with the search for origins, it dispenses with the fixing of the historian's gaze upon a single vanishing point and thus disrupts the perspectival aporia on which the optical illusion rests.[52] Of course, this approach also blurs the picture itself and leaves us with what appears to be simply a jumble of shapes that form no coherent picture at all. But in some sense, this is the point. "Is it even an advantage to replace an indistinct picture with a sharp one?" writes Wittgenstein in *Philosophical Investigations*, "Isn't the indistinct one often exactly what we need?"[53]

52. See Foucault, *The Archaeology of Knowledge*, p. 138: "Archaeological description is precisely such an abandonment of the history of ideas, a systematic rejection of its postulates and procedures, an attempt to practice a quite different history of what men have said. . . . Archaeology does not try to restore what has been thought, wished, aimed at, experienced, desired by men in the very moment at which they expressed it in discourse; it does not set out to recapture that elusive nucleus in which the author and the *oeuvre* exchange identities. . . . In other words it does not try to repeat what has been said by reaching it in its very identity. It does not claim to efface itself in the ambiguous modesty of a reading that would bring back, in all its purity, the distant, precarious, almost effaced light of the origin. . . . It is not a return to the innermost secret of the origin; it is the systematic description of the discourse object."

53. Wittgenstein, *Philosophical Investigations*, p. 34.

When we take seriously the indistinct picture of nineteenth-century Japan, we see that virtually every great insight into the history of the modern Japanese novel is also shot through with a historical blindness. This is particularly true of the most innovative recent work on the history of Meiji literature that has attempted to take seriously Karatani Kōjin's notion of "the nearness of origins." When Karatani wrote his *Origins of Modern Japanese Literature*, he was launching an attack on Nakamura Mitsuo's approach to the modern Japanese novel. But recent work has tended to trace out and even strengthen the basic critical stances that Nakamura took in his *Nihon no kindai shōsetsu*: that "contemporary Japanese novels are written based on Western notions of literature," that "the word 'novel' itself only came to be used in its present fashion under the influence of the modern Western novel"; and that "formally," the modern Japanese novel is "Western literature written in Japanese."[54]

Atsuko Ueda, for instance, in her recent dissertation "Meiji Literary Historiography," takes the position that "[Tsubouchi] Shōyō, through the very process of writing [*Shōsetsu shinzui*], constructs and configures an entity that never existed previously. . . . [T]he translation of the title naturally equates *shōsetsu* and novel, as if the term *shōsetsu* had referred to the novel all along. Yet this equation too is created through Shōyō's writing. The 'novel' was far from a familiar term or literary configuration for Meiji Japan."[55] Ueda's important insight is that we cannot treat "novel" and "*shōsetsu*" as semantic equivalents without first tracing in great detail the history of the translingual practices that underlie that seemingly natural equivalence. But we must also remember that Shōyō is himself working against the backdrop of a dense and rich semantic field and his choices and translingual transactions need to be seen within the context of this field.

I have already tried to sketch something of the rich and labyrinthine character of discourse surrounding the terms *shōsetsu* and novel from the mid-nineteenth century on.[56] But the use of the word *shōsetsu* to designate the fiction of late imperial China goes back another century.

54. See Chapter 1 of the present study.
55. Ueda, "Meiji Literary Historiography," pp. 11–12.
56. See Chapter 1 of the present study.

The *Shojaku mokuroku*, the official catalogue of books produced by the printing guilds, first used *shōsetsu* as a generic category to refer to fiction in 1754.[57] The 1772 edition of the *Shojaku mokuroku* lists Nishida Isoku's translation of the *Jin Yun Qiao*, the *Tsūzoku kin'gyōden*, under the heading of *shōsetsu*, in addition to various Japanese editions and adaptations of *Water Margin*, *Journey to the West*, *Haoqiu zhuan*, *Zui Puti*, and other works based on Chinese vernacular fiction. In the century that followed, "the name '*shōsetsu*' began to move away from its original use to refer to Chinese vernacular novels and came to center on the genre of *yomihon* and to be employed in a sense close to the present conception of '*shōsetsu*.'"[58] A passage from the preface to Gakutei Kyūzan's *Chūkō futamatagawa* (1825) gives something of the sense of early nineteenth-century discourse surrounding *shōsetsu*:

> In foreign countries, they have novels (*shōsetsu*). In our country we have tales (*monogatari*). Although their books are written in the vernacular, their plots are beautifully constructed. The books of this country are piled endlessly with the language of refinement but their structure is extremely old, very different from foreign novels (*shōsetsu*). . . . In terms of structure, the foreign novel (*shōsetsu*) appears far superior.[59]

The novel, the vernacular, and plot: more than 40 years before the Meiji Restoration, we are given a veritable catalogue of the attributes that supposedly cut off the history of Meiji literature from that which came before. And the foreign novels to which this preface refers are not those of Europe, but of China: *Water Margin*, *Journey to the West*.

To anyone familiar with the literary historiography of modern Japan, this passage is surprising because—a half century before Tsubouchi Shōyō's *Shōsetsu shinzui*—it draws a sharp contrast between an indigenous tradition and a set of foreign texts, between a native tradition of *monogatari* and a foreign tradition of *shōsetsu*. Indeed, this basic structure of identifying foreign narrative fiction—especially fiction written in the vernacular and fiction that is driven by plot—as *shōsetsu* and as distinct from an earlier Japanese narrative tradition would serve as the

57. See Nakano, *Jūhasseiki no Edo bungei*, p. 89.

58. Nakano, *Edo no hanpon*, pp. 116–17.

59. Gakutei Kyūzan, *Chūkō futamatagawa*, 1 recto.

basic framework within which, and the interpretive grid against which, all understanding of Western fiction would be developed in the Meiji period. To take *Shōsetsu shinzui* as the starting point for investigating the semantic history of *shōsetsu* in Japanese not merely severs—artificially—this history at its midpoint, it also and perhaps more importantly misrecognizes the fact that this was the framework within which Shōyō was himself, quite self-consciously, working.

Another problem raised by this 1825 preface is that of the vernacular. We have become so accustomed to narratives of Japanese literary modernization that take the *genbun itchi* movement as a central constituent of the modern novel that it is quite striking to see the vernacular raised here and discussed in relation to the example of the foreign novel, just as it would be again more than 60 years later by Futabatei Shimei in his preface to *Ukigumo*.[60] Just as the translation of European fiction would bring to the fore the problem of finding a literary language suitable for translation in the late nineteenth century, the translation of vernacular Chinese fiction raised this issue from the mid-eighteenth century onward. Indeed, the relation between the vernacular and the foreign example of the Chinese novel was of great interest to early nineteenth-century writers. Bakin, too, addresses the problem of the vernacular in a scathing critique he wrote in 1833 of Takebe Ayatari's *Honchō suikoden*, the first Japanese adaptation of *Water Margin*. Bakin's critique centered on Ayatari's use of the classical language. Writing about Ayatari's *Nishiyama monogatari* (1768), Bakin noted that "because there are many passages in the book in which he describes the realities of the present world using the language of the past, there are many points which are unintelligible." Bakin continued his critique, referencing the *Honchō suikoden*:

---

60. See Levy, "Sirens of the Western Shore," p. 76: "It is altogether too easy to lose sight of the simple fact that the call for *genbun-itchi* sprang from an awareness of the vernacular nature of Western writing which is patently obvious even from Futabatei's brief preface to *Ukigumo*"; and p. 60: "As Futabatei's preface hints and his own literary career confirms, the successful deployment of a new vernacular literature could only be achieved by means of *translating* Western vernacular literatures. Thus, although the vernacular style is discussed in terms of transparency, it is also, particularly at its inception, characterized by the opaque traces of the foreign. In other words, as a literary style, *genbun-itchi* began as an uneasy coalescence of the native body of speech with the exotic textuality of foreign letters."

And it is certainly more of a mistake still to use classical diction when you are attempting to make a story based on a foreign novel! It is precisely because when in describing human emotion in a novel, there are certain things which are difficult to grasp unless you are completely given to the vernacular that beginning with *Water Margin* and *Journey to the West*, all of the authors of the late Song, the Yuan, and the Ming dynasties wrote in the vernacular; and so even Luo Guanzhong or Gao Dongshou would be hopeless in using classical diction or literary Chinese in writing a story which takes human emotion as its theme. Even Murasaki Shikibu, had she been born today, ought surely to cast aside her brush were she to write a tale with classical diction.[61]

To anyone who has read Shōyō's *Shōsetsu shinzui*, these passages sound strikingly familiar. Shōyō repeats Bakin's remarks on Murasaki Shikibu, almost verbatim,[62] and this is not entirely surprising because we know that Shōyō read Bakin—whom he discusses at length over the course of his essay—and Kyūzan.[63] Indeed, when we read Shōyō from the perspective of the early nineteenth century, we see how little has changed, how conventional is Shōyō's essay. And yet this is the least explored and least understood aspect of an essay that is often seen as part of a movement promoting the "rapid development and westernization of Japan as a modern nation-state."[64]

When we take a long view of the problem of a written vernacular, we discover that many of the concerns harbored by—and some of the solutions proposed by—a generation of writers at the end of the nineteenth century were shared or anticipated by writers almost a century earlier. The critical place that the spoken voice of the storyteller has been accorded within the history of the modern Japanese novel also needs to be seen within the context of a dense and intimate interaction

---

61. Kyokutei Bakin, "*Honchō suikoden* wo yomu narabi hihyō," p. 319.

62. Tsubouchi Shōyō, *Shōsetsu shinzui*, p. 103: "Even the great poet Lady Murasaki would no doubt find it difficult to describe the present state of our world with her pure classical style."

63. In his *Yomihon no kenkyū*, Yokoyama Kuniharu cites a passage from a 1925 essay Tsubouchi wrote for *Waseda bungaku* in which he lists Kyūzan's *Suiko taiheiki* as one of the four greatest *yomihon* after Bakin's *Nansō satomi hakkenden*. See Yokoyama, *Yomihon no kenkyū*, p. 659 and p. 687, note 1. The preface to the *Suiko taiheiki* contains a similar passage on the use of the vernacular. See Gakutei Kyūzan, *Suiko taiheiki*, 4 recto.

64. Suzuki, *Narrating the Self*, p. 20.

between print and oral storytelling that extends back into the early years of the century. Just as the modern discourse on the relation between translation and the vernacular idiom seems to echo—perhaps unconsciously—a discourse that was already widespread in the early nineteenth century, so too does the critical place accorded to the storyteller's voice within the mythology of the origins of the modern Japanese novel seem like an almost uncanny repetition of an earlier moment. When Shōyō's protégé Futabatei Shimei discusses the origins of his own written vernacular style in his "Yo ga genbun itchi no yurai" (1906), the crucial moment of epiphany is triggered by Shōyō's suggestion: "You know [San'yūtei] Enchō's storytelling? Why not try writing like one of Enchō's stories?"[65] But, whereas looking back on the 1880s from the early years of the twentieth century, this seemingly simple suggestion to pattern the written language after the language of the storyteller appears revolutionary, the scene Futabatei recalls in his essay itself reads like a repetition of a canonical scene at the opening one of the most famous novels of the first decades of the nineteenth century, Shikitei Sanba's *Ukiyoburo*, in which Sanba recalls how he was listening to the storyteller Sanshōtei Karaku and marveling at the ease with which "his gifted tongue went right to the heart of human emotions" and lamenting "how hard it is to be even a tenth as effective on paper" when he is approached by a publisher, "greedy as ever," and "asked to put something together based on these stories of the public bath."[66] Indeed, Sanba's experimentation with language and the written transcription of the voice in the early decades of the century was deeply influenced by contemporary storytellers; in his recent biography of Sanba, Tanahashi Masahiro writes that "most of [Sanba's] comic fiction were works that built on the verbal arts like storytelling and mimicry."[67]

It is illuminating to read Futabatei's 1906 essay in the shadow of Sanba because it explains the ambivalent role that Sanba himself plays in Futabatei's retrospective narrative of those years in the 1880s, when

65. Futabatei Shimei, "Yo ga genbun itchi no yurai," p. 241.

66. See Leutner, *Shikitei Sanba and the Comic Tradition in Edo Fiction*, p. 140.

67. Tanahashi, *Shikitei Sanba*, p. 131. On the relationship between Sanba's fiction and oral storytelling see also Leutner, *Shikitei Sanba and the Comic Tradition in Edo Fiction*, esp. pp. 63–66.

he was one of a handful of young writers experimenting with a written vernacular. Sanba is the only writer to whom Futabatei acknowledges any debt, noting that he had made some "reference" to Sanba's use in his works of the colloquial language of the Fukugawa area of Edo. He describes Sanba's deployment of this language as "extremely vulgar but also *poetical*," writing that "it is in this that I believed rested the spirit of the vernacular and so this alone was of some use; but aside from this, there was nothing at all."[68] Rather than following through with this insight that Sanba had, consciously or unconsciously, discovered what Futabatei himself believed to be the spirit of the written vernacular—the existence of the poetical within the vulgar, the everyday—almost a full century earlier and a half century before the Meiji Restoration, Futabatei seems intent on instantiating a break between his own work and the textual record of the previous centuries, making no effort to understand Sanba's experimentation with the vernacular within early nineteenth-century literary discourse or practice.

"To trace the history of a revolution," writes John Pocock, "is almost of necessity, to start with a straw man. The rhetoric of the exercise compels the construction of an account of the way things stood before change began which neglects the extent to which change had begun already and the activities of men under the old regime resembled the activities which were to receive emphasis as a result of the process of transformation."[69] Within recent studies of modern Japanese literature, the end of the early modern period has become exactly this sort of "straw man." Indeed, the final century and a half before the Meiji Restoration is treated almost as an example of an Asiatic mode of literary production: monolithic and static, collapsing under the weight of its own outmoded practices. But when one turns away from the vanishing point of 1868 and looks more carefully at the historical archive, one sees immediately within the literary discourse of the late eighteenth and early nineteenth centuries a set of powerful resonances with late nineteenth-century literary discourse. "The literary establishment of the Meiji 20s and 30s, that is, at the close of the nineteenth century," the critic Miura Masashi has recently written, "were completely consumed with the

68. Futabatei Shimei, "Yo ga genbun itchi no yurai," p. 243.

69. Pocock, "Languages and Their Implications," p. 4.

topic of *genbun itchi*. They thought that only they were privileged to taste that hardship. No one thought that Kyōden and Bakin, Ikku and Sanba had themselves endured the same trials."[70]

I am not arguing that nothing changes in the Meiji period, nor am I suggesting that we can find the "origins" or the "seeds" of what we understand to be the modern novel in the final century of the early modern period. Rather, the historical record suggests that we need to abandon altogether these categories of modern and premodern and the attendant hunt for chimerical origins that inevitably leads us to privilege certain moments and texts over others. Each time we return to texts like *Shōsetsu shinzui* and *Ukigumo* to trace out the origins of modern Japanese literature, we are engaging in a solipsistic activity in which we simply offer slightly new variations on a well-rehearsed story.

To move beyond the familiar paradigms of traditional literary history, however, we need to do more than simply extend the archive back a half century or a century; we need rather to change the fundamental character of the archive itself, to take seriously modes of literary inquiry that extend beyond the close reading of a series of canonical texts. This is what is demanded by the sort of history Irokawa Daikichi puts forward in cautioning against a history which puts elites and intellectuals at the center. When we look at the history of late nineteenth-century literature from the perspective of writers such as Tsubouchi Shōyō and Futabatei Shimei, we see what they see, we see the West. But might we not imagine that there is another story to be told, the story of those readers who first encountered the West in terms of adventure and melodrama?

To pose this question is not simply to point to the outlines of a narrative as yet untold; more fundamentally, it is to cast doubt on a certain methodological approach to literary history that places discourse at the center. The study of discourse has produced some remarkable insights, but the certainty with which it has traced out the "nearness of origins" has caused it to overlook a different register of history and has tended rather to reinscribe than to challenge the more traditional narrative of closure and openness, of the rupture between the early modern and modern worlds. To move from the "intellectual" to the "cultural" is to take seriously those aporia that always separate discourse from prac-

70. Miura, *Seishun no shūen*, pp. 208–9.

tice; even more importantly, it is to take seriously the heterodox nature of discourse itself, reading texts like *Shōsetsu shinzui* not in terms of an explicit ideology—a promotion of the "rapid development and westernization of Japan as a modern nation-state"—but as complex and multivalent sites that cannot be reached through the history of ideas, but which require the force of an archaeological excavation.[71] We have too long been beguiled by the clear image presented to us of a short nineteenth century; sometimes an indistinct image is *exactly what we need.*

Let me give an example based on two pieces of nineteenth-century marginalia. The first is an anecdote in Nagatomo Chiyoji's book on early modern lending libraries. Nagatomo notes a seventeenth-century copy of Ihara Saikaku's *Kōshoku ichidai otoko*—now housed in the Waseda University Library—which had circulated in the nineteenth century as part of the collection of a commercial library run by Nakaya Shinzaemon in Kinosaki. One patron had written into the endpaper of Volume 6: "long and boring."[72] The second example is from a copy of a translation of Tolstoy's *The Kreutzer Sonata* published in 1908, now in the National Diet Library in Tokyo. Punning on the translation's title—*Chōkon*, "long resentment"—the reader had quipped: "A boring book. Where is the long resentment? The resentment is having read the book. There is no value in its being translated."

Boredom: it is a category to which literary history has devoted little attention, but one that is remarkably revealing of the ways in which readers have, historically, made sense of texts. Every act of reading is an encounter between a reader and a set of presuppositions, a *horizon of expectations*, which is often gratified, sometimes violated, perhaps occasionally subverted by the formal structures of the text, and this is why the two marginal notes are so suggestive: not simply because they allow a perspective on how these two individual texts were encountered by real historical readers, but more broadly because they are suggestive of the

71. "To move from the 'intellectual' to the 'cultural,'" Roger Chartier writes, "is . . . not only to enlarge an inquiry or change its object. Fundamentally, this movement implies casting doubt on two ideas: first, that practices can be deduced from the discourses that authorize or justify them; second, that it is possible to translate into the terms of an explicit ideology the latent meaning of social mechanisms." See Chartier, *The Cultural Origins of the French Revolution*, p. 18.

72. See Nagatomo, *Kinsei kashihon'ya no kenkyū*, p. 59 and pp. 117–18.

contours of a certain set of shared readerly presuppositions that governed—or at least guided—habits of reading across the long nineteenth century.

In the late seventeenth century, Saikaku was one of the most popular living authors; for most of the eighteenth century, his texts were widely circulated and read; by the nineteenth century, he has become already long and boring.[73] Or again, in Russia, *The Kreutzer Sonata* had caused a sensation: Tolstoy's eighth draft had circulated in manuscript and "even before it had been passed for the press hundreds, even thousands of copies . . . were made, which went from hand to hand, were translated into every language and were read everywhere with incredible passion." When the book was finally approved for publication as the thirteenth volume of Tolstoy's complete works, Pobedonostev, head of the Holy Synod, wrote to Tsar Alexander III: "On the road from Sevastopol, I saw it on sale in the station and being read in the trains. The book market is full of the thirteenth volume of Tolstoy. . . ."[74] But for an early twentieth-century Japanese reader, it is simply a boring book, unfit for translation.

A great deal separates *Kōshoku ichidai otoko* from *The Kreutzer Sonata.* Perhaps all that they share is that each had made its way into the hands of a reading public very different from that for which it had been originally produced, and each, in its own way, violates the generic conventions and expectations that had come to dominate the act of reading in nineteenth-century Japan. If there is one formal element shared by these two works that may have condemned them to the same fate at the hands of the reading public of nineteenth-century Japan, it is their digressiveness. In the case of *Kōshoku ichidai otoko*, it is what Donald Keene once called Saikaku's "seriatim construction"[75] or what Ivan Morris called a "structural weakness" in his works: "Saikaku's 'novels' lack the rigid construction that we have come to expect in the modern novel and are

73. In a passage from his *Enseki zasshi* (1811), Kyokutei Bakin describes Saikaku: "Although he was a man completely devoid of learning, he did quite well in this world and authored many works of fiction (*kesaku no sōshi*) and was for a time quite famous." See Kyokutei Bakin, *Enseki zasshi*, p. 42.

74. Quoted in McDuff, "Translator's Introduction," pp. 16–17 and p. 19.

75. Keene, *World Within Walls*, p. 182.

often close to collections of stories or sketches."[76] And of the *Kreutzer Sonata*, David McDuff makes a similar comment: "As a work of fiction it undoubtedly suffers from numerous defects—importability, long-windedness, structural weakness and much else besides."[77] It is almost uncanny that both Morris and McDuff should seize on exactly the same phrase—"structural weakness"—to describe these two books, which are in so many ways so very different. To the nineteenth-century Japanese reader, Saikaku and Tolstoy were, in a sense, equally foreign. This is why nineteenth-century Japanese fiction is such a rich terrain for a historical morphology: it is a field bordered on one end by the works of a long tradition of Japanese prose, on the other by the introduction of European forms, and yet its aesthetic and readerly sensibilities were dominated throughout by the forms of a third tradition, the Chinese novel. It is a wonderfully rich and complex field, a true *garden of literary forms*, and at its center lies that third problem raised by Kyūzan in his preface, the problem of narrative structure, the problem of plot.

When the European novel arrived in Japan in the final decades of the nineteenth century, it was, predictably, plot and sentiment that carried the day. In his *Culture of the Meiji Period*, Irokawa Daikichi has written that "the history of Meiji literature shows that during the 1880s and 1890s, writers like Shakespeare, Goethe, Wordsworth, Byron, and Heine were just being introduced to Japan, while works like *Crime and Punishment* were appreciated simply as detective stories."[78] But the history of Meiji literature also shows that hundreds of other works were known and translated in the opening decades of the Meiji period, and that authors like Bulwer-Lytton, Verne, and Dumas were avidly read. And under

76. Morris, "Introduction," p. 41. Donald Keene comments on *Kōshoku ichidai otoko*: "Judged in purely literary terms the work is a failure. The story is disjointed and the hero is a cardboard creation with scarcely a recognizable human feature." See *World Within Walls*, p. 170. Morris rightly cautions that "we must . . . avoid judging Saikaku's books by the standards of the modern novel" (p. 41); what is interesting, however, about this piece of marginalia is that it was written before the emergence of the "modern novel" in the late nineteenth century. This should lead us to problematize the uncritical use of both terms modern and novel to inscribe a break at the center of nineteenth-century literary history.

77. McDuff, "Translator's Introduction," pp. 19–20.

78. Irokawa Daikichi, *Culture of the Meiji Period*, p. 73.

the circumstances, it should perhaps not be surprising that *Crime and Punishment* was appreciated simply as a detective story: detective fiction constitutes one of the largest genres of European novels translated in the final decades of the nineteenth century.[79]

The statistical account of European translations in nineteenth-century Japan reveals that there is not a single history of European translations in nineteenth-century Japan, but rather two histories, or perhaps a fractured history. In the first several decades of the Meiji period, from the 1870s into the 1890s, the market for translations is almost entirely dominated by British and French novels. From the 1890s onward, the market begins gradually to diversify, both geographically and generically. And this structure of the market makes sense when viewed from the perspective of the long nineteenth century: the 1870s and 1880s do not really represent a break, but are rather an almost seamless continuation of the market in "foreign" books that had been developing from the eighteenth century onwards—only now the foreign books were coming from London and Paris, not from Nanjing. And the public was now weeping not for Cuiqiao, the heroine of the *Jin Yun Qiao*, but for Marguerite, the heroine of Dumas's *La Dame aux Camélias.*

But then, in the 1890s, the market fractures. There continues to be an almost unending stream of spy and detective novels, of sentiment, melodrama, and adventure fiction, but these are soon joined by the Romantics, Shakespeare, the great Russian novelists—Dostoyevsky, Tolstoy, Turgenev. Not surprisingly, this fracturing created its share of confusion. Thus for our disappointed reader of Tolstoy, the title of the translation *Chōkon* perhaps unwittingly echoes the title of one of the great sentimental novels of the mid-Meiji period, Ozaki Kōyō's *Tajō takon.* It is easy to imagine how a reader familiar with Kōyō's novel, and perhaps aware of the spate of European sentimentality translated during the Meiji period, might be disappointed by the highly complex and

79. Detective fiction was also probably one of the most widely read genres in the Meiji period. In his study of the holdings of a provincial lending library operating in Tochigi Prefecture in the early twentieth century, Asaoka Kunio notes that 28 percent of the total number of titles were detective novels, with half consisting of adaptations, and the other half of domestically produced detective novels. See Asaoka, "Meijiki kashihon kashidashi daichō no naka no dokushatachi," p. 35.

polemical *Kreutzer Sonata.* For any reader interested in plot, *The Kreutzer Sonata* is bound to disappoint.[80]

And yet, like Saikaku—and at roughly the same time—Tolstoy won admirers in early twentieth-century Japan. These two phenomena may seem unrelated, but each is, in a sense, the result of the fracturing of the book market in the 1890s and the development of a "dualist structure" similar to that described by Pierre Bourdieu for nineteenth-century France. It is not that a taste for sentiment and melodrama died out at the end of the nineteenth century, but that a new type of reading, or perhaps something of a return to an older type of reading, begins to emerge in the middle decades of the Meiji period. This moment is perfectly captured by Natsume Sōseki in his novel *Kusamakura* (1906), in a dialogue between the narrator—a painter under the spell of Shelley—and a disarming young woman, Nami.

"I see you're reading a Western book. I expect it's all about the most complicated things, isn't it?"

"Not really."

"Well then what is it about?"

"That's a difficult question. To tell you the truth I'm not absolutely sure myself."

[. . . .]

"I just lay the book open on the desk, and pick out passages to read at random."

"Do you enjoy that?"

"Yes, I enjoy it."

"Why?"

"Why? Well that's the most interesting way to read a novel."

[. . . .]

"What's wrong with reading a novel from the beginning?"

80. Writing in his *Theory of Prose*, Viktor Shklovsky notes of Tolstoy's late works (*The Kreutzer Sonatta, Hadij-Murad,* and "The Death of Ivan Ilych"): "Apparently, Tolstoy found it necessary to *eliminate plot interest* in his novels. Instead he laid great stress on analysis, on the 'details,' as he used to say. . . . What Tolstoy needed here was a new understanding of what a literary work is, a change in the usual categories of thought. *And so he renounced plot, assigning to it a merely perfunctory role.*" See Shklovsky, *Theory of Prose*, p. 102; emphasis added.

"Because if you start reading from the beginning, you have to read to the end."

"That seems a peculiar reason. What's wrong with reading to the end?"

"Nothing at all, naturally. I do it myself when I want to read the plot."

"But if you don't read the plot, what else is left?"[81]

This dialogue spells out what the numbers and graphs hint at: an emerging split in the 1890s and the first decade of the twentieth century between commercial literature and art for art's sake, between money and art, between plot and what? As Nami asks: "If you don't read the plot, what else is left?" This is a question that has essentially gone unanswered in the history of Japanese literature. As Karatani Kōjin has written: "Modern Japanese literary history has been dominated by the notion that a deepened interiority and its expression are the criteria of literary merit."[82] Unsurprisingly, then, the literature of Nami, the literature of plot, the literature of the *nineteenth century* has essentially disappeared from literary history, and there exists a long caesura between Saikaku and Tolstoy, between the works of an "indigenous tradition"—to return to Nakamura Mitsuo's terms—and those works written under the spell of Western literature, no longer works of Japanese literature in the strict sense but simply Western novels written in Japanese.

81. Natsume Sōseki, *The Three-Cornered World*, pp. 122–23. I have modified the translation for the sake of consistency.

82. Karatani, *Origins of Modern Japanese Literature*, pp. 137–38.

CHAPTER 4

The Long Road Ahead

> "I mean that I can't decide whether to take a step forward or to turn back."
> Once more, I prodded him: "Tell me, can you really turn back if you want to?"
>
> —Natsume Sōseki, *Kokoro*

Saikaku, Tolstoy, and the Serial Novel

In the fourth volume of his history of the Japanese literary world, Itō Sei tells the following anecdote about the young Tokuda Shūsei:

> One day towards the end of that year [1896], Tokuda Sueo [Shūsei] was returning from Kiryū's house and, blown about by the December wind, began to make his way up Ikidono hill next to the armory on the north side of Suidōbashi. At that point he saw on the corner an advertisement for the *Yomiuri shinbun* announcing that it would be serializing Kōyō Sanjin's [Ozaki Kōyō] new work, *Konjiki yasha*, from the beginning of the New Year. The whole advertisement was the most extraordinary looking demon enveloped in red flames. Tokuda thought "must they produce such a vulgar advertisement even for such a distinguished novelist."[1]

To Shūsei, this demon enveloped in flames was a vulgarism; but to the publisher of the *Yomiuri shinbun*—who would pay Kōyō the astounding sum of 100 yen a month for his novel—the demon enveloped in flames was a way to capitalize on art. In the mid-1890s, art and money were colliding, and at the center of this collision were two young writers:

---

1. Itō, *Nihon bundanshi*, vol. 4, p. 218.

Ozaki Kōyō and Tokutomi Roka. They would, in these years, serialize in the pages of two rival dailies—the *Yomiuri shinbun* and the *Kokumin shinbun*—the great sentimental novels that would come to define their careers as writers. But each had begun with rather different literary ambitions that would seem, in hindsight, to have been compromised by their astounding success as popular novelists.

The story is told that Awashima Kangetsu met Ishibashi Shian at the Tokyo Library in 1888. Kangetsu had the idea that he would travel to America and was working his way through the Library's collection of early modern books so he might serve as something of an ambassador of his own country's culture. Shian had, in 1885, helped to found the Ken'yūsha with Kōyō, Yamada Bimyō, and Maruoka Kyūka and had made his literary debut that same year with *Adazakura sato no yoarashi* in the second volume of *Garakuta bunko*, when that journal was still copied out in longhand by Kōyō and Bimyō and circulated in manuscript. It was through Shian's introduction that Kangetsu met Kōyō and introduced the novelist to his great discovery: Ihara Saikaku. And so the Saikaku revival began.[2]

The following year, Tokutomi Roka moved to Tokyo and began working for his elder brother Tokutomi Sohō as a proofreader for the *Kokumin shinbun*. It was in Tokyo that Roka discovered the European novel; he is said to have read *Wilhelm Meisters Lehrjahre* in three days without sleeping and to have begun a translation of Hugo's *Quatre-vingt-treize*.[3] But it was a different novelist who captured Roka's imagination: he was "le tolstoïen."[4]

2. See Itō, *Nihon bundanshi*, vol. 2, pp. 83–85.

3. See Itō, *Nihon bundanshi*, vol. 4, p. 223.

4. Koyama-Richard, *Tolstoï et le Japon*, p. 93. "Le premier nom qui vient à l'esprit des Japonais d'aujourd'hui lorsqu'on parle de ceux qui présentèrent Tolstoï à l'ère Meiji, est celui de Tokutomi Roka. Surnommé < le tolstoïen>, Roka fut non seulement un admirateur des œuvres de Tolstoï, mais abandonna tout pour aller vivre à la campagne et entendit suivre à la letter son <enseignement>." In 1896, Tokutomi Sohō enlisted Ozaki Kōyō's aid in preparing a manuscript for publication. The manuscript was Konishi Masutarō's translation of the *Kreutzer Sonata*, for which Kōyō would share credit as co-translator. See Itō, *Nihon bundanshi*, vol. 6, p. 191 and Koyama-Richard, *Tolstoï et le Japon*, p. 28. Koyama-Richard notes that of the five works of Tolstoy published by Sohō's Minyūsha, "*The Kreutzer Sonata* was undoubtedly the one to arouse the most enthusiasm and critical attention."

To the nineteenth-century Japanese reading public, Saikaku and Tolstoy may have been simply long and boring, but to the young writers of the 1880s and 1890s, Saikaku and Tolstoy seemed to offer a new departure. Kōyō felt that while other writers had a bookish learning, Saikaku had a "natural genius."[5] Roka recalled in his 1897 biography of Tolstoy the sensation of first reading *War and Peace*: "I remained for a moment without thought, at the very limits of a dream."[6] That dream would, however, be interrupted by the pressures of publishing, by the pressures of money. It is not so much that Kōyō and Roka would abandon their artistic ambitions, but that each thought it possible to compromise, to create a work that had both artistic integrity and an immense popular appeal. There was a brief moment at the end of the 1890s when this compromise seemed possible, but within a few years of the turn of the new century, it had become obvious that the dualist structure of the literary field was exacting a toll.

In part, this was because of the peculiar place that the serial novel occupied in the Meiji literary field; it was the form most directly responsive to the demands of the market.[7] These demands were particularly great in the case of Kōyō's *Konjiki yasha*, as Kōyō himself wrote in 1897, just months after he began serializing that novel:

> Japanese writers are in the pitiable situation that they must write as a trade. Pressed upon daily by the demands of earning a living, it is impossible to produce a masterpiece or really anything else. And yet, above already having to write as a trade, in the employ of a newspaper and writing serial novels, the writer must also take care. My *Konjiki yasha* has been extremely popular with

---

5. Quoted in Kōda Rohan, "Ihara Saikaku," p. 47.

6. Quoted in Koyama-Richard, *Tolstoï et le Japon*, p. 94.

7. See Bourdieu, *The Field of Cultural Production*, p. 185: "The opposition between art and money, which structures the field of power, is reproduced in the literary field in the form of the opposition between 'pure' art, symbolically dominant but economically dominated—poetry, that exemplary incarnation of 'pure' art, is not saleable—and commercial art, in its two forms, boulevard theatre . . . and industrial art: vaudeville, the popular or serialized novel [*feuilleton*], journalism, cabaret. . . . There is a chiasmatic structure . . . on the one hand, a maximal independence with regard to the demands of the market and the exaltation of the values of disinterestedness; on the other, direct dependence rewarded with immediate success, with respect to bourgeois demands, in the case of the theater, petit-bourgeois or, indeed, working-class demands in the case of vaudeville or the serialized novel."

the public—it has had so-called mass appeal—but the degree is totally different than with *Tajō takon.* Indeed, no novel I have so far serialized has been this popular. And so up 'til now, I have not received many letters from readers making demands on my novels—"how long will you write?" and so on—but only with *Konjiki yasha* have I received demands by mail from all over so I am planning on continuing but . . . but popularity is a strange thing.[8]

Popularity *is* a strange thing. Readers are enjoying the novel, but they also want a hand in its production. The mechanism of serialization invites just that intervention: first, serialization itself seems to deny the imagining of the novel as fixed, organic, and inevitable; and in turn, the newspaper soliciting letters to the editor encourages readers to become writers.[9] This blurring of the distinction between author and reader places a peculiar stress on the serial novel as a form, and it is unmistakably a hallmark of the form the novel assumes in the age of the popular press. Novelists are always and inescapably under the pressure of "demands" on their fictions; but it was the institution of the serialized novel and the letter to the editor that put reader and writer on the same page, not only figuratively, but literally as well. Such a heightened presence changed the very physics of authorship. The serial novel, Umberto Eco writes, has a "sinusoidal structure" that is "the product of an amalgamation of several plots"; it is *centrifugal* and thus creates such a tension between "market demand" (for the story to be extended) and plot structure (the need for resolution) that "at a certain point even fundamental laws of plot construction, which might have been thought inviolate for any commercial novel, are transgressed."[10]

---

8. Ozaki Kōyō, "Kōyō Sanjin wo otonau," pp. 214–15.

9. See Benjamin, "The Work of Art in the Age of Mechanical Reproduction," p. 232: "With the increasing extension of the press, which kept placing new political, religious, scientific, professional, and local organs before the readers, an increasing number of readers became writers—at first occasional ones. It began with the daily press opening to its readers space for 'letters to the editor.' And today there is hardly a gainfully employed European who could not, in principle, find an opportunity to publish somewhere or other comments on his work, grievances, documentary report or that sort of thing. Thus, the distinction between author and public is about to lose its basic character. The difference becomes merely functional; it may vary from case to case. At any moment the reader is ready to turn into writer."

10. Eco, "Rhetoric and Ideology in Eugene Sue's *Les Mystères de Paris*," p. 133. Gramsci, too, noted this tendency: "It may happen . . . that the original creator of the type makes

In a sense, early nineteenth-century writers also wrote serially, with many of the great masterpieces of the 1820s and 1830s published in annual installments just in time for the New Year. Kyokutei Bakin's *Hakkenden*, for instance, was published over 28 years between 1814 and 1842, and Bakin also complained bitterly about compromises he would make at the request of publishers. But there were not, in the first several decades of the nineteenth century, any direct channels of feedback from the reading public to the writer. If a book sold, fine; if not, it might be abandoned in the middle—which, of course, happened with serial novels in the Meiji period all the time—or it might even be taken up and finished by a different writer.[11] The tension between art and money was not new to the literary field at the end of the nineteenth century; it was exactly this tension to which Shikitei Sanba alluded in his parable of the crab and the sea cucumber. But the communication circuit, which no doubt exists in any print culture, was gradually shrinking, becoming a sort of noose around the writer's neck—or so Kōyō seemed to feel.

For Sanba, the blame lay at the feet of the lending libraries; but at the end of the nineteenth century, the lending library had, as a space of cultural consumption, all but disappeared. In 1805, there were 655 lending libraries in Edo; in 1877, there were but 64.[12] In the place of the lending library, there emerged in the late nineteenth century a new cultural institution, the newspaper reading room. By the time Kōyō broke off serializing *Konjiki yasha* in 1903, leaving the novel unfinished at the time of his death that same year, there were 93 newspaper reading rooms in Tokyo, and that number would balloon to a high of 577 in 1913 at the beginning of the Taishō era.[13]

---

his hero die and the 'sequel-writer' has him brought back to life, to the great satisfaction of the public, whose enthusiasm is revived and who recreate the hero's image, extending it with the new material offered to them. . . . Thus one finds that, for example, the contents of various novels are mixed up because the characters resemble each other. The popular storyteller brings together in one hero the adventures of many. . . ." See Gramsci, *Selections from Cultural Writings*, p. 350.

11. This happened, for instance, with Shikitei Sanba's one experiment with the genre of *yomihon*, *Akogi monogatari*, which even Sanba recognized had miserable sales, was taken up and completed by Tamenaga Shunsui. See Takagi, *Edo yomihon no kenkyū*, pp. 334–39.

12. See Maeda, *Kindai dokusha no seiritsu*, p. 82 and p. 91.

13. For the 1903 figure, see Yamamoto, *Kindai nihon no shinbun dokushasō*, p. 210; for the 1913 figure, see Nagamine, *Modan toshi no dokusho kūkan*, p. 36.

Kōyō's *Konjiki yasha* and Tokutomi Roka's *Hototogisu* were published, respectively, in the *Yomiuri shinbun* and *Kokumin shinbun,* and became the two great bestsellers of the years surrounding the turn of the twentieth century. At the end of the 1890s, the *Yomiuri* had yearly sales of over five million and the *Kokumin shinbun* had yearly sales of almost twice that.[14] A great deal had changed since the 1870s, when the first dailies appeared, amid some bewilderment among the reading public.[15] But the institution of the newspaper novel and the letter to the editor emerged in newspapers quite early. "The wicked bureaucrats," wrote Hattori Bushō in his *Tōkyō shin hanjōki* (1874), "read the newspaper in terror to see if their own crimes have been reported as news. And the wretched writing of the novelists, too, finds it hard to escape censure on the pages of the newspaper. Those wishing to give their opinions on the good and bad of the world or the strengths and weaknesses of a person can write down their ideas and send it to the newspaper; it is called a letter to the editor. Mr. Enlightenment of Nagasaki might carry out an argument with Mr. Old Fashioned of Hakodate living far away."[16] In a letter to the editor, one could write about anything one wanted, but many readers chose—in the 1890s—to write about their favorite serial novels: between 1898 and 1902, the *Yomiuri* printed 112 letters that it had received about *Konjiki yasha.* Some noted the pleasures of reading, others expressed their sympathy for the characters, but over half simply wished that the novel would continue or complained about the frequent breaks that Kōyō took from writing.[17]

Hattori's marvelous image of Mr. Enlightenment and Mr. Old Fashioned carrying out their dialogue from the two ends of an archipelago not yet conceived as the Great Japanese Empire should also remind us that

14. Yearly sales for the *Yomiuri* and the *Kokumin shinbun* between 1897 and 1899 were, respectively: 5,815,892 (Y) and 9,428,963 (K); 5,564,971 (Y) and 10,331,439 (K); 5,163,173 (Y) and 9,927,791 (K). See Yamamoto, *Kindai nihon no shinbun dokushasō*, p. 407.

15. Christiane Séguy tells the following anecdote recounted by John Black, editor of the *Nisshin shinjishi.* In 1872, Black visited a merchant in Yokohama who had agreed to sell a sample of the journal in his shop; the shopkeeper thought the idea was absurd, however, to sell the same journal every day. When Black's translator explained that each day the content was different, the merchant is said to have exclaimed: "Everyday you will have different things in the same journal? It is perfectly ridiculous!" See Séguy, *Histoire de la presse Japonaise*, p. 97.

16. Quoted in Itō, *Nihon bundanshi*, vol. 1, pp. 52–53.

17. See Seki, "*Konjiki yasha* no juyō to media mikkusu," p. 160.

along with the novel, the newspaper is the great symbol of Benedict Anderson's "imagined community" of the nation. These two tools of the imagination intersect in the serial novel, an almost literal embodiment of the nation's "homogenous, empty time." And serial novels like *Konjiki yasha* and *Hototogisu* were consumed by readers from Nagasaki to Hakodate, and increasingly, in Japanese settlements in Korea, in the concessions in northeast China, and in the new colony of Taiwan. Between 1897 and 1899, the middle years of the period between the Sino-Japanese and Russo-Japanese wars, the foreign sales of the *Yomiuri* jumped from 23,000 to almost 160,000 and those of the *Kokumin shinbun* rose from 66,000 to slightly over 70,000.[18]

In January of 1903, just months before he died, Kōyō wrote a short piece for the journal *Ekkusu* in which he complained of Japan being "too small of a stage":

> I believe this is the source of our hardship as novelists. In other words, our country is a mere 260 kilometers in breadth and just about 400 kilometers in length. And our population a mere 40 million. In places like England, Russia, Germany, France, and America, both land and population are plentiful and education widespread, so there are a great number of readers. Thus in those lands when a single work does well, the author can earn an extraordinary amount of money and so can live quite well, even if he simply enjoys himself for five or ten years. And with a bit of money to spare and without being pressed by having to worry about earning a living, one can do enough research, polish one's thoughts, think up devices, and devise a truly first-rate novel. But when you are always pressed upon simply to earn a living like Japanese writers, and must write endlessly, one simply doesn't have the room to produce a first-rate novel.[19]

Kōyō's idea was to have the new generation of Japanese writers study English and German and French, and to, quite literally, "colonize" the foreign market. It is a marvelous image, these young Japanese writers—perhaps Kōyō had in mind his students Izumi Kyōka and Tokuda Shūsei—colonizing the European literary market in search of a consuming public large enough to support a life of luxury and ease on the back of a single bestseller. But the real future of the Japanese novel as a

18. See Yamamoto, *Kindai nihon no shinbun dokushasō*, p. 407.
19. Ozaki Kōyō, "Kōyōshi no shōsetsuka dan," p. 323 and p. 325.

colonial enterprise lay closer to home, particularly in the largely untapped market of the Korean peninsula.

Konjiki yasha was translated into Korean by Cho Chung-hwan as *Changhanmong* and serialized in the *Maeil sinbo* between 1913 and 1915; when the book was published, it quickly became the "first bestseller" of the "new Korean novel."[20] The cover of the 1913 Syech'ang sŏkwan edition of the novel's first volume carries a version of the famous image of Kan'ichi and Miya at Atami—only the scene has been transposed to the bank of the Taedonggang in Pyongyang and the hero and heroine are Yi Su-il and Shim Sun-ae. Roka's *Hototogisu* also fared well in this new literary market. It was adapted three times: by Kim U-chin in 1912 under the title *Ryuhwa'u*; as *Pul'yŏgui* by Cho Chung-hwan, also in 1912; and then again by Sŏn U-il under the title *Tugyŏnsŏng*, published in two volumes by Pokŭp sŏkwan in 1912 and 1913. In these guises, it would become, like *Konjiki yasha*, one of the most widely read novels in Korea in the second decade of the twentieth century.

By that time, the better part of two decades had passed since Tokuda Shūsei had first encountered that vulgar demon on the top of Ikidono hill, and a good deal had changed. Kōyō had died in October of 1903, shortly after his final break with the *Mainichi shinbun* amidst growing tensions over his failing health and his inability—or unwillingness—to finish his novel. A year earlier, Roka had broken with the *Kokumin shinbun* amidst friction over his brother's increasingly nationalistic leanings and his tireless apologies for Japan's colonial expansion. Roka discovered socialism and rediscovered his Christianity. He spent several years traveling and in deep reflection, and on April 4, 1906, Roka set out for Yasanaya Polyana to visit the 78-year-old Tolstoy.

The Fraternization of Impossibilities

Konjiki yasha has come to be defined by a single image: Takeuchi Keishū's frontispiece to Book 1, which shows Kan'ichi violently kicking himself free of Miya on the windswept shore at Atami on the Izu peninsula. The most famous scene in this novel takes place at Atami, but the majority of the novel's action occurs in a rather different space: a small area of

20. Kim, *Han'il kundae sosŏl pigyo munhakchŏk yŏngu*, p. 212.

Tokyo between Yotsuya and the Banchō district in Kōjimachi, on either bank of the Sotobori moat as it snakes around the city center and heads south. This is the space of greed, usury, and violence; where the money lenders Wanibuchi and Akagashi live; where Kan'ichi is attacked at the end of Book 2; where the Wanibuchis meet their fiery end at the end of Book 3; and where Miya finally visits Kan'ichi to ask his forgiveness. Against this space, there is a geography of status and power: the Tomiyama family house in Akasaka; the Viscount Tazumi's villa in Hikawa in Shiba, the site of Miya and Kan'ichi's first encounter after their break; and the house in which Miya and Tomiyama Tadatsugu live in Ikenohata, on the western side of the Shinobazu pond in Ueno.

And then there are a number of other spaces, but these are less well defined: there is the Minowa's house, the site of the novel's opening chapter and the New Year's card game that proves the locus of Miya's fateful encounter with Tadatsugu; there is the house of Miya's parents, the Shigisawas, the retired bureaucrat and his wife, where Kan'ichi lives as a ward; there is Yusa's house, the site of Kan'ichi's first encounter with his old schoolmates; and there are the lodgings of the Wanibuchi's son Tadamichi—the scholar who has renounced his parents ill-gotten gains—and of Arao Jōsuke—Kan'ichi's onetime friend, a former magistrate who has been ruined by guaranteeing a bond for his benefactor.

The geography of *Konjiki yasha* is strange in that so many of its important spaces are left blank. The novel's opening, which plots Tadatsugu's arrival at the Minowa house for the New Years party, is an incredibly detailed recording of sights and sounds and even smells; on a microscopic level, the scene is exactly located, but macroscopically, there is no hint as to where this scene is set.[21] And this pattern is again repeated in Chapter 5 of Book 2 which describes, in great detail, the neighborhood surrounding Yusa's flat, but never situates this neighborhood within any larger topography of the city (p. 145). The most pronounced example of this type of peculiar geographical lacuna is Arao's almost pathological refusal to reveal the location of his residence. When Arao first reappears in Book 4, Miya asks after his lodgings: "My residence?," replies Arao, "I had better not say. The fisherman's son, as we say, has no fixed abode" (p. 302).

---

21. Ozaki Kōyō, *Konjiki yasha*, pp. 7–9. All subsequent citations to *Konjiki yasha* are to this edition and page numbers will be given in parentheses in the text.

And when Arao is again asked by Kan'ichi of his "present whereabouts" in Chapter 4 of Book 4, he again demurs: "I had better not have a usurer coming around." Kan'ichi replies, "On that day, I shall come as a *friend*." Arao retorts, "I'm afraid I have no *friends* among usurers" (p. 328).

Donald Keene has suggested that "there is much to intrigue a sociologist,"[22] in *Konjiki yasha* and perhaps the most intriguing aspect is the peculiar geography that plots the novel's social dimensions in spatial terms. The work is, in a sense, divided between one set of characters who are exactly located and another set who belong to a more abstract geography; characters who are, like Arao, everywhere and nowhere. The division between these two sets of characters—we might perhaps even say between these two classes of characters—runs along a very simple, almost allegorical, line: on the one hand, all those characters engaged in one way or another in the lending of money are exactly located;[23] and on the other hand, there are the rest of the characters. It is almost an exact topographical replica of Marx's basic description of capitalist society: the growing polarization of all members of society into capital and labor.[24]

Indeed, it is easy—perhaps too easy—to read Kōyō's novel as an allegory of capitalist society. The question is really: what sort of allegory? In the early nineteenth-century novel, money is everywhere, but everywhere, the power of money is disavowed. In *Keiseikai tora no maki*, the usurer Kiriyama can redeem Segawa, but he can never own her. The situation at the beginning of *Konjiki yasha* is reversed: the banker's scion, Tomiyama Tadatsugu, cannot purchase Miya, but in the end, he can, and does, own her. She has become, as Arao charges in Book 4, a piece of merchandise.[25]

---

22. Keene, *Dawn to the West*, p. 143.

23. Wanibuchi, Akagashi, and eventually Kan'ichi are all usurers; the Tomiyama family—whose name literally means "Mountain of Wealth"—are bankers. Most interesting of all is the Viscount Tazumi, who is completely uninterested in money, but whose fortune is, quite unbeknownst to him, being used by his head clerk, Kuroyanagi Motoe, to bankroll Wanibuchi. See Ozaki Kōyō, *Konjiki yasha*, p. 110.

24. Marx, "The German Ideology," p. 178: "Opposed to the productive forces, stands the majority of individuals . . . who, robbed of any genuine content in their lives, have therefore become abstract individuals. . . ."

25. See Ozaki Kōyō, *Konjiki yasha*, p. 295. In refusing to help Miya contact Kan'ichi, Arao suggests that since she is now Tomiyama's "property," he would be guilty of

The world of the early nineteenth-century novel has been turned on its head in *Konjiki yasha*, melodrama gone out of control, subject to the power of the purse. This, at least, is the novel's starting point, which draws heavily on the scene of Hamaji's lament from Kyokutei Bakin's *Nansō satomi hakkenden*. In Chapter 6 of Book 1, Miya and her mother have left Tokyo for Atami and Kan'ichi is left alone with Miya's father, uncomfortably awaiting word from Miya. "It may be a bit novelistic," thinks Kan'ichi, "but with Hamaji in the *Hakkenden* . . . when Shino said he would be leaving the following day, she came to him in the dead of night, in secrecy from her parents; one must have that sort of love." Kan'ichi continues, "It is strange, but my own position is similar to that of Shino. I too was separated from my parents in my youth and came here to the Shigisawas' and was betrothed to their daughter . . . yes, it's similar, very similar."

But while the starting point of this novel is indeed "similar, very similar" to this episode from the *Hakkenden*, its development could not be more different. Whereas Hamaji is the model of chastity and faithfulness, Miya acquiesces to her broken engagement and marriage to Tomiyama. She is a "depraved woman," an "adulteress" as Kan'ichi puts it at their parting in Atami. And yet, in that scene on the windswept shore at Atami, something is left unspoken:

> "Where are you going," Miya calls after Kan'ichi, "There is something I must tell you, so tonight let us go back together. Kan'ichi, please . . ."
>
> "If you have something to say, tell me here."
>
> "No, not here."
>
> "What do you have to say? Let go of me."
>
> "I shall not let go!"
>
> "If you persist, I shall kick you off."
>
> "Then kick me." (pp. 77–78)

When Kan'ichi shakes himself free "with all his might," Miya is left "pitifully" lying on the ground "without enough strength to pick herself up." The scene ends with Miya calling after Kan'ichi, the "sad sound of waves breaking" in the background.

---

damaging another's property by leading her back to her former lover: "You were merchandise sold to Tomiyama. I could not very well damage another man's merchandise."

And what is left unspoken in this scene haunts the novel. In the late eighteenth-century *Tora no maki*, money is deceiving but that deception is always external to the characters; here, the fiction is more complex and more ambivalent. In Chapter 3 of Book 1, Miya is depicted as—quite literally—calculating (p. 26). But it is Kan'ichi's unwillingness to hear Miya out, either that night at Atami or years later when she writes him over and over of her repentance and suffering, that impels the tragedy of the novel. In a recent essay on *Konjiki yasha*, Kan Satoko has suggested that Miya's letters—which occupy such an important position in Book 4 of the novel—can be seen as an attempt by Miya to narrativize her own life; she also suggests that these narratives simply replicate the narrative of herself desired by Kan'ichi, a narrative of constancy and regret.[26] But we might say further that this narrative originates neither from Kan'ichi nor Miya; it is, in fact, the "novelistic" narrative (and the term "novelistic" is, of course, Kan'ichi's own) of Hamaji and Shino that Kan'ichi imagines when he is alone at the Shigisawas' house waiting for word from Miya near the opening of the novel. It is the narrative of the early nineteenth-century novel.

When Miya encounters Arao and seeks his mediation with Kan'ichi, her plea echoes Hamaji's parting lines to Shino in the *Hakkenden*: "If you will meet Kan'ichi for me, tell him he may kill me. . . . I want for Kan'ichi to kill me" (p. 299). This is what Kan'ichi had wanted to hear that night in Atami, but it is, of course, too late. In this sense, both Miya and the novel as a whole recognize the loss of this vision of virtue from a prior age, and both try, helplessly, to rush after that vision, to recapture it. As Miya herself realizes, it is too late: "She helplessly regretted that she learned only too late which one must choose if one were not able to enjoy together both the pleasures of the body and the pleasures of the heart and one had to choose but one" (p. 216).

For releasing Miya from their betrothal, Kan'ichi has been promised an education abroad. The novel is thus set to develop along the lines of the great melodramatic novels of early Meiji: the hero will go abroad and then return sometime later, perhaps incognito or much changed as a diplomat or a member of parliament, to be reunited with his lost love in some great scene of revelation. Miya, we would discover, has—despite

26. Kan, *Media no jidai*, pp. 114–17.

her marriage to Tomiyama—remained constant to Kan'ichi; indeed, the reader might expect to learn, she had broken the engagement only so that Kan'ichi could further *his* career, that he could fulfill his father's dream of "becoming a man of learning and stand above the four classes of man" (p. 25).

As Book 2 of *Konjiki yasha* opens—following the parting at Atami—the scene is the crowded and bustling Shinbashi station. Several students board a train bound to the port city of Yokohama to see off a friend on his way to a new life. But, the reader gradually learns, the young man at the center of this scene is not Kan'ichi headed to study abroad, but Arao Jōsuke, Kan'ichi's friend and confidant who will reappear much later in the novel to assume such an important role. Kan'ichi is instead left behind on the platform, in the shadows, waving furtively goodbye. As he will tell Arao six years later: "Even if it was from the shadows, I had wanted to witness you heading off for success. I went to Shinbashi station, and when I saw what a great man you had become, I forgot everything and I wept tears of joy" (p. 326). And so the novel heads off in a very different direction.

When Kan'ichi emerges from the shadows, he is met by the "beauty usurer," Akagashi Mitsue, and he is very much changed. The contrast between Kan'ichi and Mitsue is telling, setting up Kan'ichi's emergence as an exemplar of a sort of "protestant spirit" of capitalist accumulation: frugality, temperance, abstinence, profit for profit's sake. "Her teeth were gold as was her sash ornament; her ring was gold and her armband gold; her watch was gold, and, yes, her pipe too was gold . . . 'I imagine her heart too is made of gold,' Kan'ichi could not help laughing to himself" (p. 94). "In contrast to her aristocratic trimmings," Kōyō writes of Kan'ichi, "he wore a crested *haori* made of black pongee with a lined kimono of pinstriped indigo with the rough Chichibu weave; even the white crepe tie he used in place of a sash was not new" (p. 97). In contrast to Mitsue's voracious appetite for food and alcohol, Kan'ichi is the model of temperance and abstinence.[27] But it is perhaps above all in Kan'ichi's reaction to Mitsue's proposition that his ethic is revealed:

---

27. The temperance that Kan'ichi displays throughout the latter half of the novel is in stark contrast to the scene in Chapter 4 of Book 1 in which he comes home drunk and sated after a night of revelry with his friends. See Ozaki Kōyō, *Konjiki yasha*, p. 33.

"I have decided that I shall never have a wife," Kan'ichi explains, "In truth, I would like the money you have offered to lend me; it is you, the person, for which I have no use" (pp. 103 and 105).

The opening pages of Book 2 reveal a theme that will be repeated again and again as the novel progresses: Kan'ichi's almost senseless desire for accumulation, and for accumulation for accumulation's sake: "I do not wish to torment those who sold me, to carry out such a revenge. . . . Now I have no desire for fame or love, no desire for anything but money" (p. 104). At Yusa's house, when confronted by his former classmates, Urata presses Kan'ichi to explain his motives:

> "Hazama, what is it? Your purpose?"
>
> "I just want money."
>
> "And . . . what will you do with that money?"
>
> "Such a stupid question! Can't one do anything with money? One wants money because one can do anything with it. And that is why I have come for payment." (pp. 171–72)

One wants money because one can do anything with it. This, Marx writes in the *Economic and Philosophic Manuscripts*, is the true power of money: "By possessing the *property* of buying everything, by possessing the property of appropriating all objects, *money* is thus the *object* of eminent possession."[28] Man wants money precisely because its powers are limitless, because it is the "*pimp* between man's need and the object."[29] But it is precisely this function of money that is over and over again denied by Kan'ichi; in contrast to Mitsue's "aristocratic trimmings," Kan'ichi is plain; when Kan'ichi inherits Wanibuchi's fortune after the fire, he rebuilds Wanibuchi's house exactly as it was, only "smaller and more modestly" (p. 314).

Urata's "stupid question" reverberates throughout the final three and a half volumes of *Konjiki yasha*, and it does so, of course, because it is not really a stupid question. Rather, Urata is pointing—perhaps naively—to a paradox or contradiction that lies at the heart of capitalist accumulation, a contradiction between the "logic" and "psycho-logic" of capitalism: "Although the iron law of profits is logically tight, it is

28. Marx, "Economic and Philosophic Manuscripts of 1844," p. 102.
29. Marx, "Economic and Philosophic Manuscripts of 1844," p. 102.

psycho-logically impossible. What is the point of being a capitalist, and entrepreneur, a bourgeois if there is no personal reward whatsoever?"[30] This is the riddle that lies at the heart of *Konjiki yasha*, and it is precisely this contradiction between its logic and psycho-logic that gives the novel its peculiar narrative shape as it lurches onward seemingly endlessly toward no foreseeable resolution.

Defoe had also encountered this "contradiction" in *Robinson Crusoe*: as long as Crusoe is alone on his island, he simply goes on endlessly accumulating, forever. Thus Defoe has to introduce exogenous elements: first Friday, then the Spaniards, and of course, the English, who finally rescue Crusoe. Endless accumulation becomes endless narration, and it is not very interesting. Which is why, in popular versions of *Crusoe*, the diary tends to be cut out: capitalism, when one looks too closely, is not a very interesting proposition.

In this respect, it is significant that, when Kan'ichi falls, he becomes, at first, not himself a usurer, but Wanibuchi's clerk, quite literally keeping Wanibuchi's account books. This is the capacity in which he visits Yusa, to collect his master's payment, to square his books.[31] And when Wanibuchi's house is destroyed at the end of Book 3, it is suggestive indeed that the account books are all that is left. "In one evening, the house and the warehouse had turned to smoke . . . all that had escaped unharmed was the safe that the master had installed in the living room" (p. 274):

> "I imagine everything has been burnt" Wanibuchi's son Tadamichi says to Kan'ichi.
>
> "Everything was completely burnt save one thing, the safe."
>
> "The safe has survived? And what is inside?"
>
> "There was a bit of money but mainly it was the account books and the bonds." (p. 279)

It is a remarkable image, this safe, alone amid the "reddened earth and ash," protecting the ledgers of capital even as all around it—even flesh

30. Wallerstein, "The Bourgeois(ie) as Concept and Reality," p. 146.

31. Double-entry book-keeping is also a central image in *Robinson Crusoe*. See Watt, *The Rise of the Novel*, p. 63: "All of Defoe's characters pursue money, which [Defoe] characteristically called 'the general dominating article in the world'; and they pursue it very methodically according to the profit and loss book-keeping which Max Weber considered to be the distinctive technical feature of modern capitalism."

and bone—has been turned to ash. Hidden away in this safe, here at the very center of this scene—indeed at the very center of the novel—lies the enigma of modern capital.

Capital is like a hydra: one can cut off its heads and kill the capitalists, but the capital continues to grow, unaffected, unimpeded. At the end of Book 3, as Kan'ichi and Tadamichi talk among the embers of the aftermath of the fire, it seems as if the narrative will head in a different direction. Tadamichi leaves his parents' estate to Kan'ichi, with the one request that he dissolve the bonds and leave usury. But as Book 4 opens, it becomes clear that the narrative will continue unchanged—endless accumulation, endless narration:

> If time is money, the conversion would go something like this: one could estimate one second at one *mō*; subtract the eight hours that one sleeps and each day would be a net of sixteen hours, in reality five *yen*, seven *sen*. And totaling this over the course of a 365-day year, then one would arrive at the rather considerable sum of 2,102 *yen*, 40 *sen*. (p. 286)

At the beginning of Book 4, Kan'ichi rebuilds Wanibuchi's house—*smaller, more modestly*—and then continues accumulating. Endlessly. Except that no narrative can go on forever—not even a serial novel.

Kan'ichi is torn—almost crucified—between the *endless present* of accumulation and the desire to "construct a past for the future."[32] Kan'ichi's desire is "for a sort of non-existent entity, the 'Miya of five years earlier'. . . . As Kan'ichi himself recognizes from early on, this is something which can never be recovered. And yet until the impossibility contained within this desire is resolved, the narrative of *Konjiki yasha* cannot end."[33]

A tension rises between the *endless present* of the novel and a narrative desire or impulse to *construct a past for the future*, giving the text a somewhat uncomfortable feeling, as if it were trying to do two different things at once, as if it were trying to bring together two incongruous projects. And just as the tension between these two projects puts tremendous stress on the narrative of *Konjiki yasha*, so too does a homolo-

32. On the idea of the endless present of the bourgeoisie, see Wallerstein, "The Bourgeois(ie) as Concept and Reality," p. 149: "This is what bourgeoisification is all about the end of constructing a past for the future, a condemnation to living in the present."
33. Kan, *Media no jidai*, p. 106.

gous set of tensions put a growing stress on the novelist.[34] In a piece Kōyō wrote for the journal *Bungei* in August of 1902, the author acknowledged that his novel had a "laboured style," admitting that "the labors are great and the successes few and it is not as interesting as all of that hard work merits."[35]

One begins to sense that the contradictions and entanglements within the structure of the novel are themselves part of a larger set of contradictions that broadly governed cultural production at the end of the nineteenth century and were of constant—almost pathological—concern to the author. When Kōyō wrote of his novel's hero that "in other words, Kan'ichi was himself literally to embody the struggle between love and money," the author was perhaps pointing to a larger struggle or confrontation that governed the production of his novel, a struggle not between money and love but between money and art:

> I'm of course not satisfied myself with *that* novel. You will say that I am simply pandering to the times or following the current vogue but I have never engaged in such behavior. But neither have I ignored the public simply to please myself. This is where I take pains. If one can't understand this, one cannot very well write a serial novel. . . . One must survey both one's readers and oneself and harmonize the two well. To put it simply, it is discretion. In other words, on one side, you are displaying yourself to the public and yet so as not to lose yourself in that interval, yet at the same time you are pleasing the public you must also add in your own opinions. Such discretion is neither your enemy nor is it foolish. This discretion seems to have worked with *Konjiki yasha*, for I am constantly pressed upon by my readers: quickly write Book 3, when will you put out Book 4? Usually I get fourteen or fifteen such letters but this time I have had thirty or forty.[36]

34. Itō, *Nihon bundanshi*, vol. 5, p. 171. This is Itō's description of Kōyō as he began working on Volume 5 of the novel in 1899: "Kōyō himself confronted the difficult task of giving to this popular novel a literary raison d'etre. . . . This contradiction tormented him. Each time he worked on the manuscript he would labor, writing and re-writing, piling new pages upon old with each misstep and still never achieving the desired result."

35. Ozaki Kōyō, "*Konjiki yasha* jō chū ge gappyō," p. 318. "Laboured style" is in English in the original.

36. Ozaki Kōyō, "Kōyō sanjin wo otonau," p. 215.

This was 1897, just months after he began serializing *Konjiki yasha*; by the early years of the twentieth century, however, Kōyō was no longer so assured—or so self-congratulatory—over the success of his experiment in discretion. As he began work on Book 5, it was no longer so clear that he was not, in fact, "losing himself" in the compromise. Kōyō's writings from the first years of the twentieth century are littered with the same lament, over and over again: Japanese writers must write as a profession, producing daily results, they are not paid enough, they must constantly worry about making ends meet and so are unable to write a masterpiece: "It is common knowledge that the labor of a novelist is not like the work of a laborer or a coolie in which one can see each day a certain amount of results. Without some sort of occasion—that is, without becoming absorbed in one's work, or as we say, getting into it—it is in reality impossible to create real prose or to come up with great ideas, plans, and devices."[37] It is difficult not to see in the figure of Kan'ichi something of the image of the serial novelist, daily toiling, piling up page upon page, endlessly, and for what?

As the novel progresses, this question looms larger and larger, both for Kan'ichi and for Kōyō himself. And there is no real foreseeable resolution for either. When Kōyō began writing the novel, he had a clear plan in mind: his hero would descend into the world of usury—"greed" and "cruelty"—and then, one morning, have an epiphany. He would see that love could exist beyond the power of money and save two lovers doomed to a double suicide. He would, in the end, use the vast fortune he had accumulated to save those in love. Except that, as Kan Satoko has pointed out, at some point, "*Konjiki yasha* becomes a text independent of Kōyō's 'plan,' it becomes autonomous as a text."[38] When Kan'ichi begins to awaken to his greed and cruelty—first in Chapter 5 of Book 4 and then in Book 5 itself—it feels no more a natural development of the story than if a shipload of Englishmen were to appear and whisk the hero away.

The first hint of this epiphany comes in Book 4, Chapter 5. Kan'ichi is reclining in the waiting room of Honjo station. He has just burned—unopened—a letter from Miya begging forgiveness. A pair of young

37. Ozaki Kōyō, "Kōyōshi no shōsetsuka dan," p. 322.
38. Kan, *Media no jidai*, p. 108.

lovers enter the waiting room and begin, quietly, to talk about their tragic fate.

"Even if my father and mother will not give me to you," pleads the young woman, "isn't it enough if you, Masa, will accept me."

"Please don't say such a foolish thing. You cannot know how terrible this is for me. Because of my own foolish indiscretion, I have fallen into guilt, and yet in reality, I was simply ensnared in the usurer's trap. But I have inflicted a lifelong scar on my person and my only mother . . . I have killed her. . . . And on top of that . . . our engagement has been broken. Had I known it should have come to such piteous thoughts . . . it would have been better to have died in prison." (pp. 338–39)

Kan'ichi listens furtively as he gradually realizes who the lovers are: Masayuki was put in prison for forging a countersignature on a bond for Wanibuchi and it was his mother—driven mad with resentment—who had brought Wanibuchi to his fiery end.

"Since my parents will not agree, I shall make the decision myself. Perhaps I am not being filial but, no matter what, I want to go with you, Masa, so if you are willing, please take me with you. Please do not think of me, I only want to know whether you are willing to accept me or not, please just tell me that."

More than the misfortune into which the man had plunged himself or the accompanying grief of the woman, [Kan'ichi] was most moved by the woman's spirits. His head flushed and his heart raced: "How moving! So there exists in this world a faithfulness that burns like true love!"

[. . . .]

"Even if I die, I shall never marry another."

Her body shook and she appeared to sink into tears.

"To say such a thing. What can I do?"

"Do as you must. My mind is made up."

For some time, the man did not speak, but after an interval, one began again to speak—Kan'ichi was not sure which—and after a while their hushed voices began again to leak out, but their voices were too low and Kan'ichi was unable to make out what they were saying. They whispered on for a while, neither raising their voice. Surely neither would betray their heart.

"Are you sure? Are you sure?"

The first voice he could make out was the woman's.

"If so, then I too shall be of that mind."

And then their voices lowered again. And yet they talked on and on, neither tiring. Secretly, Kan'ichi prayed for her success. He thought how overjoyed

Masayuki would be. . . . What if that girl there now were Miya? And I Masayuki? . . . Surely the faithfulness towards me that Miya had was no less than that girl's.

[. . . .]

It was Tadatsugu who destroyed my love. And their love? Who destroyed that? And now, what takes me to Chiba, is that not again to destroy? And this greed, what has it given me? (pp. 341–45)

The dramatic nature of this scene is deeply suggestive: not simply in the theatricality of the exchange, but even more so in the spectatorship inscribed in this scene, as if Kan'ichi were quite literally watching a drama—a melodrama—unfold. And for its content, this drama is drawing on precisely that idea of unconditional love and fidelity that Kan'ichi had conjured with the scene of Hamaji's lament from the *Hakkenden*: a woman willing, unconditionally, to sacrifice herself for her lover. Indeed, the whispered conversation, overheard in bits and pieces, evokes those scenes of love suicides in which the lovers resolve to flee the world and to die side by side.

The scene of Kan'ichi's epiphany in Book 5 again repeats this dramatic structure as Kan'ichi quietly watches a pair of lovers prepare for a double suicide. Aiko is a courtesan redeemed against her will by a wealthy money lender whom she despises, like Segawa in *Tora no maki*. And here, playing the role of the villainous Kiriyama, is the banker Tomiyama Tadatsugu, the man who had "bought" Miya. And so, in a scene not unlike the arrival of Magoemon at the end of Chikamatsu Hanji's *Shinjū kamiya Jihei*, Kan'ichi steps out of the shadows to save the lovers, to redeem Aiko's contract and set her free.

And so *Konjiki yasha* is torn between the endless present of accumulation and the narrative desire or impulse to construct a past; and that past is the past of the early nineteenth-century aesthetic of sentiment and melodrama. The novel returns time and time again—in both of these epiphanic scenes, but also in Miya's dialogue with Arao, in Miya's confrontation with Kan'ichi at his lodgings in Banchō, in Kan'ichi's dream of Miya's suicide at the end of Book 4—to the scene of Hamaji's seduction from Bakin's *Hakkenden*, to the scene of a beautiful young woman offering rather to end her life than to marry another. This is the "novelistic" scene for which Kan'ichi has been searching the entire novel, a way out of the endless present, a way to recover a past of innocence, of faithfulness and chastity, a world uncolored by the power of money. Except that as it emerges in the novel, the dialectic between the power of love and the power of money is much more ambiguous—and seemingly more sinister—than that found in the early nineteenth-century aesthetic of the disavowal of money. It is, after all, in a weird restaging of the *Tora no maki*, the money of a usurer, Kan'ichi, that redeems Aiko. Even the freedom of the lovers, and the purity of their love, has to be bought. But this was, in some sense, Kōyō's great dream: to earn enough writing serial novels that he could afford the luxury of writing one great masterpiece, art bought on the back of pulp, the endless present of the *feuillton* leading to a space beyond the power of money, to the space of pure art. But Kōyō would not live long enough to see this dream realized. And even in his final years, he had come to see the mendacity of his vision: that he would never earn enough to free himself from the yoke of the editor, that he would never escape the endless present of the writing life.

So how does this novel end? This is not so simple a question as it may seem. By 1902, Kōyō had finished the first five books of the novel and had begun serializing a sixth. In April of that year, at a party in Nihonbashi held by the poetry coterie Chikuhakukai, Kōyō was swamped by a group of adoring readers and castigated: "Kōyō-*sensei*, this is no time for a geography of the Shiobara spa. What on earth, *sensei*, do you plan on doing with Miya."[39] By May of that year, he had intermittently, in fits and starts, written as far as the second half of Chapter 3, but then nothing in June and July. Kōyō continued to collect his monthly salary of 100 yen—a considerable sum, Itō Sei has pointed out, noting that the *Yomiuri*'s editor-in-chief at the time, Nagai Kinjō, was making a salary of only 60 yen a month.[40]

The long simmering tension between Kōyō and his employer began to boil over. When the *Yomiuri*'s president, Motono Morimichi, learned that Kōyō was again taking a break from writing, he is said to have muttered "unbelievable, unbelievable." When Kōyō went to pick up his salary at the Ginza office of the *Yomiuri* at the beginning of August, he was confronted by a "fiftyish and pockmarked accountant, smoking a

39. Itō, *Nihon bundanshi*, vol. 6, p. 265.
40. Itō, *Nihon bundanshi*, vol. 6, p. 261.

pipe with his back to the safe," who told him, "Mr. Kōyō, your salary is at Toriizaka [at Motono's residence]. You are to pick it up there yourself, Mr. Kōyō." And so ended Kōyō's thirteen years at the *Yomiuri*.[41]

The novel was incomplete. And Kōyō would die, at the age of 37, on October 13 of that year. The novel as it stood at the time of Kōyō's death—and as it is now published today—was very much unresolved. And yet, the reading public was not satisfied, and for over a decade, sequels and continuations appeared.[42] "We might say," writes Kan Satoko, "that these were all born of the readers' desire for an 'ending' to the story."[43] The publisher Shinchōsha purchased Kōyō's manuscript, and in 1909, published a new ending for the novel, *Konjiki yasha shūhen*, written by Kōyō's student and longtime friend Oguri Fūyō. It was a tremendous commercial success: by 1914, it had gone through 20 printings.[44]

In the new "complete" version, Miya has gone mad, and after attempting suicide for a second time, divorces Tomiyama and loses her memory of the entire time she had spent as his wife. "It was as if, in reality, or at least in her own consciousness, she had been resurrected as the unblemished Miya of six years earlier, the Miya of the Shigisawa house."[45] It is with this "premise," writes Kan Satoko, "that Kan'ichi takes her back."[46] In the end, the novel abandons the *endless present* in favor of constructing a past for the future. And in order to achieve all of this, the present of the novel has to be disavowed, literally forgotten, so that Miya can return to her unspoiled state before that break at Atami. It is a little far-fetched, one thinks, a little melodramatic. But this is the point about what Hans Robert Jauss calls "culinary art," it raises difficult problems only to set them aside, reveals only to conceal once more. We might say that as a long meditation on the power of money, *Konjiki yasha* cuts the ideology of bourgeois existence to the bone and then discovers that it does not really like what it finds there. But the question remains: who does not like it? Kōyō? Or Fūyō? The novel's

---

41. Itō, *Nihon bundanshi*, vol. 6, pp. 267–68.
42. On the reaction of the reading public and the industry of sequels this spawned, see Kan, *Media no jidai*, pp. 104–08.
43. Kan, *Media no jidai*, p. 105.
44. Kan, *Media no jidai*, p. 105.
45. Oguri Fūyō, *Konjiki yasha shūhen*, quoted in Kan, *Media no jidai*, p. 107.
46. Kan, *Media no jidai*, p. 107.

publisher? Or the readers? To pursue this question is, at best, an exercise in anachronism and, more probably, hagiography. At present, Fūyō's ending is seen as something of a betrayal of Kōyō's intent, and more than that, of the artistic spirit of the novel, as if Kōyō was himself content to unveil and it was Fūyō and the publisher Shinchōsha following the demands of the readers who required that the veil be put back where it was found. We know from Kōyō's notes that the ending he had planned was quite close to what Fūyō produced, so what evidence we have does not point entirely in this direction. And to engage in this sort of speculation is really beside the point, because the protagonists of literary history are not really the authors, anyway, but the readers.

"It is the fraternization of impossibilities," Marx writes of the power of money, "it makes contradictions embrace." There is perhaps no better description of this novel—or indeed of Kōyō's life.

The Politics of Tears

In a preface he wrote in 1909 to the 100th printing of *Hototogisu*, Tokutomi Roka described his novel as "juvenile," containing elements, he admitted, that were "cheaply theatrical."[47] It was just over a decade since Roka had first started serializing the novel in his brother Tokutomi Sohō's paper *Kokumin shinbun*, but much had changed both in Roka's own life and in the larger political and social climate in Japan. *Hototogisu* ran in the *Kokumin shinbun* between November 29, 1898 and May 24, 1899 and was then published as a book by Minyūsha, the parent firm of the *Kokumin shinbun*, in 1900. In the decade that followed, *Hototogisu* would become the best-selling novel of Meiji Japan and the first Japanese novel to attract considerable attention abroad.

But the success of the novel had not always been certain. When it appeared as a serial novel in the *Kokumin shinbun*, *Hototogisu* had very limited success and never rivaled the popularity of Ozaki Kōyō's *Konjiki yasha*, serialized contemporaneously in the *Yomiuru shinbun*.[48] Roka had not even expected the novel to be turned into a book and was somewhat surprised when Watanabe Tamezō, a publisher at Minyūsha, expressed

---

47. Tokutomi Roka, "Dai hyakuban *Hototogisu* no kanshu ni," p. 3.

48. See Takagi, *Shinbun shōsetsushi: Meiji-hen*, p. 338.

interest in publishing the novel in book form. The first print run was of 2,000 copies of a much-revised version of the novel, for which Roka received a royalty of 40 *sen*, less than half of Kōyō's monthly salary at the *Yomiuri*. But within a year, the novel had run through eight printings and sold 10,000 copies in each of the following two years.[49] What had begun as a sort of speculative venture had turned out to be a spectacular commercial success. In his revision, Roka had been able to accentuate the dominant themes of the novel by eliminating many of the peripheral elements of the plot and focusing on the tragic love of the hero, Takeo, and the heroine, Namiko. In a review of the novel for the newspaper *Yorozu chōhō*, Sakai Kosen remarked that "in the dead of night, lying in bed, a stream of tears dampened the book."[50] The speculative venture begun by author and publisher was completed by the reading public: what the novel was selling—tears—had become clear for the first time, and the novel would be, even by the standard of other "tearful books," an enormous commercial success. By 1909, *Hototogisu* had gone through 100 printings, outselling even Kōyō's *Konjiki yasha*, and would go through another 100 printings by the early 1930s.

Moreover, the social life of the novel extended well beyond the covers of the book and well beyond the borders of Japan itself. *Hototogisu* had been turned into a *shinpa* play and staged continuously from the spring of 1903 on;[51] in 1909, Kinkodō published the definitive edition of the script adapted by Yanagawa Shun'yō. And in 1911, two special editions of the novel were published: an edition rendered into classical Chinese and published jointly by Chiyoda shobō in Tokyo and Sugimoto ryōkōdō in Osaka, and a deluxe picture book edition published by Sakura shobō and sold for one and a half yen, five times the price of the original Minyūsha edition, which had sold for 30 *sen*. Nine separate films were made of the novel between 1909 and 1916. And then there were the translations: first into English (1904); and then Spanish (1904); German (1905); Finnish (1906); Portuguese (1906); French (1911); Russian (1913); Chinese (1913); Italian (1921); and Czech

---

49. Takagi, *Shinbun shōsetsushi: Meiji-hen*, pp. 338–39.

50. Quoted in Takagi, *Shinbun shōsetsushi: Meiji-hen*, p. 339.

51. See Shōwa joshi daigaku kindai bungaku kenkyūshitsu, ed., *Kindai bungaku kenkyū soshō*, vol. 28, p. 51.

(1922). In Korea, two adaptations and a translation of the novel appeared between 1912 and 1913. As late as 1917, Roka noted in his diary that he had recently seen an advertisement in *Shukujo gahō* (*Ladies Illustrated*) for a new picture book edition and commented, referring to the novel's heroine, "Nami's life has been quite long indeed!"[52] But for Roka, the length of Nami's social life, which contrasts so sharply with the brevity of the fictional heroine's life within the novel, was not an entirely happy thing.

In the decade between the novel's first appearance and the time he wrote the new preface to the 100th printing, Roka had begun to have serious misgivings about *Hototogisu*. In 1909, it would still be another two years before Roka became completely disillusioned with the Meiji government in the wake of the Grand Treason Incident and before he so eloquently came to the defense of the anarchist Kōtoku Shūsui; but the feeling of "stagnation," about which the poet Ishikawa Takuboku would write, had already begun to set in among many writers and intellectuals. Roka was increasingly unnerved by the politics of late Meiji: he had embraced socialism and became estranged from his brother Sohō over the latter's nationalism and apologies for Japan's colonial expansion. Indeed, on the eve of the momentous political events of 1910 and 1911, the misgivings Roka felt towards his novel seem to take on a special significance, even a prescience, suggesting both what it meant for the sentimentalism on which this novel traded to have such continued popular appeal, but also how the central mythology of the novel might seem, in hindsight, naïve, "juvenile," even somewhat dangerous.

Roka had begun to feel unease about the success of his novel well before 1909, and some of his earliest expressions of this discomfort were occasioned by the prospect of the novel appearing in translation. When Sohō had arranged for William Turner to translate *Hototogisu* into English and publish it in America, Roka was extremely uncomfortable with the idea of his novel being seen as representative either of his own literary career, or more broadly, of Japanese fiction. In September of 1903, Roka wrote to his friend the Christian activist Miura Tōru, expressing his unease:

52. See Tokutomi Roka, *Roka nikki*, vol. 6, p. 152.

> If a work like my *Hototogisu* is translated and published abroad, it will surely be said "so *this* is an example of recent Japanese fiction." That would be most regrettable both for the Meiji novel and for my own self. If you are looking for novels worth being translated, then there are [Kōda] Rohan's *Gojū no tō* and [Ozaki] Kōyō's *Tajō takon.* And there are many other masterpieces. It was never my intention to have this childish novel be the first to be known abroad simply because my brother was an acquaintance of the translator. Of course, I have always thought I would like to write at least one work that would be remembered and it would be a dream come true to have that work translated, but to have a work like *Hototogisu*, in which I was still learning to write a story, be seen as the representative work of my life was never what I wanted.[53]

And Roka would repeat this sentiment in a letter he wrote in English to William Turner, dated January 21, 1904: "I am rather unwilling to have my story 'Hototogisu' translated and published in America. I do not speak this from modesty, but you have chosen a poor specimen while there are much finer productions here which would have more suited your purpose. But then you tell me the matter has gone too far. Well let me hope that this will be a forerunner to herald the worthier ones to come."[54] This letter was supposed to serve as "a sort of preface to the English translation of 'Hototogisu,'" but it was never published.

To take as our starting point Roka's own ambivalent feelings about his great sentimental masterpiece is to highlight two very different dimensions of this novel: its appeal to readers and success on a narrative level, on the one hand, and the way that the novel's story is deeply embedded both socially and historically in what Carol Gluck has called "a time of settlement."[55] These two facets of the novel are deeply intertwined, but not in an obvious or straightforward way. Indeed, while situating the production and consumption of this novel against a backdrop of the strengthening hold of a dualist structure in the literary field of Meiji Japan can allow us to see how this same narrative might be read in different ways at different times—or by different readers at the same time—it is only by understanding the underlying narrative logic of the novel that we can untangle the ideological shadings of *Hototogisu.*

53. Tokutomi Roka, *Roka zenshū*, vol. 20, p. 140.
54. Tokutomi Roka, *Roka zenshū*, vol. 19, pp. 367–69.
55. Gluck, *Japan's Modern Myths*, pp. 17–21.

In 1898, while summering at the resort area of Zushi, Roka met the painter Kuroda Seiki. It was now seven years since Kuroda had done his painting *Reading* (discussed above in Chapter 1) and he had become one of the leading figures of modern art. Kuroda had returned to Japan in 1893 and was at the center of a scandal in 1895 when his *Chōshō* (*Morning Bath*) was exhibited at the Fourth National Industrial Exposition held in Kyoto in honor of the 1,100th anniversary of the old capital. Kuroda had completed "Morning Bath" in Paris in 1893 while studying under Raphael Collin and the painting won the prestigious Puvis de Chavannes prize that year.[56] When the painting was exhibited in Kyoto in 1895, it caused a minor sensation and the authorities attempted to have it removed from the exposition, charging that it violated the 1872 Ishikikai'i ordinance prohibiting public nudity, mixed bathing, and lewd paintings. Kuki Ryūichi, then director of the Imperial Museum in Tokyo and a recently appointed member of the Privy Council, intervened on Kuroda's behalf to save the painting.[57] It was to Kuroda that Roka would turn in 1899 to draft the frontispiece to the Min'yūsha edition of *Hototogisu*, an image that would come to define the novel and its heroine, a beautiful young woman suffering from tuberculosis. Like Takeuchi Keishū's frontispiece for the first volume of Kōyō's *Konjiki yasha*, Kuroda's *Namiko* was set against the rough sea around the Izu peninsula, depicting the tubercular heroine of Roka's novel sitting in solitude at the spot where she and her husband had pledged to one another undying love, but where she now contemplated—as the reader would later learn—jumping to her death in the breaking waves below.

At the same resort and in that same summer, Roka also met a woman who had come to Zushi to recover from an illness. One evening, Roka recalled almost a decade later, the woman began to tell him a "tragic story":

> A woman, "Nami-san," divorced because of tuberculosis; the sorrow of "Takeo"; the anger of Lieutenant General Kataoka and his reclaiming of his daughter; the setting up of a place of convalescence for the stricken woman; the Lieutenant General taking "Nami-san" on a farewell tour of the Kyoto and

56. See Takashina, "Inshōha to kindai no Nihon kaiga," pp. 126–27.

57. See Satō, *'Nihon bijutsu' no tanjō*, pp. 133–38.

Osaka area; the rejection of the flowers sent to the funeral by the Kawashima family; these were the basic facts of the story. Despite her congestion, the woman spoke earnestly. I listened resting against a pillar in the alcove. My wife hung her head. The sun had set without our realizing it. It had become dim in the old country house and only the summer kimono of the woman was whitely visible. When she spoke of the pathos of the moment of the young woman's death, she began to say "it is said that these were her final words—never again should such a thing as a woman be born" but choked with tears her sentence broke off. Something raced down my spine like a flash of lightning. . . . The impression from the story never left me. . . . I had to do something. . . . And so I took the skeleton of that story and freely fleshed it out, roughly drafting a novel and publishing it in the *Kokumin shinbun*; what was later published as a single volume by Minyūsha is this novel, *Hototogisu*.[58]

A woman dying of consumption, divorced by her husband's family against his will and without his knowledge, stigmatized by her illness and doomed to die without meeting her true love again—this is the 'skeleton' of Roka's first novel *Hototogisu* and the kernel of what would become one of the dominant mythologies of the late Meiji period.

In Roka's telling of his first encounter with the story in the 1909 preface to the 100th edition, there is a particular moment at which he experiences the sensationalism of the story, a moment punctuated by the narrator's tears: the deathbed scene. "When she spoke of the pathos of Nami-san's moment of death . . . [she was] choked with tears [and] her sentence broke off. Something raced down my spine like a flash of lightning." And in Roka's rendering of Namiko's story in the novel itself, the young heroine's deathbed scene becomes the central dramatic moment in which the constitutive elements of the mythology rendered by the novel are produced:

Namiko closed her mouth and her eyes and the shadow of death began gradually to envelop her face. Her father approached—"Nami, is there nothing more you wish to say?—be strong . . ." She was brought back by the familiar voice and her barely opened eyes concentrated on the figure of the Viscountess Kataoka. Taking Namiko's hand she said "Nami-san, I shall do whatever you wish. Be at ease and go to your mother's side . . ." And just as a faint smile rose upon her lips, she closed her eyelids and her breathing ceased as if she

58. Tokutomi Roka, "Dai hyakuban *Hototogisu* no kanshu ni," p. 4.

had fallen asleep. The moonlight that seeped into the room shone upon her pale countenance and the smile still floated upon her lips. But Namiko had begun her eternal sleep.[59]

The death of the young and beautiful heroine: this is the crucial moment of pathos in the novel, the moment at which the reader is brought to tears and at which much of the work of the novel is accomplished. The heroine is surrounded by family and friends; her mother, who had died when Namiko was only eight, waits for her daughter in death. Namiko's husband, from whom she has been separated by a scheming mother-in-law, is away at war, unaware that his wife is about to die. He will return to see her, but at a point already too late. Namiko takes her final breath in the company of her stepmother and closest maidservant, unaware that Takeo has always been faithful and will return for her following the armistice.

The reader is moved to tears, not only because Namiko has died so young, but because she was never able to see Takeo again, despite his final words: "I shall soon return" (p. 118). The deathbed scene is the climactic moment at which the reader is moved to tears, but the scene cannot accomplish this work by itself. Rather, the scene of Namiko's beautiful death depends for much of its efficacy on a failed encounter between Namiko and Takeo in the chapter by which it is immediately preceded.

Takeo has returned from Manchuria after the capture of Port Arthur and attempts to see his wife at her place of convalescence at Zushi. His parting words to Namiko, over a year before, had been "I shall soon return"; in the meantime, his mother has fallen prey to the machinations of Takeo's cousin Chijiwa and the "merchant prince" (*shinshō*) Yamaki, and has divorced her son from his wife against his wishes. When Takeo returns from war the first time, it is already too late: "It is too much, it is really too much" Takeo protests to his mother. "It is too late now," she responds, "her family has agreed and taken her back. What more can you do?" In a moment of frustration Takeo charges: "Mother, you have killed Nami, and on top of that you have killed me. I shall never

59. Tokutomi Roka, *Hototogisu*, p. 218. All subsequent citations to *Hototogisu* are to this edition and page numbers will be given in parentheses in the text.

see you again" (p. 140), and the hero heads back to war. When Takeo returns from Manchuria the second time and attempts to see Namiko at Zushi, he again arrives too late: "She returned to Tokyo before her father returned from China," Takeo is informed by the groundskeeper at Zushi. "It seems that after that, she went to Kyoto with her father and they have probably not yet returned to Tokyo" (p. 204). Takeo is set to return to sea but misses the train to the naval base at Yokosuka, and so has to meet up with the ship at Kure in Hiroshima. The scene is now set for the final failed encounter between Takeo and Namiko:

Although she felt great pathos towards her father, the man whom she loved was her husband, Takeo. She had only heard that Takeo had saved her father's life at Port Arthur, but there was no one who could tell her whether after that he was living or dead; her love was scattered and they met in her dreams but she knew not where he now was. I want to see him, she thought, I want to see him once, once before I die, I want to see him but once more. . . . When they arrived in Yamashina, they boarded the eastbound train. There was no one in the first class compartment and Namiko sat by the open window and her father sat beside her with the newspaper open. At that moment, a train heading for Kobe came up from the East spitting smoke and shaking the ground and pulled up alongside Namiko's own train just as it was about to depart. And just as one began to hear the opening and closing of doors and the voice of a porter walking along the gravel platform calling out "Yamashina! Yamashina!" the whistle of the train blew and it began slowly to move. Sitting by the open window, Namiko casually looked at the train which they were passing. Just as her carriage came before a second class compartment, she came face to face with a man in western dress resting his cheek against his hand in the window. "It's you!"

"Oh, Nami-san!" It was Takeo. The carriages began to pass. Namiko leaned out the window as if she were mad and threw to him the violet handkerchief which she had clasped in her hand. The car passed—ten meters, twenty meters. Namiko, leaning out until she was about to fall and looking back, saw Takeo waving the handkerchief as if he were mad and calling something. The rails curled around a mountain. On both sides, there was nothing but verdant mountains. . . . Namiko covered her face and buried her head in her father's lap. (pp. 210–11)

The deathbed scene is set up by this failed encounter—the two trains pulling away from each other, one taking the heroine back to Tokyo, the other taking the hero off to war; and this scene is itself but the final in a series of failed encounters in which the hero always arrives too late. When Takeo returns from his first absence, the divorce has already been completed; when he returns the second time and attempts to see Namiko at Zushi, he is again too late—she has returned to Tokyo; and in the end, when he has returned for the third time, she has already died. The novel's every maneuver is structured in the same way, and the novel's final scene—an encounter between Takeo and Namiko's father, Lieutenant General Kataoka, over Namiko's grave—again replays this structure:

> Takeo stood in front of the grave, forgetting himself and weeping. Visions of these three years floated up before him in a haze of tears. The day of their marriage; their sojourn in Ikaho; their pledge to one another at the Fudō Shrine; the evening they parted at the villa in Zushi; and that day when they last saw each other at Yamashina; these visions appeared in his heart one after another like a flashes of lightning. Although the words "come back soon" lingered in his ears, when he had returned the first time she was already no longer his wife, and when he had returned the second time she was no longer among those in this world.
>
> [. . . .]
>
> The two men stood clasping one another's hands, shedding tears at the foot of her grave. Gradually, the Lieutenant General wiped away his tears. Patting Takeo on the shoulder, he spoke—"Takeo, even now that Nami has died, I am still your father. I ask you to be strong. The journey ahead of us is long. It has been a long time, Takeo-san, tell me of Taiwan." (pp. 224–26)

A series of failed encounters in which the hero arrives too late; the beautiful death of the young heroine consumed by tuberculosis; the final scene of reconciliation over the heroine's grave in which the woman's father and her husband prepare for "the long journey ahead." Alone, in the dead of night, the reader is moved to tears. But why? Or rather, once we come to understand why the reader is moved to tears, why was it that, 30 years on from the Meiji Restoration, tears continued to be such an important part of the literary and social economy of Japan? And why, a decade later, would these tears come to seem to the author who first elicited them suspect, both aesthetically and ideologically?

In his *Origins of Modern Japanese Literature*, Karatani Kōjin began an ideological critique of *Hototogisu*, arguing that "the popularity of this novel was due not merely to its depiction of Meiji mores, but to a 'contagious' inversion condensed within it."[60] And indeed, the "inversion" contained within the novel—the ascription to illness of metaphorical value, of meaning—is, of course, central to the narrative. But the mere presence of this inversion can no more explain the popularity of the novel than can an argument based the novel's depiction of "Meiji mores." The problem becomes clear when we situate *Hototogisu* within the literary field of the late Meiji period and within what Fukuda Mahito has called "the process of romanticization" of tuberculosis in that period. In his cultural history of tuberculosis, Fukuda has noted that *Hototogisu* was not the first novel in which tuberculosis played a central role. The disease appeared as a peripheral aspect of the plot in several novels of the early 1880s, including Suehiro Tetchō's *Setchūbai*, one of the most popular political novels of the time. And then, in 1889, the disease became a central theme of Hirotsu Ryūrō's *Zangiku* which depicts a young wife dying of consumption while her husband is away in Europe; but when the husband returns at the end of the novel, the wife recovers from her illness, overcome by joy. And then there were the translations of Alexandre Dumas fils's *La Dame aux Camélias*: by the time *Zangiku* was published at the end of the 1880s, three translations or adaptations of the story had appeared and, by 1902, the novel had been rendered in Japanese four more times including translations by Uchida Roan and Mori Ōgai. *Hototogisu* was, of course, part of—and central to—the "process of romanticization" of tuberculosis;[61] but as Karatani himself has noted, "to try to dispense with [the] issue by using the label 'romanticism' is to lose sight of the problem. For what we find in condensed form in late nineteenth-century Japan is an inversion typical of Western culture, of which romanticism is only one part."[62]

The problem central to understanding the constitutive mythology of *Hototogisu* and the widespread currency of this mythology is the relationship between tears on the one hand and this "inversion" on the other. The "inversion" does not produce the tears, but the two worked together to erect a social mythology that attempted to make

60. Karatani, *Origins of Modern Japanese Literature*, pp. 99–100.
61. See Fukuda, *Kekkaku no bunkashi*, p. 101, p. 107, and p. 372.
62. Karatani, *Origins of Modern Japanese Literature*, p. 103.

sense of an ideological moment of "a time of settlement." And the scene of beautiful death is the central moment both of sentiment and of this "inversion" in which a metaphorical meaning is ascribed to the brute fact of death by adapting certain conventions from nineteenth-century European literature.[63] The death is rendered beautiful by the adaptation of these conventions to produce an "inversion" in which sickness accrues sentimentalized meaning as beautiful. But the inversion does not produce the popularity of the novel; rather, it is a sort of secret sharer that capitalizes on the novel's production of sentiment to create a dominant mythology for this "time of settlement."

In his essay on "moving literature" in *Signs Taken for Wonders*, Franco Moretti has argued that the function of the protagonist's death in tear-jerkers is "to show that time is *irreversible*." At the end of such novels:

> A universal consensus has been re-established but to no avail. Even if everybody is now in a position to share the same values, nothing guarantees any longer that they can materialize in the world, that they can turn into facts. This state of affairs arises from what we have called the "too late," and what could simply be called time. . . . But time does not stop, and it does not heed anyone's bidding. Still less does it turn back and allow us to use it differently. This is what the protagonist's death is for: to show that time is *irreversible*. And this irreversibility is perceived that much more clearly if there are no doubts about the *different direction* one would like to impose on the course of events. This is what makes one cry.[64]

What makes *Hototogisu* so interesting is not just that it employs this rhetoric of "too late" to produce tears; rather, it is that the novel uses this rhetoric to erect a social mythology which succeeds, even against the expectations of the author, in capturing the imagination of a generation of readers, and so allows us to situate this rhetoric of "too late" within a broader social landscape. The rhetoric of "too late" is one thing when we understand it as the central formal element of this novel, the device that produces tears; it is another thing entirely when we understand it as the central constitutive element of a social mythology which

---

63. On the trope of the beautiful death in nineteenth-century European literature see Bronfen, *Over Her Dead Body*, p. 77.
64. Moretti, "Kindergarten," p. 162.

situates the rhetoric of "too late" at the center of an ideological process of "settlement."

Hototogisu sits at the end of a series of tearjerkers that span the long nineteenth century; at the same time, it participates in an ideological moment quite different from the one in which the myths of Segawa, Agemaki, and Yonehachi were produced. This is why Hirotsu Ryūrō's *Zangiku* is so striking in relation to *Hototogisu*: in this novel of the late 1880s, the "inversion" through which tuberculosis accrues meaning is already present; but when the heroine recovers at the end, the sentimental movement is short-circuited. Although Ryūrō was most likely aware of and responding to the mythology surrounding Marguerite Gautier, the protagonist of *La Dame aux Camélias*—translated by Katō Shihō as *Tsubaki no hanataba* and serialized in the *Yomiuri shinbun* the year before Hirotsu's own work appeared—it is as if he had failed to realize the centrality of the heroine's death for the constitution of that mythology. Or perhaps the heroine's death had not been necessary in the late 1880s—the "inversion" functioning in a different way in this text—and it was only after another decade had elapsed that the importance of death, both narrative and ideological, became apparent. After all, it would have been quite unthinkable for Tamenaga Shunsui to have one of his heroines die, and Shunsui went so far as to resurrect Segawa as a ghost in his sequel to Tanishi Kin'gyo's *Tora no maki*.

By the turn of the twentieth century, compromise and reconciliation were no longer as straightforward as they had been in the previous decades. Compromise is effected at the end of *Hototogisu*, but at a price: the death of the heroine, not unlike the compromise proposed in *Tora no maki* over a century earlier. The melodramatic novels of the 1870s and 1880s often brought to bear on their seemingly modern plots narrative strategies borrowed from the fiction of the early nineteenth century; thus, in these novels the hero and heroine were separated, their love subjected to a series of ordeals, but they were eventually reconciled By the turn of the twentieth century, this plot became, in some respects, inadequate to an altered ideological context. In 1889, Ryūrō had traded on one aspect of the mythology of Marguerite Gautier; a decade later, Roka had traded on another. What had appeared at an earlier ideological moment as incidental, indeed simply mistaken—the heroine's death, the tragic ending—had emerged at another moment as crucial. Although the two texts share many themes, the ideological work each effects is quite different.

In her study of Japan's modern myths, Carol Gluck has argued that:

> The ideological seizure at the end of the [1880s] was partly a response to what one contemporary commentator described as the 'thunderboltism' of the first two post-Restoration decades. The late Meiji period was less a time of upheaval than one of settlement, less of structural drama than functional adjustment. . . . By 1890, too much had changed; there was no possibility of going home again. It was partly because so many recognized this—some with fear, others with anticipation, that the ideological momentum gathered as it did in the late 1880s."[65]

In Gluck's account of ideology in the late Meiji period, 1890 serves as a sort of double watershed: even as the promulgation of the Constitution of the Empire of Japan in 1889 and the opening of the Diet and the first general elections in 1890 marked a euphoric moment of promise in which anything seemed possible, already the possibilities were beginning to be foreclosed.[66] And we see in Roka's *Hototogisu* precisely this double movement of possibility and foreclosure that offers both the rhetoric of possibility and then a strategy for dealing with the frustration of foreclosure, a strategy for laying to rest the idealism of the first two decades of the Meiji period and preparing for, as Namiko's father puts it in the final sentence of the novel, the long journey ahead.

How does the novel do this work? First, the novel erects an ideal that lies beyond the world of sociability and in defiance of that world—the love of Takeo and Namiko; then, through the heroine's death, the tension created by this ideal is resolved: "The death of the protagonist manages to rebuild the community of those who remain. Through communal weeping, all rancor, all injustice, all blame is abolished. It is a

---

65. Gluck, *Japan's Modern Myths*, pp. 20–21.

66. Gluck, *Japan's Modern Myths*, p. 60: "In the ideological construction of the political universe as it came to exist in the government's presentation after 1890, politics retained its negative connotation of private interest and conflict while any positive civic value it may have had was usurped and absorbed by the word 'nation'. . . . With regard to politics, the combined ideological result in 1890 cannot be described as apolitical, or as anti-political either. Rather, what the government had achieved was essentially to poison the pot. By adding something to the political to make it patriotically unpalatable, politics was denatured even as the constitutional system was beginning to function."

ritual of reciprocal collective absolution."[67] The tearjerker takes a potentially tragic situation and diffuses it: the "denaturing of politics" thus becomes not a defeat, not a betrayal of the idealism of the People's Rights Movement and its call for a democratic politics, but a "compromise," a pragmatic reconciliation of that idealism with the demands of the newly formed constitutional monarchy and the nation that this institution had come to represent. The tears that gripped Japan in the years around the opening of the twentieth century were a way both to acknowledge the sacrifices demanded of that idealism and to lay the idealism quietly to rest and move beyond it in preparation for "the long journey ahead." Tears are constant across the nineteenth century, but of course the function of tears is not. There is thus continuity and discontinuity to the practices of the sentimental imagination across this century, and it is by historically locating the latter within the longer history of sentiment and melodrama that we can begin to understand the true ideological implication of the form. When the tearjerker is at the center of the literary field, it is because tears are, for whatever reason, necessary; in the late Meiji period, tears were necessary to acknowledge the losses entailed by compromise but also to keep those losses from becoming constitutive of a tragic vision of the modern world.

Hototogisu, then, offers a symbolic compromise effected over the dead body of the heroine; at the heart of this symbolic compromise is a narrative movement that gravitates toward tragedy, but that always doubles back, short-circuiting its tragic impulses and concealing behind a wall of sentimentality the ambiguous truths underwriting this compromise. By the first decade of the twentieth century, however, something had changed. Roka's ambition had always been to be a great artist, a Tolstoy in his own right and the very success of this tearful novel and the sentimental myth that it peddled had come to seem something of an embarrassment. The symbolic compromise offered by the novel had come to seem—to its author at least—"juvenile." And juvenile is an apt description of a literary form that at once acknowledges the sadness of loss and distances itself from that sadness, erecting a wall of sentimentality around the pain of loss. As Franco Moretti argues, death by natural causes is crucial to "moving literature" and "its one great lie. . . . Nature

67. Moretti, "Kindergarten," p. 173.

is demonized in order to absolve society by showing its sad powerlessness."[68] And here we see how *Hototogisu* contrasts so sharply with the late eighteenth-century *Tora no maki* in which the culpability of society, while reduced to the figure of the usurer and his henchman, is still acknowledged.

For Roka, by the early years of the twentieth century, the fraudulence of this "great lie" had become increasingly exposed; to continue to absolve society of its guilt had become increasingly untenable. Although *Hototogisu* would continue to sell well into the twentieth century, a new fiction had already begun to emerge in the first decades of the twentieth century, a fiction taking as its central motif not compromise but betrayal. The great novel of this theme would be Natsume Sōseki's *Kokoro*, serialized in the *Tokyo asahi shinbun* between April and August, 1914. "Can you really go back?"—that is the central question at the heart of *Kokoro*. The novel ends with the narrator reading Sensei's letter on the train that links his hometown and Tokyo, not just two different spaces, but two different times. And the question remains unanswered. It resounds through the history of modern Japanese literature, posed over and again by most of the great writers of the twentieth century: Akutagawa, Tanizaki, Kobayashi Hideo, Kawabata, Mishima, and Ōe.

68. Moretti, "Kindergarten," p. 181.

EPILOGUE

Commodities of the Imagination

"It would be absurd to claim that the literature of a country is capable of producing a *Betrothed* or a *Sepolcri* once a year or even once every ten years," Gramsci writes in his *Prison Notebooks*:

> [T]hat is why normal critical activity . . . cannot but be a criticism of 'trends' if it is not to become a continuous massacre. . . . A consistently negative criticism, based on slashing evaluations and demonstrations of "non-poetry" rather than "poetry," would become tedious and revolting. The choice would look like a man-hunt. . . . It seems clear that criticism must always have a positive function, in the sense that it must point to the positive value in the work being studied. If this aspect cannot be artistic, perhaps it can be cultural, in which case the individual work (except in rare instances) will not be as important as groups of works placed in series according to cultural tendency.[1]

Once again we are confronted with the problem of the relationship between the individual case and the broader field or series in which that case is situated. Numbers can help us identify "cultural tendencies," they can tell us where within a cultural field to focus; formal analysis can then help identify *how* the field operates; but then, we need to work outward, to situate these individual works and individual readings back within the larger literary landscape, within a series. But as Gramsci suggests, we will then have moved away from "art" or "beauty" or "poetry" as the central determinant of value and instead have attempted to understand the "cultural" *work* that these texts do: how they operate within a field, how they relate to other works within a

1. Gramsci, *Selections from Cultural Writings*, p. 113.

series, and how we might relate these works to larger historical, ideological, and political contexts. Let us now return to the graphs from Chapter 3, and place *Konjiki yasha* and *Hototogisu* back into a literary series, back into the larger cultural framework in which these two novels—conspicuous for their "success"—were produced and consumed.

When we return to Figure 9, "The Rise of the Novel" from Chapter 3, we see three lines representing three separate "traditions": early modern fiction, translations, and modern novels. To this we could add a fourth line, Chinese novels, but only a handful are published each year and the line would lie flat across the bottom of the graph. Three lines, four lines, neatly separated out; but, of course, the life of books is far more complex, because all of these works are participating in a literary market, a *single* literary market, even if this market fractures around 1890 and there emerges a sort of dualist structure between what would later be called *junbungaku* ("pure" literature) and *taishū bungaku* ("popular" literature), a structure that is still very much in place today.

The catalogues of late nineteenth- and early twentieth-century lending libraries are revealing because they begin to situate these "lines," these "tendencies," back in the real historical space of their consumption; that is to say, the catalogues begin to reveal the shape of the literary market as a whole even if we can only glimpse it in fragments here and there where the fleeting evidence of consumption remains. In a recent essay in the journal *Shoseki bunkashi*, Asaoka Kunio has analyzed one such catalogue produced in 1891 by a commercial lending library in Osaka.[2] The catalogue contains 704 titles in two volumes. The first volume contains a large selection of early modern novels, *sokkibon* of *rakugo* and *kōdan*, Meiji political novels, and translations. Sixteen of the titles were written by Kyokutei Bakin and another sixteen titles were collections of stories told by the famous nineteenth-century raconteur San'yūtei Enchō. Among Bakin's novels are his masterpieces—the *Hakkenden*, *Yumi harizuki*, *Bishōnenroku*—and also, strikingly, his adaptation of the *Jin Yun Qiao*, *Fūzoku kin'gyoden*, attesting to the remarkable social afterlife this Chinese novel continued to have until the close of the nineteenth century. The volume also contains works by Meiji novelists and translators like Kuroiwa Ruikō and Udagawa Bunkai,

2. Asaoka, "Meijiki Ōsaka no kashihon mokuroku," pp. 23–30.

by Tsubouchi Shōyō, Hattori Bushō, and Saganoya Omuro, as well as several works by the great Meiji translator Inoue Tsutomu.

Volume 2 contains more political novels and translations as well as other titles related to philosophy, history, religion, politics, economics, law, and society. Novels constitute roughly a third of the 355 titles in this second volume, with ten works by Sudō Nansui, eight by Inoue Tsutomu (including several translations of Jules Verne and his 1883 translation of *Robinson Crusoe*), five by the political novelist Suehiro Tetchō (including *Setchūbai* and its sequel *Kakan'ō*), six by Tsubouchi Shōyō (including *Tōsei shosei katagi* and under Shōyō's name Futabatei Shimei's *Ukigumo*), and four works by the translator Morita Shiken (including several more works by Verne). "Above all," notes Asaoka about this second volume, "what stand out are political novels and translations."[3]

One of the most striking features of the two-volume catalogue is that, as Asaoka points out, it is utterly unclear on what basis the catalogue is divided.[4] Writers such as Tsubouchi Shōyō, Kuroiwa Ruikō, Hattori Bushō, and Inoue Tsutomu appear in both volumes; even within one volume, the system of classification seems almost arbitrary. For example, a couple of pages from the second volume of the catalogue reproduced in Asaoka's article are telling. Page 38 begins with Saganoya Omuro's *Ajikinaki* then—extending onto page 39—lists eleven translations (one by Ozaki Yukio, one by Nakane Kiyoshi, five by Inoue Tsutomu including *Robinson Crusoe*, one by Fukuda Naohiko, and another two by Inoue Tsutomu), then another ten novels, including Ozaki Kōyō's early *Fūryū kyōnin'gyō* (originally published in *Garakuta bunko*) and Kuroiwa Ruikō's *Muzan*. The entry for "author/translator/publisher" distinguishes between "authors" and "translators" and within specific pages there seems to be a loose grouping or clustering of translations together with other translations and so on, but this order, where it exists, is only loose—why, after all, does Fukuda's translation break up the entries for Inoue?

Of course, title catalogues can only tell us so much. We do not have circulation records, so we do not know which books were checked out and with what frequency. We do not know whether a reader of Bakin

3. Asaoka, "Meijiki Ōsaka no kashihon mokuroku," p. 28.
4. Asaoka, "Meijiki Ōsaka no kashihon mokuroku," p. 28.

might also have borrowed works by Shōyō, who had criticized Bakin in his *Shōsetsu shinzui.* We do not know whether a fan of Enchō's wit might also have enjoyed the political novels of Tetchō or Tōkai Sanshi or if a reader knew—or cared—whether his book was original, an adaptation, or a translation. This is the cultural field, the literary market, within which both *Konjiki yasha* and *Hototogisu* emerged, and so, not surprisingly, each bears the imprint of this market.

Roka, "le tolstoïen," writes a great sentimental novel in the vein of Dumas fils. But as Tokuda Teru has pointed out, that "famous scene," which above all others "brought rosy tears to girls all over"—Takeo and Namiko passing each other at Yamashina Station—is borrowed, almost exactly, and somewhat self-consciously, from a scene in the early nineteenth-century *Asagao nikki*, except in that novel, the handkerchief was a fan and the trains two boats on the Uji river. And—one imagines almost inevitably—*Asagao nikki* was itself largely based on two Chinese novels: *Taohua shan* and the *Jin Yun Qiao.*[5]

For his part, Kōyō's writings were described, even during his lifetime, as "Genroku literature in Western clothes."[6] He helped to rediscover Saikaku and helped to translate Tolstoy, but his *kanbun* preface to Book 4 of *Konjiki yasha* describes a different literary pedigree. He writes that in his youth he had read "Kyōden, Sanba, and Ikku; Kyokutei, Ryūtei, Shunsui and others." Later on, he continued, he would read *Water Margin*, *Journey to the West*, *Jin Ping Mei*, *Romance of the Three Kingdoms*, and *Dream of the Red Chamber*; *Genji monogatari*, *Taketori monogatari*, and *Utsuho monogatari.* The novel borrows heavily from the story of Shino and Hamaji from Kyokutei Bakin's *Hakkenden* but—as he confided to friends—the "hint" for the novel had come from a different source, a novel called *White Lily* by an American woman novelist. Through a marvelous piece of literary detective work, Hori Keiko has recently tracked down this novel, except that its title is not *White Lilly*, but *Weaker Than a Woman*, and both the gender and the nationality of the author are somewhat more complex than Kōyō could have known.[7]

---

5. Tokuda, *Nihon kinsei shōsetsu to Chūgoku shōsetsu*, pp. 628–55.

6. This was Kunikida Doppo's description of Kōyō in "Kōyō sanjin" quoted in Noyama, *Kindai shōsetsu no seiritsu*, p. 85.

7. Hori, "*Konjiki yasha* no ranpon," pp. 189–201.

The author of *Weaker Than a Woman*, one Bertha M. Clay, was, in fact, a fictive persona first invented in the 1870s by the *New York Weekly* as the author of a series of novels that had been pirated from the *Family Herald* of London, originally written by Charlotte M. Brame. In America, the name "Bertha M. Clay" was soon used for a variety of novels not originally written by Brame, romances published by Street & Smith, "written by the same house novelists who wrote the Nick Carter and Frank Merriwell stories: John R. Coyrell, Frederick V. Dey, Gilbert Patten, William J. Banners, and William Wallace Cook."[8]

When one reflects on the problem of "authorship" in *Konjiki yasha*, a serial novel left unfinished and completed by a different hand, it is striking indeed that it should have begun with a "hint" from a dime novel, a genre that Michael Denning describes in his *Mechanic Accents* as "best considered an essentially anonymous, 'unauthored' discourse."[9] It is a testament to how little understood Kōyō's novel has been, and indeed, how little understood the late nineteenth-century literary market has been, that *Konjiki yasha* is even now reprinted only in the "original version" as Kōyō left it—incomplete, darkly foreboding—and that Oguri Fūyō's ending, in which Kan'ichi and Miya are happily reunited, should have been erased from literary history as a sort of betrayal of authorial intent, an unorthodox, almost heretical, attempt to bring a forced closure to a work of art. Although we know that Kōyō's intent, as he started the novel, was very much in line with what Fūyō would write after his mentor's death, perhaps the very categories of intention and authorship are highly problematic for an unfinished serial novel based on an American dime novel written by anonymous men masquerading as women. To view a novel like *Konjiki yasha* as an organic, integral whole born of a single mind is a deep misconstrual of the nature of this kind of object, a devoutly misplaced belief in the unity of the author and of the work.

When we shift attention away from the site of literary production and turn instead to the sites of literary and cultural consumption, we can begin to piece together the outlines of the literary market of late nineteenth-century Japan and to see that this market was itself part of a

---

8. Denning, *Mechanic Accents*, pp. 23–24.
9. Denning, *Mechanic Accents*, p. 24.

larger literary market that was becoming, by the turn of the twentieth century, truly global, a market of novels as commodities, "commodities of the imagination."

In *Mechanic Accents*, Michael Denning writes of one of Bertha M. Clay's early twentieth-century readers: "Sadie Frowne, a Polish Immigrant and New York garment worker in a sweat shop, says . . . 'she's a grand writer and makes things just like real to you. You feel as if you were the poor girl yourself going to get married to a rich duke.'"[10] And Abraham Bisno, a Jewish immigrant from Russia who worked in the garment district, wrote in his autobiography of his own reading habits as a young man:

> A man named Shomer wrote a great many Jewish romances copied from the French with a change only of names and habits from the French to the Jewish. He wrote a great many of them and I would read three or four a week, absorb their contents enthusiastically and eagerly. The stories went like this: a poor girl, but very beautiful, fell in love with a rich young man, whose parents would not permit a marriage. Tragedy would follow. The boy would talk of suicide, the girl was miserable, until something happened where the girl was found out really to be an heiress, the family smiled on her, they married and lived happily ever after. In a great many of them, there was an intriguing character who would cause either the boy or girl to distrust the other by false tale bearing. He would be found out in his lies, and the differences were patched up again. Some tales of adventure and enterprise, but most of them about romantic love, the difficulties besetting the path of love, the difficulties ensuing, marriage, and everlasting happiness. But for me these were great finds. When there was no work I read them day and night and would tell about them to any who would listen.[11]

Shomer, whose works were published in Vilna and Warsaw at the end of the nineteenth century, had no doubt never read Santō Kyōden's late *gōkan*, but Bisno's inventory of Shomer's plots is almost an exact replica of that given for Kyōden's works by Mizuno Minoru. And it is, of course, the same pattern one finds in the "scholar-beauty romances" of late imperial China or in Shunsui's *ninjōbon*.[12] Indeed, it is easy to

---

10. Quoted in Denning, *Mechanic Accents*, p. 35.

11. Quoted in Denning, *Mechanic Accents*, pp. 36–37.

12. Robert Hegel describes the "scholar-beauty romances" as "probably the most popular books during the last centuries of imperial rule" and writes that "they narrate the adven-

imagine that Bisno would quite have enjoyed the story of Tanjirō and O-Chō and Yonehachi; provided, of course, that "names and habits" had become Jewish, a change, one imagines, that would have meant that the novel ended in monogamy.

We tend to think of the novel and the nation state as mapping onto each other; but here, we can see that the geography of the novel is considerably more complex—Bisno is, after all, a Russian immigrant reading French novels in Yiddish in New York—and *much* larger. In the late nineteenth century, perhaps for the first time, it becomes possible to speak of a global history of the novel, to speak, indeed, of the emergence of "world literature," in which "sensational novels were translated back and forth from English, French, German, and Yiddish, translated not to be faithful to the 'original', but, as in the case of Shomer, to be adapted to local names, geography, and customs."[13]

Reflecting on the treaty of March 31, 1854 that "opened" Japanese ports, and markets, to America, Commodore Matthew Perry wrote that "Japan has been opened to the nations of the West" and that "as prejudice gradually vanishes, we may hope to see the future negotiation of commercial treaties more and more liberal, for the benefit not of ourselves only, but of all of the maritime powers of Europe, for the advancement of Japan, and for the upward progress of our common humanity."[14] Perry did not, one imagines, have the publishers of cheap fiction and dime novels in mind as one of the primary beneficiaries of

tures of talented and virtuous young men and women who are destined for marriage with each other despite the obstacles and machinations created by the lustful villains who want the young women for themselves. Major characters tend to be lacking in moral ambiguity and develop little through their experiences. All are brilliant, virtuous, and brave in the face of both adversity and temptation. They are the scions of good houses, although not all are particularly well placed in society; they earn the recognition and wealth they enjoy in the end through their moral steadfastness and literary talent." Hegel, *Reading Illustrated Fiction in Late Imperial China*, p. 49 and p. 48.

13. Denning, *Mechanic Accents*, p. 37. Denning writes that "the similarity of plots, together with the absence of an international copyright agreement until 1891 made for a kind of 'world literature.'" The history of "world literature"—and its possibilities as an analytical category—has attracted renewed interest in recnt years. See Moretti, "Conjectures of World Literature," Arac, "Anglo-Globalism?," and Apter, "Global *Translatio*: The 'Invention' of Comparative Literature, Istanbul, 1933."

14. Quoted in W. G. Beasley "The foreign threat and the opening of the ports," p. 270.

his opening of new markets. But his timing was impeccable. A year after Perry wrote of *the upward progress of our common humanity*, Robert Bonner began his story paper, the *New York Ledger*, and in 1859, Street & Smith began the *New York Weekly*, the story paper that would first introduce "Bertha M. Clay." In 1860, Beadle and Adams began publishing Beadle's Dime Novels, and by the eve of the Meiji Restoration, they had published four million dime novels, each with sales in the tens of thousands.[15] This is what Kōyō had in mind when, at the end of the century, he dreamed of the fertile plains and vast expanses of readers to be had in Europe and the Americas.

To understand the world of literary commerce within which both Kōyō and Roka were operating, we might repeat something of the odd genealogy of a book like *Konjiki yasha*. Charlotte M. Brame writes stories for the London *Family Herald*; some of these novels are then pirated and reprinted in the *New York Weekly*, and a new "author" is born: Bertha M. Clay, whose novels were "ground out by men who were versatile enough to befool women readers, with a feminine style."[16] Clay's *Weaker Than a Woman* makes its way to Japan and becomes the kernel of Kōyō's *Konjiki yasha*, which is unfinished at the time of Kōyō's death in 1903 and is completed by Oguri Fūyō. *Konjiki yasha* is then translated back into English and into Korean in 1913. In Korean, it becomes an immediate literary success: "by offering such novels" as *Changhanmong* (the Korean version of *Konjiki yasha*) writes Cho Dong-il, "the *Maeil sinbo*—the organ of the Governor General's Office—increased its circulation, the publishers made money, and the authors divvied up the profits." Cho continues: "As Readers turned their attention to popular novels, there appeared, over the course of the 1920s and into the 1930s, a constant stream of novels with tears in their titles (*nucha sosŏl*) such as *Tears of Love*, *Tears of the Devil*, and *Tears of Cruelty*, and weeping novels (*nunmul sosŏl*) such as *Don't Cry Hong-do!*, *Fooled in Love*, *Weeping over Money*, and *That Woman's Tears*, which broadly captured the bottom of the novel market."[17]

15. Denning, *Mechanic Accents*, p. 11.
16. Quoted in Denning, *Mechanic Accents*, p. 25.
17. Cho, *Hanguk munhak t'ongsa*, p. 386.

Although Kōyō's novel had immediate success in and lasting impact on the literary market of colonial Korea, it was Roka's *Hototogisu* that would come closest to achieving the sort of "colonial" conquest of the Western literary market that Kōyō had envisioned. The novel was published in Boston in 1904, "presented in English dress, though not exactly an English translation" as A. Lloyd put it in his preface, "re-written" in English, "in a word, to make the book a little more Anglo-Saxon." The English translation was an immediate success and was quickly re-translated: into Swedish, French, and German, Spanish and Portuguese. The geography of the novel is simply stunning. The Chinese version published by Shang wu yin shu guan in 1906 was translated *from the English* by Lin Shu and Zeng Zonggong, who had teamed up to translate *Robinson Crusoe* in 1905–1906.[18] But Lin Shu is, of course, best known for his translation of Dumas fils' *La Dame aux Camélias* with Wang Shouchang, during the translation of which "they wept so profusely that they could be heard even outside the house."[19] The Spanish version of *Hototogisu*, which ends with a wonderful image of Takeo weeping by Namiko's grave, was published in 1904 simultaneously by Casa Editorial Maucci in Barcelona and Maucci Hermanos in Buenos Aires. To get some sense of where *Hototogisu* fits into the world of the novel at the turn of the century, we can look at the other works published by Casa Editorial Maucci and Maucci Hermanos in the years surrounding their first printing of *Nami-ko: novela popular japonesa.*

The Maucci publishing house, which had offices in Mexico City and Genoa as well as Barcelona and Buenos Aires, published hundreds of titles in the first decade of the twentieth century. They published two editions of *Don Quixote* in 1900 and 1902, and in 1910 published both the ninth *and* the tenth printings of *María* by the great Colombian novelist Jorge Isaacs. Maucci also published works by the Portuguese novelist Eça de Queiroz such as *O Mandarim* and *O Primo Basílio* and both of José Rizal's novels, *Noli Me Tángere* and its sequel *Il filibusterismo.* There were popular Spanish novels such as *Mariquita León: novella origi-*

18. For a discussion of Lin and Zeng's translation of *Crusoe* see Liu, "Robinson Crusoe's Earthenware Pot," pp. 728–57.

19. Chow, *Woman and Chinese Modernity*, p. 121. See also Lee, *The Romantic Generation of Modern Chinese Writers*, pp. 44–45.

nal by José Nogales y Nogales (with illustrations by J. Diéguez, the illustrator of *Nami-ko*) and dozens of translations from Italian writers like Emilio Salgari and Carolina Invernizio. In 1906, the Mauccis published the third edition *Azucena; novela escrita en ingles* by Charlotte M. Brame—the original "Bertha M. Clay"—and they published a Spanish edition of Lew Wallace's *Ben-Hur*. They published the works of Polish novelist Henryk Sienkiewicz (*Quo Vadis* in 1900 and 1902, *Liliana* in 1901) in the years before he won the Nobel Prize and Flaubert's *Salambó* and *Madame Bovary*, both in 1903.

In *Imagined Communities*, Benedict Anderson writes of Rizal's *Noli Me Tángere* that "right from the start the image (wholly new to Filipino writing) of a dinner-party being discussed by hundreds of unnamed people, who do not know each other, in quite different parts of Manila, in a particular month in a particular decade, immediately conjures up the imagined community."[20] Yes, so far so good, but then Anderson continues, "and in the phrase 'a house on Anloague Street' which 'we shall describe in such a way that it may still be recognized,' the would-be recognizers are we-Filipino readers."[21] But who were the readers of Rizal's novel? It was, after all, in Berlin in 1886 that *Noli Me Tángere: Novela tagala* was originally published in Spanish by Berliner Buchdruckerei-Actien-Gesellschaft. The novel was then published in Manila, but not until 1899 by Chofré; but it was also published at that time in Paris (1899) and New York (1900), in addition to Berlin, Madrid, Barcelona, and Buenos Aires. In 1891, F. Meyer-Van Loo published *Noli*'s sequel *El filibusterismo* in Spanish in Ghent. And Yamada Bimyō, Ozaki Kōyō's onetime friend and colleague in the Ken'yūsha and *Garakuta bunko* and a veteran of the Philippine War of Independence, translated *Noli* into Japanese in 1906 under the title *Chi no namida* (*Tears of Blood*).

Of course, *Noli Me Tángere* was read in Manila and no doubt elsewhere on the archipelago and perhaps by Philippine nationals living abroad in Europe and the Americas; but Rizal's novel was also read by American and French, Spanish and Argentine and Japanese readers. We can talk about an "imagined world conjured up by the author in his

20. Anderson, *Imagined Communities*, p. 27.
21. Anderson, *Imagined Communities*, p. 27.

readers' minds,"[22] but is this *imagined world*, this *imagined community*, the nation? It seems to me that the answer to this question is probably yes and no. Yes, the novel *is* the great instrument of the national imagination, but it is also something else, and it is something else precisely because it is riddled by the same contradictions that riddle the nation form. "Of all forms of government and organizations of people," Hannah Arendt writes in *The Origins of Totalitarianism*, "the nation-state is least suited for unlimited growth"; of course, "unlimited growth," a phrase that immediately conjures up the essence of capitalism, is precisely, perhaps in spite of itself, what the nation-state has undertaken over the course of the nineteenth and twentieth centuries. This is one example—perhaps the prime example—of what Arendt calls "the absurd disparities between cause and effect which have become the hallmark of modern history," producing a "wild confusion of modern historical terminology."[23]

Historical terminology is confused because history itself is confused; or, at least, it appears that way, as long as the nation is thought to be—should we say *imagined* to be?—constant with itself, of a single purpose. But the history of nation-states, and the history of the nation form, has continually contradicted this assumption. Indeed, the very contradiction is inherent in Anderson's work on the nation precisely because of the centrality he gives to print capitalism as one of the hallmarks of the national imagination. Print capitalism, *as a form of capitalism*, is always striving to transcend the boundaries of the nation-state. And there is no better example of the "world literary market" of the late nineteenth century than the history of publishers like the Mauccis or indeed than the printing history of *Noli Me Tángere* itself.

Nothing more clearly suggests this double life of the novel than the history of translations, which by their very nature are born of one literary tradition, only to quite literally "transcend" the boundaries of the nation-state and the national language. In approaching translation, literary history and theory have tended to vacillate between two very different ideas of what translation is—or should be. Walter Benjamin describes translation as the transmission of the inessential, and this is

---

22. Anderson, *Imagined Communities*, p. 26.
23. Arendt, *The Origins of Totalitarianism*, p. 126 and p. 131.

true especially when translation "undertakes to serve the reader."[24] Claude Lévi-Strauss takes almost the opposite approach: for him, what is essential, "the mythical value of the myth," is preserved "even through the worst translation. Whatever our ignorance of the language and the culture of the people where it originated, a myth is still felt as a myth by any reader anywhere in the world. Its substance does not lie in its style, its original music, or its syntax, but in the *story* which it tells."[25] Two very different approaches, because literature encompasses two very different elements: form and content, discourse and story, *sjuzet* and *fabula*. And, we might add, every literary form is made up of both, but in *unequal amounts*.

Both Benjamin's and Lévi-Strauss's ideas about translation are useful, but useful for different objects. For Benjamin, the "story" is inessential, even misleading; attention to the story is the very hallmark of bad translation. For Lévi-Strauss, on the other hand, the "story" is the very *substance* of translation, preserved even in the worst translation. If we recall here our Meiji reader of *The Kreutzer Sonata* who found the work so boring, unfit for translation, we might allow that what we encounter in translation are not simply two aspects of literature, but, perhaps more fundamentally still, two aspects of reading in which the "story" functions quite differently. It is striking—and certainly telling—that both Benjamin and Lévi-Strauss should mention the reader, the one as a caution, the other almost as a criterion.

And where does the novel fit into this discussion? The novel too is made up of a story and a discourse, but the history of translation suggests that these elements are present in very unequal proportions. There is no better expression of the primacy of the story, of the mythological nature of the novel than the "world literature" of the late nineteenth century, which was "translated not to be faithful to the 'original', but . . . to be adapted to local names, geography and customs," which presented European novels with Japanese characters and Japanese novels "in English dress," not unlike Bakin's adaptation of the *Jin Yun Qiao* in which his Japanese characters stare into mirrors in which are reflected their Chinese "originals."

---

24. Benjamin, "The Task of the Translator," p. 69 and p. 70.
25. Lévi-Strauss, *Structural Anthropology*, p. 210.

Myth, as Roland Barthes writes in *Mythologies*, "has an imperative, buttonholing character";[26] it is a wonderful image, and one quite suited to the novel. It recalls on the one hand Umberto Eco's description of novels as "inflexible projects" and on the other brings to mind Jacques Lacan's notion of "*points de caption*," or "quilting points" as Slavoj Žižek puts it: "The 'quilting' performs the totalization by means of which this free floating of ideological elements is halted, fixed—that is to say, by means of which they become parts of a structured network of meaning."[27] But here, again, we run up against the odd double nature of the novel. If novels perform a sort of ideological quilting function in which they provide particular answers to local ideological problems, how is it that the same novel can *work* in very different ideological circumstances, how is it that novels travel so well? One would have to imagine that everywhere it went, the novel encountered the same problems, or perhaps more unlikely still, that the same answers solved many different problems, that the nineteenth-century novel provided a sort of master key which could open—or more likely close—a vast array of ideological doors.

And what do we make of the fact that very similar forms have emerged in historically very different ideological and cultural circumstances? How do we explain the fact that "scholar-beauty romances" emerge in China at almost exactly the same time the sentimental novel emerges in Europe, or why these novels should be so well received in early modern Japan? Perhaps the novel leads a sort of double life: it is extremely historically and culturally specific (it emerges from and is consumed by historically specific social formations), but it also partakes in some other larger history, "*forever* disintegrating, *forever* being

---

26. Barthes, *Mythologies*, p. 124.

27. Žižek, *The Sublime Object of Ideology*, p. 87. See also Žižek, *For They Know Not What They Do*, pp. 16–20. As Elisabeth Roudinesco notes in her biography of Lacan, "Lacan uses the term *point de caption*—button tie (an upholsterer's stitch)—to denote the point in a chain at which a signifier and a signified are knotted together to give birth to a meaning. See Roudinesco, *Jacques Lacan*, p. 272. It should be pointed out that Barthes's original—"le myth a un caractère impératif, interpellatoire"—less readily recalls Lacan's *point de caption* than Althusser's notion of ideology as *hailing* or *interpolating*. See Barthes, *Mythologies*, p. 197. I will return to Althusser's theory of ideology below.

rebuilt."[28] It is a paradoxical, seemingly impossible, situation. But it is also reminiscent of Althusser's famous dictum that "*ideology has no history*." Ideology "is endowed with a structure and a functioning such as to make it a non-historical reality, i.e. an *omni-historical* reality, in the sense in which that structure and functioning are immutable, present in the same form throughout what we call history." And, Althusser continues, that "ideology has no history, can and must . . . be related directly to Freud's proposition that the *unconscious is eternal*, i.e. that it has no history. . . . *Ideology is eternal*, exactly like the unconscious. And I add that I find this comparison theoretically justified by the fact that the eternity of the unconscious is not unrelated to the eternity of ideology in general."[29]

The novel's double life, then, emerges not in spite of its ideological character, but precisely the opposite: *because of* its ideological character. Because the novel is ideological, it partakes of two histories at once: one local and occasional and the other "eternal" or, what seems to me more precise, "omni-historical." After all, the novel responds to quite local palates and hungers but the "hunger for redundancy" is itself rather eternal, as is the ideological quilting process in which the novel partakes—even if the bits of fabric which are stitched together are quite local.

In 1827, at almost exactly the same time Bakin was adapting the *Jin Yun Qiao* half a world away, Goethe too was reading a Chinese novel. "I like to look about me in foreign nations," Goethe told his young friend Eckermann, "and advise everyone to do the same. National literature is now a rather unmeaning term; the epoch of World-literature is at hand, and everyone must strive to hasten its approach."[30] And yet, in the almost two centuries that have passed since Goethe made these remarks, "national literature" has become, if anything, a stronger, less

---

28. Shklovsky, *Theory of Prose*, pp. 17–18. "Fortuitous coincidences are impossible," Shklovsky writes, "coincidences can be explained only by the existence of special laws of plot formation. Even the admission of borrowings does not explain the existence of identical stories separated by thousands of years and tens of thousands of miles. . . . Such stories are forever disintegrating and forever being rebuilt in accordance with special laws of plot formation still unknown to us."

29. Althusser, "Ideology and Ideological State Apparatuses," p. 161.

30. Goethe, *Conversations of Goethe with Johann Peter Eckermann*, pp. 164–66.

flexible concept. And just as those two centuries were the great era of the nation, so too were they the great era of national literature. And yet, the history of nineteenth-century Japanese literature suggests that such an approach to literature is often blind to the subtleties and complexities of literary history. If we are to recover this history, we must acknowledge and come to terms with two seemingly contradictory facets of literary history. Readers have encountered texts differently at different moments and places throughout history and we must begin to learn to read historically, attuning ourselves to ways of reading now lost. But at the same time, we must also learn that to historicize a particular moment of reading or writing does not mean to isolate it, to sever it from the rest of history and from other histories in a sort of controlled experiment. After all, to acknowledge historical difference is also to disavow absolute difference. "A Chinese novel, that must look strange enough," Eckermann responded. "Not so much as you might think," said Goethe.[31]

31. Goethe, *Conversations of Goethe with Johann Peter Eckermann,* p. 164.

Reference Matter

Character List

Adazakura sato no yoarashi 仇桜遊里廼夜嵐
"Aiqing zhuan" 愛卿傳
Ajikinaki 無味気
akahon 赤本
Akogi monogatari 阿古義物語
Akutagawa Ryūnosuke 芥川龍之介
Asagao nikki 朝顔日記
"Asaji ga yado" 浅茅が宿
Awashima Kangetsu 淡島寒月

bakufu 幕府
bunshō 文章

Chikamatsu Hanji 近松半二
Chikamatsu Monzaemon 近松門左衛門
Chikubetsu 築別
Chikuhakukai 竹柏会
Chi no namida 血の涙
Chinsetsu yumi harizuki 椿説弓張月
Chōkon 長恨
Chōshō 朝妝
chūhon 中本
Chūkō futamatagawa 忠孝水水川
Chūshin suikoden 忠臣水滸伝

Daisō 大惣
Dokusho 読書

"E-awase" 絵合
Edo hanjōki 江戸繁昌記
ehon banzuke 絵本番付
Ehon sayo shigure 絵本小夜時雨
Enseki zasshi 燕石雑志

Feng Menglong 馮夢龍
Fuji no Karamaro 富士唐麿
Fukuda Naohiko 福田直彦
Fūryū kyōnin'gyō 風流京人形
Futabatei Shimei 二葉亭四迷
Fūzoku kin'gyoden 風俗金魚伝

Gakutei Kyūzan 岳亭丘山
Garakuta bunko 我楽多文庫
Gedai kagami 外題鑑
Geisha yobukodori 妓者呼子鳥

genbun itchi 言文一致
Genji monogatari 源氏物語
Genji monogatari tama no ogushi 源氏物語玉の小櫛
Gesaku hyōban hana no origami 戯作評判花折紙
gōkan 合巻
Gozonji no shōbaimono 御存商売物

Hachimonjiya 八文字屋
haikai 俳諧
"Hankechi" 手巾
Harutsugedori 春告鳥
Hattori Bushō 服部撫松
Hayami Shun'gyōsai 速水春暁斎
Hirotsu Ryūrō 広津柳浪
hōgaku 邦楽
Honchō suikoden 本朝水滸伝
Hototogisu 不如帰

Iezakura tsugiho no hachiue 家桜継穂鉢植
Ihara Saikaku 井原西鶴
Ikuta Kizan 生田葵山
Inō Hidenori 伊能頴則
Inoue Tsutomu 井上勤
Ise monogatari 伊勢物語
Ishibashi Shian 石橋思案
Ishikawa Takuboku 石川啄木
Ishikikai'i 違式詿違
Itako zekkushū 潮来絶句集
Itō Sei 伊藤整
Itozakura shunchō kien 糸桜春蝶奇縁
Izumi Kyōka 泉鏡花

Jiandeng xinhua 剪燈新話
Jin Ping Mei 金瓶梅
Jin Yun Qiao 金雲翹
Jippensha Ikku 十返舎一九
jitsurokutai shōsetsu 実録体小説
jōruribon 浄瑠璃本
junbungaku 純文学

Kakan'ō 花間鶯
Kamiko jitate ryōmen kagami 紙子仕立両面鑑
kanshibun 漢詩文
Katō Shihō 加藤紫芳
Katsu Kokichi 勝小吉
Katsushika Hokusai 葛飾北斎
Keisei hangonkō 傾城反魂香
Keiseikai shijūhatte 傾城買四十八手
Keiseikai tora no maki 契情買虎之巻
Kejō suigen maku no soto 戯場粋言幕乃外
Ken'yūsha 硯友社
kibyōshi 黄表紙
Kinosaki 城ノ崎
Kinsei mono no hon Edo sakusha burui 近世物之本江戸作者部類
Kinsei setsu bishōnenroku 近世説美少年録
kiritsukebon 切附本
Kitagawa Morisada 喜田川守貞
Kojiki 古事記
kokkeibon 滑稽本
Kokoro こころ
Konjiki yasha 金色夜叉
Konjiki yasha shūhen 金色夜叉終編
Kōshoku ichidai otoko 好色一代男

Kōtoku Shūsui 幸徳秋水
Kōyō Sanjin 紅葉山人
Kuki Ryūichi 九鬼隆一
Kuroda Seiki 黒田清輝
Kuroiwa Ruikō 黒岩涙香
Kusamakura 草枕
kusazōzhi 草双紙
Kyōhō 享保
kyōka 狂歌
Kyokutei Bakin 曲亭馬琴

Lin Shu 林紓

Maruoka Kyūka 丸岡九華
Matsuzawa Gohei
松沢五兵衛
Meiji 明治
Min'yūsha 民友社
Mitsukuri Genpo 箕作阮甫
Miura Tōru 三浦徹
monogatari 物語
Mori Ōgai 森鴎外
Morita Shiken 森田思軒
Motono Morimichi 本野盛亨
Motoori Norinaga 本居宣長
Murasaki Shikibu 紫式部
Musui dokugen 夢酔独言
Muzan 無惨

Nagai Kafū 永井荷風
Naimushō keihokyoku
内務省警保局
Nakae Chōmin 中江兆民
Nakane Kiyoshi 中根淑
Nakaya Shinzaemon
中屋甚左衛門
Nansō satomi hakkenden
南総里見八犬伝
Naobi no mitama 直毘霊
Natsume Sōseki 夏目漱石
Nihonga 日本画
ninjōbon 人情本
Nishida Isoku 西田維則
Nishiyama monogatari 西山物語
Nitobe Inazō 新渡户稲造
nukihon 抜本

Oguri Fūyō 小栗風葉
Oka Hakku 岡白駒
ōraimono 往来物
Ōta Nanpo 大田南畝
Ozaki Kōyō 尾崎紅葉

riron 理論
Robinson hyōkōkiryaku
魯敏遜漂行紀略
Ryūtei Tanehiko 柳亭種彦

Sagabon 嵯峨本
Saganoya Omuro
嵯峨の屋お室
Sakurahime zenden akebono sōshi
桜姫全伝曙草紙
Sanshōtei Karaku 三笑亭可楽
Santō Kyōden 山東京伝
Santō Kyōzan 山東京山
San'yūtei Enchō 三遊亭圓朝
Setchūbai 雪中梅
sharebon 洒落本
Shibai kinmōzui
戯場訓蒙図彙
Shikitei Sanba 式亭三馬
Shinjū kamiya Jihei
心中紙屋治兵衛
Shinjū ten no Amijima
心中天網島
Shojaku mokuroku 書籍目録
shōsetsu 小説
Shōsetsu shinzui 小説神髄
Shukujo gahō 淑女画報

Shunshoku megumi no hana 春色恵之花
Shunshoku tatsumi no sono 春色辰巳園
Shunshoku umegoyomi 春色梅児譽美
Sono no yuki 園の雪
sōshi monogatari 册子物語
Sudō Nansui 須藤南翠
Suehiro Tetchō 末広鉄腸
Suga Sensuke 菅専助
Suiko taiheiki 水滸太平記
Suisen tanzen 水仙丹前
Sumiyoshi monogatari 住吉物語

Taishō 大正
taishū bungaku 大衆文学
Tajō takon 多情多恨
Takarabune kogane no hobashira 宝船黄金桅
Takebe Ayatari 建部綾足
Taketori monogatari 竹取物語
Takeuchi Keishū 武内桂舟
Tamenaga Shunsui 為永春水
Tanishi Kin'gyo 田螺金魚
Taohua shan 桃花扇
Terakado Seiken 寺門静軒
Tōkaidōchū hizakurige 東海道中膝栗毛
Tōkai Sanshi 東海散士
Tokuda Shūsei 徳田秋声
Tokutomi Roka 徳冨蘆花
Tokutomi Sohō 徳富蘇峰
Tōkyō shin hanjōki 東京新繁昌記
Tōri Sanjin 東里山人
Tōsei shosei katagi 当世書生気質
Tsubouchi Shōyō 坪内逍遥
Tsurezuregusa 徒然草
Tsutaya Jūzaburō 蔦谷重三郎
Tsūzoku kin'gyōden 通俗金翹伝
Tsūzoku sekijōkien 通俗赤縄奇縁

Uchida Roan 内田魯庵
Udagawa Bunkai 宇田川文海
Ueda Akinari 上田秋成
Ugetsu monogatari 雨月物語
Ukigumo 浮雲
Ukiyoburo 浮世風呂
Ukiyodoko 浮世床
ukiyozōshi 浮世草子
Utagawa Kuniyasu 歌川国安
Utsuho monogatari 宇津保物語

Vita Sexualis ヰタ・セクスアリス

waka 和歌
Wang Shouchang 王壽昌
Watanabe Tamezō 渡辺為蔵

Xingshi hengyan 醒世恆言

Yamada Bimyō 山田美妙
Yamamichi no Takahiko 山道高彦
Yanagawa Shun'yō 柳川春葉
Yano Ryūkei 矢野龍渓
Yokoyama Yoshikiyo 横山由清
yomihon 読本

Zangiku 残菊
zappai 雑俳
Zeng Zonggong 曾宗鞏
Zhuangzi 莊子

Works Cited

Akutagawa Ryūnosuke 芥川龍之介. "Hankechi" 手巾. *Akutagawa Ryūnosuke zenshū* 芥川龍之介全集. Vol. 1. Tokyo: Iwanami shoten, 1995, pp. 265–77.

Althusser, Louis. "Ideology and Ideological State Apparatuses (Notes towards an Investigation)." In *Lenin and Philosophy and Other Essays*, translated by Ben Brewster. New York: Monthly Review Press, 1971, pp. 127–86.

Anderson, Benedict. *Imagined Communities: Reflections on the Origin and Spread of Nationalism*. Revised Edition. London: Verso, 1991.

Anderson, Perry. *Passages from Antiquity to Feudalism*. London: Verso, 1996.

Aoki Kōichirō 青木宏一郎. *Meiji Tōkyō shomin no tanoshimi* 明治東京庶民の楽しみ. Tokyo: Chūō kōron shinsha, 2004.

Apter, Emily. "Global *Translatio*: The 'Invention' of Comparative Literature, Istanbul, 1933." *Critical Inquiry* 29, no. 2 (winter 2003): 253–81.

Arac, Jonathan. "Anglo-Globalism?" *New Left Review*, no. 16 (July-August 2002): 35–45.

Araki, James T. "*Sharebon*: Books for Men of Mode." *Monumenta Nipponica* 24, no. 1 (1969): 49–64.

Arendt, Hannah. *The Origins of Totalitarianism*. New Edition. San Diego: Harcourt Brace, 1973.

Asaoka Kunio 浅岡邦雄. "Meijiki kashihon kashidashi daichō no naka no dokushatachi" 明治期貸本貸出台帳のなかの読者たち. *Nihon shuppan shiryō* 日本出版史料, no. 4 (March 1999): 1–46.

——. "Meijiki Ōsaka no kashihon mokuroku" 明治期大阪の貸本目録. *Shoseki bunkashi* 書籍文化史 2 (January 2001): 23–30.

Auerbach, Erich. *Mimesis: The Representation of Reality in Western Literature*. Translated by Willard Trask. Princeton: Princeton University Press, 1953.

Bakhtin, M. M. "Epic and Novel." In *The Dialogic Imagination: Four Essays*, translated by Caryl Emerson and Michael Holquist. Austin: University of Texas Press, 1981, pp. 3–40.

Balibar, Etienne. "The Nation Form." In *Race, Nation, Class: Ambiguous Identities*, by Etienne Balibar and Immanuel Wallerstein. London: Verso, 1991, pp. 86–106.

Balibar, Etienne and Pierre Macherey. "On Literature as an Ideological Form." In *Marxist Literary Theory: A Reader*, edited by Terry Eagleton and Drew Milne. Oxford: Blackwell, 1996, pp. 275–95.

Balibar, Etienne and Immanuel Wallerstein. *Race, Nation, Class: Ambiguous Identities*. London: Verso, 1991.

Barthes, Roland. "The Death of the Author." In *The Rustle of Language*, translated by Richard Howard. Berkeley: University of California Press, 1989, pp. 49–55.

——. "History or Literature?". In *On Racine*, translated by Richard Howard. Berkeley: University of California Press, 1992, pp. 153–72.

——. *Mythologies*. Paris: Éditions du Seuil, 1957.

——. *Mythologies*. Translated by Annette Lavers. New York: Hill and Wang, 1972.

——. *The Pleasure of the Text*. Translated by Richard Miller. New York: Hill and Wang, 1975.

——. "Rhetorical Analysis." In *The Rustle of Language*, translated by Richard Howard. Berkeley: University of California Press, 1989, pp. 83–89.

Beasley, W. G. "The Foreign Threat and the Opening of the Ports." In *The Cambridge History of Japan*. Vol. 5. Edited by Marius Jansen. Cambridge, Eng.: Cambridge University Press, 1988.

Benjamin, Walter. "Chambermaids' Romances of the Past Century." Translated by Rodney Livingstone. In *Walter Benjamin: Selected Writings*. Vol. 2. Edited by Michael Jennings, Howard Eiland, and Gary Smith. Cambridge, Mass.: Harvard University Press, Belknap Press, 1999, pp. 225–31.

——. "Critique of Violence." Translated by Edmund Jephcott. In *Walter Benjamin: Selected Writings*. Vol. 1. Edited by Marcus Bullock and Michael Jennings. Cambridge, Mass.: Harvard University Press, Belknap Press, 1999, pp. 236–52.

——. "The Work of Art in the Age of Mechanical Reproduction." Translated by Harry Zohn. In *Illuminations*. New York: Shocken Books, 1968, pp. 217–51.

Bijker, Weibe. *Of Bicycles, Bakelites, and Bulbs: Toward a Theory of Sociotechnical Change*. Cambridge, Mass.: The MIT Press, 1995.

Bourdieu, Pierre. *The Field of Cultural Production*, edited by Randal Johnson. New York: Columbia University Press, 1993.

——. *The Logic of Practice*. Translated by R. Nice. Stanford: Stanford University Press, 1990.

——. *The Rules of Art*. Translated by Susan Emanuel. Stanford: Stanford University Press, 1996.

Braudel, Fernand. "History and the Social Sciences: The *Longue Durée*." In *On History*, translated by Sarah Matthews. Chicago: University of Chicago Press, 1980, pp. 25–54.

——. *The Structures of Everyday Life*. Translated by Siān Reynolds. Vol. 1 of *Civilization and Capitalism, 15th–18th Century*. Berkeley: University of California Press, 1992.

Bronfen, Elisabeth. *Over Her Dead Body: Death, Femininity, and the Aesthetic*. New York: Routledge, 1992.

Brooks, Peter. *The Melodramatic Imagination: Balzac, Henry James, Melodrama, and the Mode of Excess*. New Haven: Yale University Press, 1976.

Burke, Kenneth. *The Philosophy of Literary Form: Studies in Symbolic Action*. Berkeley: University of California Press, 1973.

Chartier, Roger. *The Cultural Origins of the French Revolution*. Translated by Lydia G. Cochrane. Durham, N.C.: Duke University Press, 1991.

——. "Du Livre au Lire." In *Pratiques de la lecture*, edited by Roger Chartier. Paris: Editions Rivages, 1993, pp. 79–113.

——. *The Order of Books*. Translated by Lydia G. Cochrane. Stanford: Stanford University Press, 1994.

——. "Popular Appropriations: Readers and their Books." In *Forms and Meanings: Texts, Performances, and Audiences from Codex to Computer*. Philadelphia: University of Pennsylvania Press, 1995, pp. 83–97.

——. "Representations of the Written Word." In *Forms and Meanings: Texts, Performances, and Audiences from Codex to Computer*. Philadelphia: University of Pennsylvania Press, 1995, pp. 6–24.

Chatterjee, Partha. *Nationalist Thought and the Colonial World*. Minneapolis: University of Minnesota Press, 1996.

Chikamatsu Hanji 近松半二. "Shinjū kamiya Jihei" 心中紙屋治兵衛. In *Nihon gikyoku meisaku taikei* 日本戯曲名作大系. Vol. 3. Tokyo: Shuhōkaku, 1925.

Chikamatsu Monzaemon. "The Love Suicides at Amijima." In *Four Major Plays of Chikamatsu*, edited and translated by Donald Keene. New York: Columbia University Press, 1961.

Cho Dong-il 조동일. "Chungguk, Hanguk, Ilbon 'sosŏl' ui gaenyŏm" 중국・한국・일본 '小說' 의개념. In *Han'guk munhak kwa segye munhak* 한국문학과 세계문학. Seoul: Chisik sanŏpsa, 1991, pp. 310–49.

——. *Hanguk munhak t'ongsa* 한국문학통사. 3rd Edition. Vol. 4. Seoul: Chisik sanŏpsa, 2002.

Chow, Rey. *Woman and Chinese Modernity: The Politics of Reading between West and East.* Minneapolis: University of Minnesota Press, 1991.

Clark, T. J. *The Painting of Modern Life: Paris in the Art of Manet and his Followers.* Princeton: Princeton University Press, 1984.

Clunas, Craig. *Pictures and Visuality in Early Modern China.* Princeton: Princeton University Press, 1997.

Cohen, Margaret. *The Sentimental Education of the Novel.* Princeton: Princeton University Press, 1999.

Courant, Maurice. *Bibliographie Coréenne.* Paris: Publications de L'École des langues Orientales vivantes, 1894.

Curtius, Ernst Robert. *European Literature and the Latin Middle Ages.* Translated by Willard Trask. Princeton: Princeton University Press, 1983.

Darnton, Robert. *The Forbidden Best-Sellers of Pre-Revolutionary France.* New York: Norton, 1996.

——. *The Great Cat Massacre and Other Episodes in French Cultural History.* New York: Vintage Books, 1984.

——. *The Kiss of Lamourette: Reflections in Cultural History.* New York: Norton, 1990.

de Certeau, Michel. *The Practice of Everyday Life.* Translated by Steven F. Rendall. Berkeley: University of California Press, 1984.

Defoe, Daniel. *Robinson Crusoe.* London: Penguin Books, 1985.

Denning, Michael. *Mechanic Accents: Dime Novels and Working Class Culture in America.* Revised Edition. London: Verso, 1998.

Derrida, Jacques. *Of Grammatology.* Translated by Gayatri Spivak. Baltimore: The Johns Hopkins University Press, 1997.

Doody, Margaret. *The True Story of the Novel.* New Brunswick, N.J.: Rutgers University Press, 1996.

Duara, Prasenjit. *Rescuing Hisory from the Nation: Questioning Narratives of Modern China.* Chicago: University of Chicago Press, 1995.

Eco, Umberto. *The Role of the Reader: Explorations in the Semiotics of Texts.* Bloomington: Indiana University Press, 1979.

Etō Jun 江藤淳. " Riarizumu no genryū" リアリズムの源流. *Shinchō* 新潮 68, no. 11 (1971): 217–40.

Febvre, Lucien and Henri-Jean Martin. *The Coming of the Book: The Impact of Printing, 1450–1900.* Translated by David Gerard. London: Verso, 1997.

Felski, Rita. "Love, God, and the Orient." In *The Gender of Modernity*. Cambridge, Mass.: Harvard University Press, 1995.

Ford, George H. *Dickens and His Readers: Aspects of Novel Criticism*. New York: W. W. Norton & Co., 1965.

Foucault, Michel. *The Archaeology of Knowledge and the Discourse on Language*. Translated by A. M. Sheridan Smith. New York: Pantheon Books, 1972.

Freud, Sigmund. *Beyond the Pleasure Principle*. Translated by James Strachey. New York: Norton, 1961.

——. *Civilization and its Discontents*. Translated by James Strachey. New York: Norton, 1961.

Fukuda Mahito 福田真人. *Kekkaku no bunkashi* 結核の文化史. Nagoya: Nagoya daigaku shuppankai, 1995.

Furet, François. "Quantitative History." In *In the Workshop of History*, translated by Jonathan Mandelbaum. Chicago: University of Chicago Press, 1984, pp. 40–53.

Futabatei Shimei 二葉亭四迷. "Yo ga genbun itchi no yurai" 余が言文一致の由来. In *Heibon/Watashi wa kaigiha da* 平凡・私は懐疑派だ. Tokyo: Kōdansha, 1997, pp. 241–44.

Gakutei Kyūzan 岳亭丘山. *Chūkō futamatagawa* 忠孝水水川. Edo: 1825.

——. *Suiko taiheiki* 水滸太平記. Osaka: Okada Mohci, undated.

Gernet, Jacques. *A History of Chinese Civilization*. Translated by J. R. Foster. Cambridge, Eng.: Cambridge University Press, 1982.

Gesaku hyōban hana no origami 戯作評判花折紙. *Sharebon taisei*. 洒落本大成. Vol. 22. Tokyo: Chūō kōronsha, 1984, pp. 135–82.

Ginzburg, Carlo. *The Cheese and the Worms: The Cosmos of a Sixteenth Century Miller*. Translated by John and Anne Tedeschi. Baltimore: The Johns Hopkins University Press, 1980.

Girard, René. *Deceit, Desire, and the Novel: Self and Other in Literary Structure*. Translated by Yvonne Freccero. Baltimore: The Johns Hopkins University Press, 1965.

Gluck, Carol. *Japan's Modern Myths*. Princeton: Princeton University Press, 1985.

Goethe, Johann Wolfgang von. *Conversations of Goethe with Johann Peter Eckermann*. Translated by John Oxenford. New York: Da Capo Press, 1998.

Gramsci, Antonio. *The Modern Prince & Other Writings*. Translated by Louis Marks. New York: International Publishers, 1992.

——. *Selections from Cultural Writings*. Translated by William Boelhower. Cambridge, Mass.: Harvard University Press, 1985.

Greimas, A.-J. *Structural Semantics: An Attempt at a Method*. Translated by Danielle McDowell, Ronald Schleifer, and Alan Velie. Lincoln, Neb.: University of Nebraska Press, 1983.

Habermas, Jürgen. *The Structural Transformation of the Public Sphere: An Inquiry into a Category of Bourgeois Society*. Translated by Thomas Burger. Cambridge, Mass.: The MIT Press, 1993.

Hamada Keisuke 濱田啓介. "Bakin wo meguru shoshi/sakusha/dokusha no mondai" 馬琴をめぐる書肆・作者・読者の問題. In *Kinsei shōsetsu: ei'i to yōshiki ni kansuru shiken* 近世小説・営為と様式に関する私見. Kyoto: Kyōto daigaku gakujutsu shuppankai, 1993.

Han Won-yŏng 韓元永. *Hangug kŭndae sinmun yŏnchae sosŏl 1910 nyŏn butŏ 1945 nyŏn kkaji* 韓國近代新聞連載小説研究 1910 년부터 1945 년까지. Seoul: Yihwi ch'ulpansa, 1996.

Hegel, Robert. *Reading Illustrated Fiction in Late Imperial China*. Stanford: Stanford University Press, 1998.

Hockley, Allen. *The Prints of Isoda Koryūsai: Floating World Culture and its Consumers in Eighteenth-Century Japan*. Seattle: University of Washington Press, 2003.

Hori Keiko 堀啓子. "*Konjiki yasha* no ranpon: Bertha M. Clay wo megutte" 『金色夜叉』の藍本：Bertha M. Clay をめぐって. *Bungaku* 文学 1, no. 6 (November-December 2000): 189–201.

Horkheimer, Max and Theodor W. Adorno. *Dialectic of Enlightenment*. Translated by John Cumming. New York: Continuum, 1972.

Ichiko Natsuo 市古夏生 and Fujie Mineo 藤江峰夫, eds. *Ihara Saikaku* 井原西鶴. Tokyo: Perikansha, 1989.

Ikeda Mayumi 池田真由美. "Shimōsa no kuni Katsushika-gun Onigoe-mura Matsuzawa Gohei no Bunka gonen kara jūnen 'shoseki arimonochō'." 下総国葛飾郡鬼越村松沢五兵衛の文化五〜一〇年「書籍有物帳」. In *Yomihon kenkyū shinshū* 読本研究新集. Vol. 4. Tokyo: Kanrin shobō, 2003, pp. 166–95.

Inouye, Charles Shirō. "Japanese Books in Perspective." *Harvard Journal of Asian Studies* 60, no. 1 (2000): 229–58.

International House of Japan Library, ed. *Modern Japanese Literature in Translation: A Bibliography*. Tokyo: Kodansha International, 1979.

Irokawa Daikichi. *The Culture of the Meiji Period*. Princeton: Princeton University Press, 1985.

Isomae Jun'ichi 磯前順一. "Kindai ekurichūru no tōitsu" 近代エクリチュールの統一. *Gendai shisō* 現代思想 24, no. 9 (August 1996): 170–81.

Itami Chin'en 伊丹椿園. *Kara nishiki* 唐錦. In *Tsuga Teishō/Itami Chin'en shū* 都賀庭鐘・伊丹椿園集, edited by Inada Atsunobu, Kigoshi Osamu, and Fukuda Yasunori. Edo kai'i kisō bungei taikei 江戸怪異綺想文芸大系. Vol. 2. Tokyo: Kokusho kankōkai, 2001, pp. 551–614.

Itō Sei 伊藤整. *Nihon bundanshi* 日本文壇史. 24 vols. Tokyo: Kōdansha, 1953–1978.

Jameson, Frederic. *The Political Unconscious: Narrative as a Socially Symbolic Act.* Ithaca: Cornell University Press, 1981.

Jardine, Lisa and Anthony Grafton. "'Studied for Action': How Gabriel Harvey Read His Livy." *Past and Present* 129 (November 1990): 30–78.

Jauss, Hans Robert. "Literary History as a Challenge to Literary Theory." In *Toward an Aesthetic of Reception*, translated by Timothy Bahti. Minneapolis: University of Minnesota Press, 1982, pp. 3–45.

Jinbō Kazuya 神保五彌 "Kaseido/Tenpōki no Edo shōsetsu sakusha to dokusha" 化政度・天保期の江戸小説作者と読者. *Bungaku* 文学 26, no. 5 (1958): 95–108.

——. "Makki sharebon no isō" 末期洒落本の位相. *Kokubungaku kenkyū* 国文学研究, no. 2 (1950): 72–82.

Johns, Adrian. *The Nature of the Book: Print and Knowledge in the Making.* Chicago: University of Chicago Press, 1998.

Kaempfer, Engelbert. *Kaempfer's Japan*, edited and translated by Beatrice Bodart-Bailey. Honolulu: University of Hawai'i Press, 1998.

Kan Satoko 菅聡子. *Media no jidai: Meiji bungaku wo meguru jōkyō.* メディアの時代：明治文学をめぐる状況. Tokyo: Sōbunsha, 2001.

Karatani Kōjin. *Origins of Modern Japanese Literature.* Durham, N.C.: Duke University Press, 1993.

Keene, Donald. *Dawn to the West: Japanese Literature in the Modern Era.* New York: Holt, Rinehart, and Winston, 1984.

——. *World Within Walls: Japanese Literature of the Pre-Modern Era, 1600–1867.* New York: Columbia University Press, 1999.

Kern, Adam. "Blowing Smoke: Tobacco Pouches, Literary Squibs, and Authorial Puffery in the Pictorial Comic Fiction (*Kibyōshi*) of Santō Kyōden (1761–1816)." Ph.D. diss., Harvard University, 1997.

Kim Sun-chŏn 김순전. *Han'il kundae sosŏl ui pigyo munhakchŏk yŏngu* 韓日近代小說의比較文學的硏究. Seoul: T'aehaksa, 1998.

Kimura Ki 木村毅. *Meiji hon'yaku bungakushū* 明治翻訳文学集. Tokyo: Chikuma shobō, 1972.

Kitagawa Morisada 喜田川守貞. *Kinsei fūzokushi* 近世風俗志. 5 vols. Tokyo: Iwanami shoten, 2001.

Kōda Rohan 幸田露伴. "Ihara Saikaku" 井原西鶴. In *Ihara Saikaku*, edited by Ichiko Natsuo and Fujie Mineo. Tokyo: Perikansha, 1989, pp. 45–51.

Kokuritsu gekijō chōsa shiryōka 国立劇場調査資料課 ed. *Shinrei Yaguchi no watashi/Natsu matsuri Naniwa kagami/Shinjū ten no Amijima.* 心霊矢口渡・夏祭難波鑑・心中天網島. Tokyo: Nihon geijutsu bunka shinkōkai, 2002.

Kokuritsu gekijō geinō chōsashitsu 国立劇場芸能調査室 ed. *Jōruri sakuhin yōsetsu* 浄瑠璃作品要説. Vol. 4. Tokyo: Kokuritsu gekijō, 1986.

Kokuritsu kokkai toshokan 国立国会図書館. *Meijiki kankō tosho mokuroku* 明治期刊行図書目録. Tokyo: Kokuritsu kokkai toshokan, 1989.

Komori Yōichi 小森陽一. "Shōsetsu gensetsu no seisei" 小説言説の生成. In *Kōzō toshite no katari* 構造としての語り. Tokyo: Shin'yōsha, 1988, pp. 3–81.

Komori Yōichi 小森陽一, Kōno Kensuke 紅野謙介, and Takahashi Osamu 高橋修, eds. *Media/hyōshō/ideorogii: Meiji sanjūnendai no bunka kenkyū* メディア・表象・イデオロギー：明治三十年代の文化研究. Tokyo: Ozawa shoten, 1997.

Kōno Kensuke 紅野謙介. *Shomotsu no kindai* 書物の近代. Tokyo: Chikuma bungei bunko, 1999.

Kornicki, Peter. *The Book in Japan: A Cultural History from the Beginnings to the Nineteenth Century*. Leiden: Brill, 1998.

——. "*Nishiki no Ura*: An Instance of Censorship and the Structure of a Sharebon." *Monumenta Nipponica* 32, no. 2 (1977): 153–88.

——. "The Survival of Tokugawa Fiction in the Meiji Period." *Harvard Journal of Asiatic Studies* 41, no. 2 (December 1981): 461–82.

Koselleck, Reinhart. "Representation, Event, and Structure." In *Futures Past: On the Semantics of Historical Time*, translated by Keith Tribe. Cambridge, Mass.: The MIT Press, 1985, pp. 105–15.

Koyama-Richard, Brigitte. *Tolstoï et le Japon*. Paris: Publications Orientalistes de France, 1990.

Kracauer, Siegfried. "On Bestsellers and Their Audience." In *The Mass Ornament: Weimar Essays*, translated by Thomas Levin. Cambridge, Mass.: Harvard University Press, 1995, pp. 89–105.

Kuhn, Thomas S. *The Structure of Scientific Revolutions*. 2nd Edition. Chicago: University of Chicago Press, 1970.

Kyokutei Bakin 曲亭馬琴. "Chosakudō zakki shō" 著作堂雑記抄. In *Kyokutei ikō* 曲亭遺稿. Tokyo: Kokusho kankōkai, 1911.

——. *Enseki zasshi* 燕石雑志. In *Ihara Saikaku*, edited by Ichiko Natsuo and Fujie Mineo. Tokyo: Perikansha, 1989, pp. 42–44.

——. *Fūzoku kin'gyoden* 風俗金魚伝. 3 vols. Edo: Izumiya Ichibei, 1829–32.

——. "*Haishi gedai kagami* hihyō" 稗史外題鑑批評. In *Kyokutei ikō* 曲亭遺稿. Tokyo: Kokusho kankōkai, 1911.

——. "*Honchō suikoden* wo yomu narabi ni hihyō" 本朝水滸伝を読む並批評. In *Kyokutei ikō* 曲亭遺稿. Tokyo: Kokusho kankōkai, 1911.

——. *Kinsei mono no hon Edo sakusha burui* 近世物之本江戸作者部類. Tokyo: Yagi shoten, 1988.

——. *Kyokutei ikō* 曲亭遺稿. Tokyo: Kokusho kankōkai, 1911.

Lacan, Jacques. *The Ethics of Psychoanalysis: The Seminar of Jacques Lacan, Book VII*. New York: Norton, 1992.

Lee, Leo Ou-fan. *The Romantic Generation of Modern Chinese Writers.* Cambridge, Mass.: Harvard University Press, 1973.

Leroi-Gourham, André. *Gesture and Speech.* Translated by Anna Bostock Berger. Cambridge, Mass.: The MIT Press, 1993.

Leutner, Robert. *Shikitei Sanba and the Comic Tradition in Edo Fiction.* Cambridge, Mass.: Council on East Asian Studies, Harvard University, 1985.

Lévi-Strauss, Claude. "The Sorcerer and His Magic." In *Structural Anthropology.* Translated by Claire Jacobson and Brooke Grundfest Schoepf. New York: Basic Books, 1963, pp. 167–85.

——. "The Stuctural Study of Myth." In *Structural Anthropology.* Translated by Claire Jacobson and Brooke Grundfest Schoepf. New York: Basic Books, 1963, pp. 206–31.

Levy, Indra. "Sirens of the Western Shore." Ph.D. diss., Columbia University, 2001.

Li Takanori 李孝徳. *Hyōshōkūkan no kindai* 表象空間の近代. Tokyo: Shin'yōsha, 1996.

Liu, Lydia H. "Robinson Crusoe's Earthenware Pot." *Critical Inquiry* 25, no. 4 (summer 1999): 728–57.

Lotman, Yuri M. *Universe of the Mind: A Semiotic Theory of Culture.* Translated by Ann Shukman. Bloomington, Indiana: Indiana University Press, 1990.

Luhmann, Niklas. *Love as Passion: The Codification of Intimacy.* Translated by Jeremy Gaines and Doris L. Jones. Stanford: Stanford University Press, 1998.

——. *Social Systems.* Translated by John Bednarz. Stanford: Stanford University Press, 1995.

Maeda Ai 前田愛. *Bungaku tekusuto nyūmon* 文学テクスト入門. Tokyo: Chikuma shobō, 1996.

——. *Kindai dokusha no seiritsu* 近代読者の成立. Tokyo: Chikuma shobō, 1989.

Mandrou, Robert. *De la Culture populaire aux 17e et 18e siècles.* Paris: Editions Imago, 1999.

Manguel, Alberto. *The History of Reading.* New York: Penguin Books, 1996.

Marcuse, Herbert. *Eros and Civilization: A Philosophical Inquiry into Freud.* Boston: Beacon Press, 1966.

Martin, Henri-Jean. *The History and the Power of Writing.* Translated by Lydia G. Cochrane. Chicago: University of Chicago Press, 1994.

Marx, Karl. *Capital: Volume I.* Translated by Ben Fowkes. London: Penguin, 1990.

——. "Economic and Philosophic Manuscripts of 1844." In *The Marx-Engels Reader,* edited by Robert C. Tucker. New York: Norton, 1978, pp. 66–125.

——. "The German Ideology." In *Marx: Early Political Writings*, edited by Joseph O'Malley. Cambridge, Eng.: Cambridge University Press, 1994, pp. 119–81.

May, Ekkehard. *Die Kommerzialisierung der japanischen Literatur in der späten Edo-Zeit (1750–1868)*. Weisbaden: Otto Harrassowitz, 1983.

McDuff, David. Introduction to *The Kreutzer Sonata and Other Stories*, by Leo Tolstoy. London: Penguin, 1985.

McKenzie, D. F. *Bibliography and the Sociology of Texts*. Cambridge, Eng.: Cambridge University Press, 1999.

Metz, Christian. *Film Language: A Semiotics of Cinema*. Translated by Michael Taylor. Chicago: University of Chicago Press, 1991.

Mitamura En'gyo 三田村鳶魚. "Chikamatsu no shinjūmono: jiyūren'ai no fukkatsu" 近松の心中物・自由恋愛の復活. *Chikamatsu shinjūmono: onna no ryūkō* 近松心中物・女の流行. En'gyo bunko. Vol. 31. Tokyo: Chūō kōronsha, 1999.

Miura Masashi 三浦雅士. *Seishun no shūen* 青春の終焉. Tokyo: Kōdansha, 2001.

Mizuno Minoru 水野稔. *Edo shōsetsu ronsō* 江戸小説論叢. Tokyo: Chūō kōronsha, 1974.

Moretti, Franco. *Atlas of the European Novel 1800–1900*. London: Verso, 1998.

——. "Conjectures on World Literature." *New Left Review*, no. 1 (January-February 2000): 54–68.

——. "Modern European Literature: A Geographical Sketch." *New Left Review*, no. 206 (July-August 1994): 86–109.

——. "Kindergarten." In *Signs Taken for Wonders: Essays in the Sociology of Literary Forms*. London: Verso, 1997, pp. 157–81.

——. *Signs Taken for Wonders: Essays in the Sociology of Literary Forms*. Translated by Susan Fischer, David Forgacs, and David Miller. London: Verso, 1997.

——. "The Slaughterhouse of Literature." *Modern Language Quarterly* 61, no. 1 (2000): 207–27.

——. "The Soul and the Harpy." In *Signs Taken for Wonders: Essays in the Sociology of Literary Forms*. London: Verso, 1997, pp. 1–41.

——. "The Spell of Indecision." In *Signs Taken for Wonders: Essays in the Sociology of Literary Forms*. London: Verso, 1997, pp. 240–48.

Morris, Ivan. Introduction to *The Life of an Amorous Woman and Other Writings*, by Ihara Saikaku. Translated by Ivan Morris. New York: New Directions, 1969.

Morris-Suzuki, Tessa. "The Frontiers of Japanese Identity." In *Asian Forms of the Nation*, edited by Stein Tønneson and Hans Antlöv. Surrey: Curzon, 1996, pp. 41–66.

Moses, Michael Valdez. *The Novel and the Globalization of Culture*. Oxford: Oxford University Press, 1995.

Motoori Norinaga 本居宣長. *Genji monogatari tama no ogushi* 源氏物語玉の小櫛. In *Motoori norinaga* 本居宣長, edited by Ishikawa Jun. Nihon no meicho 日本の名著. Vol. 21. Tokyo: Chūō kōronsha, 1970.

———. *Naobi no mitama* 直毘霊, In *Motoori Norinaga shū*, edited by Yoshikawa Kōjirō. Nihon no shisō 日本の思想. Vol. 15. Tokyo: Chikuma shobō, 1969, pp. 279–312.

Murasaki Shikibu. *The Tale of Genji*. Translated by Edward Seidensticker. New York: Alfred A. Knopf, 1999.

Nagamine Shigetoshi 永嶺重敏. *Modan toshi no dokusho kūkan* モダン都市の読書空間. Tokyo: Nihon editāsukūru shuppanbu, 2001.

———. *Zasshi to dokusha no kindai* 雑誌と読者の近代. Tokyo: Nihon editāskūru shuppanbu, 1997.

Nagata Seiji 永田生慈. *Hokusai no kyōka ehon* 北斎の狂歌絵本. Tokyo: Iwasaki bijutsusha, 1988.

Nagatomo Chiyoji. 長友千代治. *Edo jidai no shomotsu to dokusho* 江戸時代の書物と読書. Tokyo: Tōkyōdō shuppan, 2001.

———. *Kinsei Kamigata jōruribon shuppan no kenkyū* 近世上方浄瑠璃本出版の研究. Tokyo: Tōkyōdō shuppan, 1999.

———. *Kinsei kashihon'ya no kenkyū* 近世貸本屋の研究. Tokyo: Tōkyōdō shuppan, 1982.

Najita, Tetsuo. *Visions of Virtue in Tokugawa Japan: The Kaitokudo Merchant Academy of Osaka*. Chicago: University of Chicago Press, 1987.

Nakae Chōmin 中江兆民. "Nishikaigan nite no kankaku" 西海岸にての感覚. In *Sabetsu no shosō* 差別の諸相, edited by Hirota Masaki. Nihon kindai shisō taikei 日本近代思想体系. Vol. 22. Tokyo: Iwanami shoten, 1990, pp. 35–41.

Nakamura Mitsuo 中村光夫. *Nihon no kindai shōsetsu*. 日本の近代小説. Tokyo: Iwanami shoten, 1995.

Nakamura Yukihiko 中村幸彦. "Ninjōbon to chūhonkata yomihon" 人情本と中本型読本. In *Nakamura Yukihiko chojutsushū* 中村幸彦著述集. Vol. 5. Tokyo: Chūō kōronsha, 1984.

———. "Tsūzokumono zatsudan" 通俗物雑談. In *Nakamura Yukihiko chojutsushū* 中村幸彦著述集. Vol. 7. Tokyo: Chūō kōronsha, 1984.

———. "Yomihon hassei ni kansuru shomondai" 読本発生に関する諸問題. In *Nakamura Yukihiko chojutsushū* 中村幸彦著述集. Vol. 5. Tokyo: Chūō kōronsha, 1984.

Nakano Mitsutoshi 中野三敏 *Edo no hanpon* 江戸の版本. Tokyo: Iwanami shoten, 1995.

——. *Jūhasseiki no Edo bungei* 十八世紀の江戸文芸. Tokyo: Iwanami shoten, 1999.

Natsume Sōseki. *Kokoro.* Translated by Edwin McClellan. Chicago: H. Regnery Co., 1957.

——. *The Three-Cornered World.* Translated by Alan Turney. Tokyo: Charles E. Tuttle Company, 1968.

Nishida Isoku 西田維則. *Tsūzoku kin'gyōden* 通俗金翹伝. Osaka: Fujiya Yahei, 1763. Photo-reproduction in *Kinsei hakuwa shōsetsu hon'yaku shū* 近世白話小説翻訳集, edited by Nakamura Yukihiko. Vol. 2. Tokyo: Kyūko shoin, 1984.

Noyama Kashō 野山嘉正. *Kindai shōsetsu no seiritsu: Meiji no seishun* 近代小説の成立：明治の青春. Tokyo: Iwanami shoten, 1997.

Ōba Osamu 大庭脩. *Edo jidai ni okeru Chūgoku bunka juyō no kenkyū* 江戸時代における中国文化受容の研究. Kyoto: Dōhōsha shuppan, 1984.

——. *Edo jidai ni okeru Tōsen mochiwatarisho no kenkyū* 江戸時代における唐船持渡書の研究. Suita: Kansai daigaku tōzai gakujutsu kenkyūjo, 1981.

——. *Kanseki yunyū no bunkashi* 漢籍輸入の文化史. Tokyo: Kenbun shuppan, 1997.

Ōta Nanpo 大田南畝. *Ōta Nanpo zenshū* 大田南畝全集. 21 vols. Tokyo: Iwanami shoten, 1985–2000.

Ōtsuka Hidetaka 大塚秀高. *Zōho Chūgoku tsūzoku shōsetsu mokuroku* 増補中国通俗小説目録. Tokyo: Kyūko shoin, 1987.

Ozaki Kōyō 尾崎紅葉. *Konjiki yasha* 金色夜叉. Tokyo: Shinchōsha, 1969.

——. "*Konjiki yasha* jō chū ge gappyō" 金色夜叉上中下合評. *Kōyō zenshū* 紅葉全集. Vol. 10. Tokyo: Iwanami shoten, 1994, pp. 317–18.

——. "Kōyō sanjin wo otonau" 紅葉山人を訪ふ. *Kōyō zenshū* 紅葉全集. Vol. 10. Tokyo: Iwanami shoten, 1994, pp. 209–18.

——. "Kōyōshi no shōsetsuka dan" 紅葉氏の小説家談. *Kōyō zenshū* 紅葉全集. Vol. 10. Tokyo: Iwanami shoten, 1994, pp. 322–25.

Ozaki Shunsuke 尾崎俊介. *Kamihyōshi no yūwaku: Amerikan pēpābakku rabirinsu* 紙表紙の誘惑：アメリカン・ペーパーバック・ラビリンス. Tokyo: Kenkyūsha, 2002.

Pocock, J. G. A. "Concepts and Discourses: A Difference in Culture?" In *The Meaning of Historical Terms and Concepts*, edited by H. Lehmann and M. Richter. Washington, D.C.: German Historical Institute, 1996, pp. 47–58.

——. "Empire, Revolution, and the End of Early Modernity. " In *The Varieties of British Political Thought 1500–1800*, edited by J. G. A. Pocock. Cambridge, Eng.: Cambridge University Press, 1993, pp. 283–317.

——. "Languages and Their Implications." In *Politics, Language, and Time: Essays on Political Thought and History*. Chicago: University of Chicago Press, 1989.

———. "Texts as Events: Reflections on the History of Political Thought." In *Politics of Discourse*, edited by K. Sharpe and S. Zwicker. Berkeley: University of California Press, 1987, pp. 21–34.

Propp, Vladimir. *Morphology of the Folktale*. Translated by Laurence Scott. Austin: University of Texas Press, 1996.

Qu Yu 瞿佑. "Aikei no monogatari" 愛卿のものがたり. In *Sentō shinwa* 剪灯新話, translated by Iizuka Akira. Tokyo: Heibonsha, 1997, pp. 151–166.

Radway, Janice. *Reading the Romance: Women, Patriarchy, and Popular Literature*. Chapel Hill: University of North Carolina Press, 1984.

Rath, Eric. *The Ethos of Noh*. Cambridge, Mass.: Harvard University Asia Center, 2005.

Raven, James. "Introduction: The Practice and Representation of Reading in England." In *The Practice and Representation of Reading in England*, edited by James Raven, Helen Small, and Naomi Tadmor. New York: Cambridge University Press, 1996.

Roudinesco, Elisabeth. *Jacques Lacan*. Translated by Barbara Bray. New York: Columbia University Press, 1997.

Santō Kyōden 山東京伝. *Chūshin suikoden* 忠臣水滸伝. *Santō Kyōden zenshū* 山東京伝全集. Vol. 15. Tokyo: Perikansha, 1994.

Santō Kyōden 山東京伝 and Santō Kyōzan 山東京山. *Iezakura tsugiho no hachiue* 家桜継穂鉢植. In *Santō Kyōzan denki shōsetsushū* 山東京山伝奇小説集, edited by Takagi Gen. Tokyo: Kokusho kankōkai, 2003.

Sartre, Jean-Paul. *Sketch for a Theory of the Emotions*. Translated by Philip Mairet. London: Routledge 1994.

Satō Dōshin 佐藤道信. *"Nihon bijutsu" no tanjō* 「日本美術」の誕生. Tokyo: Kōdansha, 1996.

Satō Yukiko 佐藤至子. *Edo no e'iri shōsetsu: gōkan no sekai* 江戸の絵入小説：合巻の世界. Tokyo: Perikansha, 2001.

Séguy, Christiane. *Histoire de la presse Japonaise*. Paris: Publications Orientalistes de France, 1993.

Seki Hajime 関肇. *Konjiki yasha* no juyō to media mikkusu" 『金色夜叉』の受容とメディアミックス. In *Media/hyōshō/ideorogii: Meiji sanjūnendai no bunka kenkyū*, edited by Komori Yōichi, Kōno Kensuke, and Takahashi Osamu. Tokyo: Ozawa shoten, 1997.

Sharpe, Kevin. *Reading Revolutions: The Politics of Reading in Early Modern England*. New Haven: Yale University Press, 2000.

Sherman, Stuart. *Telling Time: Clocks, Diaries, and English Diurnal Form, 1660–1785*. Chicago: University of Chicago Press, 1996.

Shikitei Sanba 式亭三馬. *Kejō suigen maku no soto* 戯場粋言幕乃外 in *Ukiyoburo/Kejō suigen maku no soto/Daisen sekai gakuyasagashi* 浮世風呂・戯場粋言

幕乃外・大千世界楽屋探. Shin Nihon koten bungaku taikei 新日本古典文学体系. Vol. 86. Tokyo: Iwanami shoten, 1989, pp. 275–356.

Shimizu Isao 清水勲, ed. *Kindai nihon manga hyakusen* 近代日本漫画百選. Tokyo: Iwanami shoten, 1997.

Shirane, Haruo. *Sōzōsareta koten: kanon keisei, kokumin kokka, Nihon bungaku* 創造された古典：カノン形成・国民国家・日本文学. Tokyo: Shin'yōsha, 1999.

Shklovsky, Viktor. *Theory of Prose*. Translated by Benjamin Sher. Elmwood Park, Ill.: Darkley Archive Press, 1990.

Shōwa joshi daigaku kindai bungaku kenkyūshitsu 昭和女子大学近代文学研究室, ed. *Kindai bungaku kenkyū sōsho* 近代文学研究叢書. Vol. 28. Tokyo: Shōwa joshi daigaku, 1968.

Suzuki, Tomi. *Narrating the Self: Fictions of Japanese Modernity*. Stanford: Stanford University Press, 1996.

Suzuki Toshiyuki 鈴木俊幸 et al. *Kinsei kōki ni okeru shomotsu/sōshi nado no shuppan/ryūtsū/kyōju ni tsuite no kenkyū: Kiso Tsumago Hayashike zōsho oyobi Kiso Uematsu Rinsenji shozō hangi no chōsa wo chūshin ni* 近世後期における書物・草紙等の出版・流通・享受についての研究—木曾妻籠林家蔵書、及び、木曾上松臨川寺所蔵版木の調査を中心に. Hachiōji: Chūō daigaku bungakubu 3833 kenkyūshitsu, 1996.

Takagi Gen 高木元. *Edo yomihon no kenkyū: jūkyū seiki shōsetsu yōshikikō* 江戸読本の研究：十九世紀小説様式攷. Tokyo: Perikansha, 1995.

Takagi Takeo 高木健夫. *Shinbun shōsetsushi: Meiji-hen* 新聞小説史：明治篇. Tokyo: Kokusho kankōkai, 1974.

Takashina Shūji 高階秀爾. "Inshōha to kindai no Nihon kaiga" 印象派と近代日本の絵画. In *Kuroda Seiki* 黒田清輝, edited by Kagesato Tetsurō. Tokyo: Chuō kōronsha, 1975.

Tamenaga Shunsui 為永春水. *Harutsugedori* 春告鳥. In *Sharebon/kokkeibon/ninjōbon* 洒落本・滑稽本・人情本, edited by Nakano Mitsutoshi, Jinbō Kazuya, and Maeda Ai. Tokyo: Shogakukan, 2000.

——. *Shunshoku umegoyomi* 春色梅児誉美. In *Umegoyomi* 梅暦. Vol. 1. Edited by Furukawa Hisashi. Tokyo: Iwanami shoten, 1951, pp. 17–183.

——. *Zōho gedai kagami* 増補外題鑑. Osaka: Izumi shoin, 1985.

Tanahashi Masahiro 棚橋正博. *Shikitei Sanba: Edo no gesakusha* 式亭三馬：江戸の戯作者. Tokyo: Perikansha, 1994.

Tanishi Kin'gyo 田螺金魚. *Keiseikai tora no maki* 契情買虎之巻. In *Sharebon taisei* 洒落本大成. Vol. 7. Tokyo: Chūō kōronsha, 1980, pp. 303–30.

Terakado Seiken 寺門静軒. *Edo hanjōki* 江戸繁昌記. In *Edo hanjōki/Yanagibashi shinshi* 江戸繁昌記・柳橋新誌, edited by Hino Tatsuo. Shin Nihon koten bungaku taikei 新日本古典文学体系. Vol. 100. Tokyo: Iwanami shoten, 1989.

Tokuda Takeshi 徳田武. *Nihon kinsei shōsetsu to Chūgoku shōsetsu* 日本近世小説と中国小説. Tokyo: Seishōdō shoten, 1987.

Tokutomi Roka 徳冨蘆花. "Dai hyakuban Hototogisu no kanshu ni." 第百版不如帰の巻首に. In *Hototogisu* 不如帰. Tokyo: Iwanami shoten, 1994.

——. *Hototogisu* 不如帰. Tokyo: Iwanami shoten, 1994.

——. *Roka nikki* 蘆花日記. 7 vols. Tokyo: Chikuma shobō, 1985–86.

——. *Roka zenshū* 蘆花全集. 20 vols. Tokyo: Roka zenshū kankōkai, 1929–30.

Tolstoy, Leo. *The Kreutzer Sonata and Other Stories.* Translated by David McDuff. London: Penguin Books, 1985.

Totman, Conrad. *Early Modern Japan.* Berkeley: University of California Press, 1993.

Tsien Tsuen-hsuin. *Paper and Printing.* Science and Civilization in China. Vol. 5, part 1. Edited by Joseph Needham. Cambridge, Eng.: Cambridge University Press, 1985.

Tsubouchi Shōyō 坪内逍遥. *Shōsetsu Shinzui* 小説神髄. Meiji bungaku zenshū. 明治文学全集. Vol. 16. Tokyo: Chikuma shobō, 1969.

Ueda Akinari 上田秋成. *Ugetsu monogatari* 雨月物語. 2 vols. Tokyo: Kōdansha, 1997.

Ueda, Atsuko. "Meiji Literary Historiography: The Production of Modern Japanese Literature." Ph.D. diss., University of Michigan, 1999.

Vincent-Buffault, Anne. *The History of Tears: Sensibility and Sentimentality in France, 1700–1900.* Translated by Teresa Bridgeman. New York: St. Martin's Press, 1991.

Wallerstein, Immanuel. "The Bourgeois(ie) as Concept and Reality." In *Race, Nation, Class: Ambiguous Identities,* by Etienne Balibar and Immanuel Wallerstein. London: Verso, 1991, pp. 135–52.

Washburn, Dennis. "Ghostwriters and Literary Haunts: Subordinating Ethics to Art in *Ugetsu Monogatari.*" *Monumenta Nipponica* 45, no. 1 (spring 1990): 39–74.

Watt, Ian. *The Rise of the Novel: Studies in Defoe, Richardson and Fielding.* Berkeley: University of California Press, 1957.

Wellek, René. "The Crisis of Comparative Literature." In *Concepts of Criticism.* New Haven: Yale University Press, 1965, pp. 282–95.

Williams, Raymond. *The City and the Country.* New York: Oxford University Press, 1973.

——. "Culture and Technology." In *The Politics of Modernism.* London: Verso, 1996, pp. 119–39.

Wittgenstein, Ludwig. *Philosophical Investigations.* Translated by G. E. M. Ascombe. London: Blackwell, 2001.

Yamaguchi Kyōko 山口恭子. "Hosoai Hansai to shoshi Fujiya Yahei: Takimotoryū chūkō no haikei" 細合半斎と書肆·藤屋弥兵衛—滝本流中興の背景—. *Nihon bungaku shiyō* 日本文学誌要, no. 63 (2001): 26–37.

Yamamoto Taketoshi 山本武利. *Kindai nihon no shinbun dokushasō* 近代日本の新聞読者層. Tokyo: Hōsei daigaku shuppankyoku, 1981.

Yamazaki Fumoto 山崎麓. *Nihon shōsetsu shomoku nenpyō* 日本小説書目年表. Tokyo: Yumani shobō, 1977.

Yayoshi Mitsunaga 彌吉光長. *Mikan shiryō ni yoru Nihon shuppan bunka* 未刊史料による日本出版文化. Vol. 5. Tokyo: Yumani shobō, 1990.

Yokota Fuyuhiko 横田冬彦. *Tenka taihei* 天下泰平. Nihon no rekishi. 日本の歴史. Vol. 16. Tokyo: Kōdansha, 2002.

Yokoyama Kuniharu 横山邦治. *Yomihon no kenkyū* 読本の研究. Tokyo: Kazama shobō, 1974.

Yokoyama Yoshikiyo 横山由清. *Fukkokuban Robinson hyōkōkiryaku* 復刻版魯敏遜漂行紀略. Tokyo: Marui kōbunsha, 1975.

Žižek, Slavoj. *For They Know Not What They Do: Enjoyment as a Political Factor.* London: Verso, 1991.

———. *The Sublime Object of Ideology*. London: Verso, 1989.

Index

Harvard East Asian Monographs
(* out-of-print)

*1. Liang Fang-chung, *The Single-Whip Method of Taxation in China*
*2. Harold C. Hinton, *The Grain Tribute System of China, 1845–1911*
3. Ellsworth C. Carlson, *The Kaiping Mines, 1877–1912*
*4. Chao Kuo-chün, *Agrarian Policies of Mainland China: A Documentary Study, 1949–1956*
*5. Edgar Snow, *Random Notes on Red China, 1936–1945*
*6. Edwin George Beal, Jr., *The Origin of Likin, 1835–1864*
7. Chao Kuo-chün, *Economic Planning and Organization in Mainland China: A Documentary Study, 1949–1957*
*8. John K. Fairbank, *Ching Documents: An Introductory Syllabus*
*9. Helen Yin and Yi-chang Yin, *Economic Statistics of Mainland China, 1949–1957*
10. Wolfgang Franke, *The Reform and Abolition of the Traditional Chinese Examination System*
11. Albert Feuerwerker and S. Cheng, *Chinese Communist Studies of Modern Chinese History*
12. C. John Stanley, *Late Ching Finance: Hu Kuang-yung as an Innovator*
13. S. M. Meng, *The Tsungli Yamen: Its Organization and Functions*
*14. Ssu-yü Teng, *Historiography of the Taiping Rebellion*
15. Chun-Jo Liu, *Controversies in Modern Chinese Intellectual History: An Analytic Bibliography of Periodical Articles, Mainly of the May Fourth and Post-May Fourth Era*
*16. Edward J. M. Rhoads, *The Chinese Red Army, 1927–1963: An Annotated Bibliography*
*17. Andrew J. Nathan, *A History of the China International Famine Relief Commission*
*18. Frank H. H. King (ed.) and Prescott Clarke, *A Research Guide to China-Coast Newspapers, 1822–1911*
*19. Ellis Joffe, *Party and Army: Professionalism and Political Control in the Chinese Officer Corps, 1949–1964*

*20. Toshio G. Tsukahira, *Feudal Control in Tokugawa Japan: The Sankin Kōtai System*
*21. Kwang-Ching Liu, ed., *American Missionaries in China: Papers from Harvard Seminars*
*22. George Moseley, *A Sino-Soviet Cultural Frontier: The Ili Kazakh Autonomous Chou*
23. Carl F. Nathan, *Plague Prevention and Politics in Manchuria, 1910–1931*
*24. Adrian Arthur Bennett, *John Fryer: The Introduction of Western Science and Technology into Nineteenth-Century China*
*25. Donald J. Friedman, *The Road from Isolation: The Campaign of the American Committee for Non-Participation in Japanese Aggression, 1938–1941*
*26. Edward LeFevour, *Western Enterprise in Late Ching China: A Selective Survey of Jardine, Matheson and Company's Operations, 1842–1895*
27. Charles Neuhauser, *Third World Politics: China and the Afro-Asian People's Solidarity Organization, 1957–1967*
*28. Kungtu C. Sun, assisted by Ralph W. Huenemann, *The Economic Development of Manchuria in the First Half of the Twentieth Century*
*29. Shahid Javed Burki, *A Study of Chinese Communes, 1965*
30. John Carter Vincent, *The Extraterritorial System in China: Final Phase*
31. Madeleine Chi, *China Diplomacy, 1914–1918*
*32. Clifton Jackson Phillips, *Protestant America and the Pagan World: The First Half Century of the American Board of Commissioners for Foreign Missions, 1810–1860*
*33. James Pusey, *Wu Han: Attacking the Present Through the Past*
*34. Ying-wan Cheng, *Postal Communication in China and Its Modernization, 1860–1896*
35. Tuvia Blumenthal, *Saving in Postwar Japan*
36. Peter Frost, *The Bakumatsu Currency Crisis*
37. Stephen C. Lockwood, *Augustine Heard and Company, 1858–1862*
38. Robert R. Campbell, *James Duncan Campbell: A Memoir by His Son*
39. Jerome Alan Cohen, ed., *The Dynamics of China's Foreign Relations*
40. V. V. Vishnyakova-Akimova, *Two Years in Revolutionary China, 1925–1927,* tr. Steven L. Levine
41. Meron Medzini, *French Policy in Japan During the Closing Years of the Tokugawa Regime*
42. Ezra Vogel, Margie Sargent, Vivienne B. Shue, Thomas Jay Mathews, and Deborah S. Davis, *The Cultural Revolution in the Provinces*
43. Sidney A. Forsythe, *An American Missionary Community in China, 1895–1905*
*44. Benjamin I. Schwartz, ed., *Reflections on the May Fourth Movement.: A Symposium*
*45. Ching Young Choe, *The Rule of the Taewŏngun, 1864–1873: Restoration in Yi Korea*
46. W. P. J. Hall, *A Bibliographical Guide to Japanese Research on the Chinese Economy, 1958–1970*
47. Jack J. Gerson, *Horatio Nelson Lay and Sino-British Relations, 1854–1864*

48. Paul Richard Bohr, *Famine and the Missionary: Timothy Richard as Relief Administrator and Advocate of National Reform*
49. Endymion Wilkinson, *The History of Imperial China: A Research Guide*
50. Britten Dean, *China and Great Britain: The Diplomacy of Commercial Relations, 1860–1864*
51. Ellsworth C. Carlson, *The Foochow Missionaries, 1847–1880*
52. Yeh-chien Wang, *An Estimate of the Land-Tax Collection in China, 1753 and 1908*
53. Richard M. Pfeffer, *Understanding Business Contracts in China, 1949–1963*

*54. Han-sheng Chuan and Richard Kraus, *Mid-Ching Rice Markets and Trade: An Essay in Price History*

55. Ranbir Vohra, *Lao She and the Chinese Revolution*
56. Liang-lin Hsiao, *China's Foreign Trade Statistics, 1864–1949*

*57. Lee-hsia Hsu Ting, *Government Control of the Press in Modern China, 1900–1949*

*58. Edward W. Wagner, *The Literati Purges: Political Conflict in Early Yi Korea*

*59. Joungwon A. Kim, *Divided Korea: The Politics of Development, 1945–1972*

60. Noriko Kamachi, John K. Fairbank, and Chūzō Ichiko, *Japanese Studies of Modern China Since 1953: A Bibliographical Guide to Historical and Social-Science Research on the Nineteenth and Twentieth Centuries, Supplementary Volume for 1953–1969*
61. Donald A. Gibbs and Yun-chen Li, *A Bibliography of Studies and Translations of Modern Chinese Literature, 1918–1942*
62. Robert H. Silin, *Leadership and Values: The Organization of Large-Scale Taiwanese Enterprises*
63. David Pong, *A Critical Guide to the Kwangtung Provincial Archives Deposited at the Public Record Office of London*

*64. Fred W. Drake, *China Charts the World: Hsu Chi-yü and His Geography of 1848*

*65. William A. Brown and Urgrunge Onon, translators and annotators, *History of the Mongolian People's Republic*

66. Edward L. Farmer, *Early Ming Government: The Evolution of Dual Capitals*

*67. Ralph C. Croizier, *Koxinga and Chinese Nationalism: History, Myth, and the Hero*

*68. William J. Tyler, tr., *The Psychological World of Natsume Sōseki,* by Doi Takeo

69. Eric Widmer, *The Russian Ecclesiastical Mission in Peking During the Eighteenth Century*

*70. Charlton M. Lewis, *Prologue to the Chinese Revolution: The Transformation of Ideas and Institutions in Hunan Province, 1891–1907*

71. Preston Torbert, *The Ching Imperial Household Department: A Study of Its Organization and Principal Functions, 1662–1796*
72. Paul A. Cohen and John E. Schrecker, eds., *Reform in Nineteenth-Century China*
73. Jon Sigurdson, *Rural Industrialism in China*

74. Kang Chao, *The Development of Cotton Textile Production in China*
75. Valentin Rabe, *The Home Base of American China Missions, 1880–1920*
*76. Sarasin Viraphol, *Tribute and Profit: Sino-Siamese Trade, 1652–1853*
77. Ch'i-ch'ing Hsiao, *The Military Establishment of the Yuan Dynasty*
78. Meishi Tsai, *Contemporary Chinese Novels and Short Stories, 1949–1974: An Annotated Bibliography*
*79. Wellington K. K. Chan, *Merchants, Mandarins and Modern Enterprise in Late Ching China*
80. Endymion Wilkinson, *Landlord and Labor in Late Imperial China: Case Studies from Shandong by Jing Su and Luo Lun*
*81. Barry Keenan, *The Dewey Experiment in China: Educational Reform and Political Power in the Early Republic*
*82. George A. Hayden, *Crime and Punishment in Medieval Chinese Drama: Three Judge Pao Plays*
*83. Sang-Chul Suh, *Growth and Structural Changes in the Korean Economy, 1910–1940*
84. J. W. Dower, *Empire and Aftermath: Yoshida Shigeru and the Japanese Experience, 1878–1954*
85. Martin Collcutt, *Five Mountains: The Rinzai Zen Monastic Institution in Medieval Japan*
86. Kwang Suk Kim and Michael Roemer, *Growth and Structural Transformation*
87. Anne O. Krueger, *The Developmental Role of the Foreign Sector and Aid*
*88. Edwin S. Mills and Byung-Nak Song, *Urbanization and Urban Problems*
89. Sung Hwan Ban, Pal Yong Moon, and Dwight H. Perkins, *Rural Development*
*90. Noel F. McGinn, Donald R. Snodgrass, Yung Bong Kim, Shin-Bok Kim, and Quee-Young Kim, *Education and Development in Korea*
*91. Leroy P. Jones and Il SaKong, *Government, Business, and Entrepreneurship in Economic Development: The Korean Case*
92. Edward S. Mason, Dwight H. Perkins, Kwang Suk Kim, David C. Cole, Mahn Je Kim et al., *The Economic and Social Modernization of the Republic of Korea*
93. Robert Repetto, Tai Hwan Kwon, Son-Ung Kim, Dae Young Kim, John E. Sloboda, and Peter J. Donaldson, *Economic Development, Population Policy, and Demographic Transition in the Republic of Korea*
94. Parks M. Coble, Jr., *The Shanghai Capitalists and the Nationalist Government, 1927–1937*
95. Noriko Kamachi, *Reform in China: Huang Tsun-hsien and the Japanese Model*
96. Richard Wich, *Sino-Soviet Crisis Politics: A Study of Political Change and Communication*
97. Lillian M. Li, *China's Silk Trade: Traditional Industry in the Modern World, 1842–1937*
98. R. David Arkush, *Fei Xiaotong and Sociology in Revolutionary China*
*99. Kenneth Alan Grossberg, *Japan's Renaissance: The Politics of the Muromachi Bakufu*
100. James Reeve Pusey, *China and Charles Darwin*

101. Hoyt Cleveland Tillman, *Utilitarian Confucianism: Chen Liang's Challenge to Chu Hsi*
102. Thomas A. Stanley, *Ōsugi Sakae, Anarchist in Taishō Japan: The Creativity of the Ego*
103. Jonathan K. Ocko, *Bureaucratic Reform in Provincial China: Ting Jih-ch'ang in Restoration Kiangsu, 1867–1870*
104. James Reed, *The Missionary Mind and American East Asia Policy, 1911–1915*
105. Neil L. Waters, *Japan's Local Pragmatists: The Transition from Bakumatsu to Meiji in the Kawasaki Region*
106. David C. Cole and Yung Chul Park, *Financial Development in Korea, 1945–1978*
107. Roy Bahl, Chuk Kyo Kim, and Chong Kee Park, *Public Finances During the Korean Modernization Process*
108. William D. Wray, *Mitsubishi and the N.Y.K, 1870–1914: Business Strategy in the Japanese Shipping Industry*
109. Ralph William Huenemann, *The Dragon and the Iron Horse: The Economics of Railroads in China, 1876–1937*
*110. Benjamin A. Elman, *From Philosophy to Philology: Intellectual and Social Aspects of Change in Late Imperial China*
111. Jane Kate Leonard, *Wei Yüan and China's Rediscovery of the Maritime World*
112. Luke S. K. Kwong, *A Mosaic of the Hundred Days:. Personalities, Politics, and Ideas of 1898*
*113. John E. Wills, Jr., *Embassies and Illusions: Dutch and Portuguese Envoys to K'ang-hsi, 1666–1687*
114. Joshua A. Fogel, *Politics and Sinology: The Case of Naitō Konan (1866–1934)*
*115. Jeffrey C. Kinkley, ed., *After Mao: Chinese Literature and Society, 1978–1981*
116. C. Andrew Gerstle, *Circles of Fantasy: Convention in the Plays of Chikamatsu*
117. Andrew Gordon, *The Evolution of Labor Relations in Japan: Heavy Industry, 1853–1955*
*118. Daniel K. Gardner, *Chu Hsi and the "Ta Hsueh": Neo-Confucian Reflection on the Confucian Canon*
119. Christine Guth Kanda, *Shinzō: Hachiman Imagery and Its Development*
*120. Robert Borgen, *Sugawara no Michizane and the Early Heian Court*
121. Chang-tai Hung, *Going to the People: Chinese Intellectual and Folk Literature, 1918–1937*
*122. Michael A. Cusumano, *The Japanese Automobile Industry: Technology and Management at Nissan and Toyota*
123. Richard von Glahn, *The Country of Streams and Grottoes: Expansion, Settlement, and the Civilizing of the Sichuan Frontier in Song Times*
124. Steven D. Carter, *The Road to Komatsubara: A Classical Reading of the Renga Hyakuin*
125. Katherine F. Bruner, John K. Fairbank, and Richard T. Smith, *Entering China's Service: Robert Hart's Journals, 1854–1863*
126. Bob Tadashi Wakabayashi, *Anti-Foreignism and Western Learning in Early-Modern Japan: The "New Theses" of 1825*

127. Atsuko Hirai, *Individualism and Socialism: The Life and Thought of Kawai Eijirō (1891–1944)*
128. Ellen Widmer, *The Margins of Utopia: "Shui-hu hou-chuan" and the Literature of Ming Loyalism*
129. R. Kent Guy, *The Emperor's Four Treasuries: Scholars and the State in the Late Chien-lung Era*
130. Peter C. Perdue, *Exhausting the Earth: State and Peasant in Hunan, 1500–1850*
131. Susan Chan Egan, *A Latterday Confucian: Reminiscences of William Hung (1893–1980)*
132. James T. C. Liu, *China Turning Inward: Intellectual-Political Changes in the Early Twelfth Century*
*133. Paul A. Cohen, *Between Tradition and Modernity: Wang T'ao and Reform in Late Ching China*
134. Kate Wildman Nakai, *Shogunal Politics: Arai Hakuseki and the Premises of Tokugawa Rule*
*135. Parks M. Coble, *Facing Japan: Chinese Politics and Japanese Imperialism, 1931–1937*
136. Jon L. Saari, *Legacies of Childhood: Growing Up Chinese in a Time of Crisis, 1890–1920*
137. Susan Downing Videen, *Tales of Heichū*
138. Heinz Morioka and Miyoko Sasaki, *Rakugo: The Popular Narrative Art of Japan*
139. Joshua A. Fogel, *Nakae Ushikichi in China: The Mourning of Spirit*
140. Alexander Barton Woodside, *Vietnam and the Chinese Model.: A Comparative Study of Vietnamese and Chinese Government in the First Half of the Nineteenth Century*
*141. George Elison, *Deus Destroyed: The Image of Christianity in Early Modern Japan*
142. William D. Wray, ed., *Managing Industrial Enterprise: Cases from Japan's Prewar Experience*
*143. T'ung-tsu Ch'ü, *Local Government in China Under the Ching*
144. Marie Anchordoguy, *Computers, Inc.: Japan's Challenge to IBM*
145. Barbara Molony, *Technology and Investment: The Prewar Japanese Chemical Industry*
146. Mary Elizabeth Berry, *Hideyoshi*
147. Laura E. Hein, *Fueling Growth: The Energy Revolution and Economic Policy in Postwar Japan*
148. Wen-hsin Yeh, *The Alienated Academy: Culture and Politics in Republican China, 1919–1937*
149. Dru C. Gladney, *Muslim Chinese: Ethnic Nationalism in the People's Republic*
150. Merle Goldman and Paul A. Cohen, eds., *Ideas Across Cultures: Essays on Chinese Thought in Honor of Benjamin L Schwartz*
151. James M. Polachek, *The Inner Opium War*
152. Gail Lee Bernstein, *Japanese Marxist: A Portrait of Kawakami Hajime, 1879–1946*
*153. Lloyd E. Eastman, *The Abortive Revolution: China Under Nationalist Rule, 1927–1937*

154. Mark Mason, *American Multinationals and Japan: The Political Economy of Japanese Capital Controls, 1899–1980*
155. Richard J. Smith, John K. Fairbank, and Katherine F. Bruner, *Robert Hart and China's Early Modernization: His Journals, 1863–1866*
156. George J. Tanabe, Jr., *Myōe the Dreamkeeper: Fantasy and Knowledge in Kamakura Buddhism*
157. William Wayne Farris, *Heavenly Warriors: The Evolution of Japan's Military, 500–1300*
158. Yu-ming Shaw, *An American Missionary in China: John Leighton Stuart and Chinese-American Relations*
159. James B. Palais, *Politics and Policy in Traditional Korea*

*160. Douglas Reynolds, *China, 1898–1912: The Xinzheng Revolution and Japan*

161. Roger R. Thompson, *China's Local Councils in the Age of Constitutional Reform, 1898–1911*
162. William Johnston, *The Modern Epidemic: History of Tuberculosis in Japan*
163. Constantine Nomikos Vaporis, *Breaking Barriers: Travel and the State in Early Modern Japan*
164. Irmela Hijiya-Kirschnereit, *Rituals of Self-Revelation: Shishōsetsu as Literary Genre and Socio-Cultural Phenomenon*
165. James C. Baxter, *The Meiji Unification Through the Lens of Ishikawa Prefecture*
166. Thomas R. H. Havens, *Architects of Affluence: The Tsutsumi Family and the Seibu-Saison Enterprises in Twentieth-Century Japan*
167. Anthony Hood Chambers, *The Secret Window: Ideal Worlds in Tanizaki's Fiction*
168. Steven J. Ericson, *The Sound of the Whistle: Railroads and the State in Meiji Japan*
169. Andrew Edmund Goble, *Kenmu: Go-Daigo's Revolution*
170. Denise Potrzeba Lett, *In Pursuit of Status: The Making of South Korea's "New" Urban Middle Class*
171. Mimi Hall Yiengpruksawan, *Hiraizumi: Buddhist Art and Regional Politics in Twelfth-Century Japan*
172. Charles Shirō Inouye, *The Similitude of Blossoms: A Critical Biography of Izumi Kyōka (1873–1939), Japanese Novelist and Playwright*
173. Aviad E. Raz, *Riding the Black Ship: Japan and Tokyo Disneyland*
174. Deborah J. Milly, *Poverty, Equality, and Growth: The Politics of Economic Need in Postwar Japan*
175. See Heng Teow, *Japan's Cultural Policy Toward China, 1918–1931: A Comparative Perspective*
176. Michael A. Fuller, *An Introduction to Literary Chinese*
177. Frederick R. Dickinson, *War and National Reinvention: Japan in the Great War, 1914–1919*
178. John Solt, *Shredding the Tapestry of Meaning: The Poetry and Poetics of Kitasono Katue (1902–1978)*

179. Edward Pratt, *Japan's Protoindustrial Elite: The Economic Foundations of the Gōnō*
180. Atsuko Sakaki, *Recontextualizing Texts: Narrative Performance in Modern Japanese Fiction*
181. Soon-Won Park, *Colonial Industrialization and Labor in Korea: The Onoda Cement Factory*
182. JaHyun Kim Haboush and Martina Deuchler, *Culture and the State in Late Chosŏn Korea*
183. John W. Chaffee, *Branches of Heaven: A History of the Imperial Clan of Sung China*
184. Gi-Wook Shin and Michael Robinson, eds., *Colonial Modernity in Korea*
185. Nam-lin Hur, *Prayer and Play in Late Tokugawa Japan: Asakusa Sensōji and Edo Society*
186. Kristin Stapleton, *Civilizing Chengdu: Chinese Urban Reform, 1895–1937*
187. Hyung Il Pai, *Constructing "Korean" Origins: A Critical Review of Archaeology, Historiography, and Racial Myth in Korean State-Formation Theories*
188. Brian D. Ruppert, *Jewel in the Ashes: Buddha Relics and Power in Early Medieval Japan*
189. Susan Daruvala, *Zhou Zuoren and an Alternative Chinese Response to Modernity*
*190. James Z. Lee, *The Political Economy of a Frontier: Southwest China, 1250–1850*
191. Kerry Smith, *A Time of Crisis: Japan, the Great Depression, and Rural Revitalization*
192. Michael Lewis, *Becoming Apart: National Power and Local Politics in Toyama, 1868–1945*
193. William C. Kirby, Man-houng Lin, James Chin Shih, and David A. Pietz, eds., *State and Economy in Republican China: A Handbook for Scholars*
194. Timothy S. George, *Minamata: Pollution and the Struggle for Democracy in Postwar Japan*
195. Billy K. L. So, *Prosperity, Region, and Institutions in Maritime China: The South Fukien Pattern, 946–1368*
196. Yoshihisa Tak Matsusaka, *The Making of Japanese Manchuria, 1904–1932*
197. Maram Epstein, *Competing Discourses: Orthodoxy, Authenticity, and Engendered Meanings in Late Imperial Chinese Fiction*
198. Curtis J. Milhaupt, J. Mark Ramseyer, and Michael K. Young, eds. and comps., *Japanese Law in Context: Readings in Society, the Economy, and Politics*
199. Haruo Iguchi, *Unfinished Business: Ayukawa Yoshisuke and U.S.-Japan Relations, 1937–1952*
200. Scott Pearce, Audrey Spiro, and Patricia Ebrey, *Culture and Power in the Reconstitution of the Chinese Realm, 200–600*
201. Terry Kawashima, *Writing Margins: The Textual Construction of Gender in Heian and Kamakura Japan*
202. Martin W. Huang, *Desire and Fictional Narrative in Late Imperial China*

203. Robert S. Ross and Jiang Changbin, eds., *Re-examining the Cold War: U.S.-China Diplomacy, 1954–1973*
204. Guanhua Wang, *In Search of Justice: The 1905–1906 Chinese Anti-American Boycott*
205. David Schaberg, *A Patterned Past: Form and Thought in Early Chinese Historiography*
206. Christine Yano, *Tears of Longing: Nostalgia and the Nation in Japanese Popular Song*
207. Milena Doleželová-Velingerová and Oldřich Král, with Graham Sanders, eds., *The Appropriation of Cultural Capital: China's May Fourth Project*
208. Robert N. Huey, *The Making of 'Shinkokinshū'*
209. Lee Butler, *Emperor and Aristocracy in Japan, 1467–1680: Resilience and Renewal*
210. Suzanne Ogden, *Inklings of Democracy in China*
211. Kenneth J. Ruoff, *The People's Emperor: Democracy and the Japanese Monarchy, 1945–1995*
212. Haun Saussy, *Great Walls of Discourse and Other Adventures in Cultural China*
213. Aviad E. Raz, *Emotions at Work: Normative Control, Organizations, and Culture in Japan and America*
214. Rebecca E. Karl and Peter Zarrow, eds., *Rethinking the 1898 Reform Period: Political and Cultural Change in Late Qing China*
215. Kevin O'Rourke, *The Book of Korean Shijo*
216. Ezra F. Vogel, ed., *The Golden Age of the U.S.-China-Japan Triangle, 1972–1989*
217. Thomas A Wilson, ed., *On Sacred Grounds: Culture, Society, Politics, and the Formation of the Cult of Confucius*
218. Donald S. Sutton, *Steps of Perfection: Exorcistic Performers and Chinese Religion in Twentieth-Century Taiwan*
219. Daqing Yang, *Technology of Empire: Telecommunications and Japanese Expansionism, 1895–1945*
220. Qianshen Bai, *Fu Shan's World: The Transformation of Chinese Calligraphy in the Seventeenth Century*
221. Paul Jakov Smith and Richard von Glahn, eds., *The Song-Yuan-Ming Transition in Chinese History*
222. Rania Huntington, *Alien Kind: Foxes and Late Imperial Chinese Narrative*
223. Jordan Sand, *House and Home in Modern Japan: Architecture, Domestic Space, and Bourgeois Culture, 1880–1930*
224. Karl Gerth, *China Made: Consumer Culture and the Creation of the Nation*
225. Xiaoshan Yang, *Metamorphosis of the Private Sphere: Gardens and Objects in Tang-Song Poetry*
226. Barbara Mittler, *A Newspaper for China? Power, Identity, and Change in Shanghai's News Media, 1872–1912*
227. Joyce A. Madancy, *The Troublesome Legacy of Commissioner Lin: The Opium Trade and Opium Suppression in Fujian Province, 1820s to 1920s*

228. John Makeham, *Transmitters and Creators: Chinese Commentators and Commentaries on the Analects*
229. Elisabeth Köll, *From Cotton Mill to Business Empire: The Emergence of Regional Enterprises in Modern China*
230. Emma Teng, *Taiwan's Imagined Geography: Chinese Colonial Travel Writing and Pictures, 1683–1895*
231. Wilt Idema and Beata Grant, *The Red Brush: Writing Women of Imperial China*
232. Eric C. Rath, *The Ethos of Noh: Actors and Their Art*
233. Elizabeth Remick, *Building Local States: China During the Republican and Post-Mao Eras*
234. Lynn Struve, ed., *The Qing Formation in World-Historical Time*
235. D. Max Moerman, *Localizing Paradise: Kumano Pilgrimage and the Religious Landscape of Premodern Japan*
236. Antonia Finnane, *Speaking of Yangzhou: A Chinese City, 1550–1850*
237. Brian Platt, *Burning and Building: Schooling and State Formation in Japan, 1750–1890*
238. Gail Bernstein, Andrew Gordon, and Kate Wildman Nakai, eds., *Public Spheres, Private Lives in Modern Japan, 1600–1950: Essays in Honor of Albert Craig*
239. Wu Hung and Katherine R. Tsiang, *Body and Face in Chinese Visual Culture*
240. Stephen Dodd, *Writing Home: Representations of the Native Place in Modern Japanese Literature*
241. David Anthony Bello, *Opium and the Limits of Empire: Drug Prohibition in the Chinese Interior, 1729–1850*
242. Hosea Hirata, *Discourses of Seduction: History, Evil, Desire, and Modern Japanese Literature*
243. Kyung Moon Hwang, *Beyond Birth: Social Status in the Emergence of Modern Korea*
244. Brian R. Dott, *Identity Reflections: Pilgrimages to Mount Tai in Late Imperial China*
245. Mark McNally, *Proving the Way: Conflict and Practice in the History of Japanese Nativism*
246. Yongping Wu, *A Political Explanation of Economic Growth: State Survival, Bureaucratic Politics, and Private Enterprises in the Making of Taiwan's Economy, 1950–1985*
247. Kyu Hyun Kim, *The Age of Visions and Arguments: Parliamentarianism and the National Public Sphere in Early Meiji Japan*
248. Zvi Ben-Dor Benite, *The Dao of Muhammad: A Cultural History of Muslims in Late Imperial China*
249. David Der-wei Wang and Shang Wei, eds., *Dynastic Crisis and Cultural Innovation: From the Late Ming to the Late Qing and Beyond*
250. Wilt L. Idema, Wai-yee Li, and Ellen Widmer, eds., *Trauma and Transcendence in Early Qing Literature*
251. Barbara Molony and Kathleen Uno, eds., *Gendering Modern Japanese History*

252. Hiroshi Aoyagi, *Islands of Eight Million Smiles: Idol Performance and Symbolic Production in Contemporary Japan*
253. Wai-yee Li, *The Readability of the Past in Early Chinese Historiography*
254. William C. Kirby, Robert S. Ross, and Gong Li, eds., *Normalization of U.S.-China Relations: An International History*
255. Ellen Gardner Nakamura, *Practical Pursuits: Takano Chōei, Takahashi Keisaku, and Western Medicine in Nineteenth-Century Japan*
256. Jonathan W. Best, *A History of the Early Korean Kingdom of Paekche, together with an annotated translation of* The Paekche Annals *of the* Samguk sagi
257. Liang Pan, *The United Nations in Japan's Foreign and Security Policymaking, 1945–1992: National Security, Party Politics, and International Status*
258. Richard Belsky, *Localities at the Center: Native Place, Space, and Power in Late Imperial Beijing*
259. Zwia Lipkin, *"Useless to the State": "Social Problems" and Social Engineering in Nationalist Nanjing, 1927–1937*
260. William O. Gardner, *Advertising Tower: Japanese Modernism and Modernity in the 1920s*
261. Stephen Owen, *The Making of Early Chinese Classical Poetry*
262. Martin J. Powers, *Pattern and Person: Ornament, Society, and Self in Classical China*
263. Anna M. Shields, *Crafting a Collection: The Cultural Contexts and Poetic Practice of the* Huajian ji 花間集 *(Collection from Among the Flowers)*
264. Stephen Owen, *The Late Tang: Chinese Poetry of the Mid-Ninth Century (827–860)*
265. Sara L. Friedman, *Intimate Politics: Marriage, the Market, and State Power in Southeastern China*
266. Patricia Buckley Ebrey and Maggie Bickford, *Emperor Huizong and Late Northern Song China: The Politics of Culture and the Culture of Politics*
267. Sophie Volpp, *Worldly Stage: Theatricality in Seventeenth-Century China*
268. Ellen Widmer, *The Beauty and the Book: Women and Fiction in Nineteenth-Century China*
269. Steven B. Miles, *The Sea of Learning: Mobility and Identity in Nineteenth-Century Guangzhou*
270. Lin Man-houng, *China Upside Down: Currency, Society, and Ideologies, 1808–1856*
271. Ronald Egan, *The Problem of Beauty: Aesthetic Thought and Pursuits in Northern Song Dynasty China*
272. Mark Halperin, *Out of the Cloister: Literati Perspectives on Buddhism in Sung China, 960–1279*
273. Helen Dunstan, *State or Merchant? Political Economy and Political Process in 1740s China*
274. Sabina Knight, *The Heart of Time: Moral Agency in Twentieth-Century Chinese Fiction*

275. Timothy J. Van Compernolle, *The Uses of Memory: The Critique of Modernity in the Fiction of Higuchi Ichiyō*
276. Paul Rouzer, *A New Practical Primer of Literary Chinese*
277. Jonathan Zwicker, *Practices of the Sentimental Imagination: Melodrama, the Novel, and the Social Imaginary in Nineteenth-Century Japan*